SIMAMA

—— BREAKING FAMILY STRONGHOLDS ——

MURIITHI & CAROL WANJAU

Published by Edenica Ltd.

P.O. Box 27583-00506,

Nairobi, Kenya.

Cover by: Art Creative Ltd | +254 (0) 706 243 297 | www.artcreativeltd.com

Design and Layout: Zing Press | +254 (0) 722364691 | thezingpress@gmail.com

Print, Production & Publishing Consultants: BlackRain Ltd.

Edited by: Top Tier Books | +254 (0) 720 758617 | consult@toptier.co.ke

CONTENTS

DEDICATION

To our children. May you exceed us in every way!

Once, a mutual friend, at the end of yet another failed relationship, in lament, shared with us a quote which at the time best captured for him the nature of relationships. He told us, "Relationships are like a cigarette. They start with a flame but end up in ashes!"

What a thing to say! But, it really got us thinking about the negative patterns we see in our relationships. Why do so many people find themselves trapped in a cycle of bad relationships? Why, despite their best intentions, do people find themselves in abusive relationships, even after they swear that they will not be like their parents? Why do others continue in relationships even when partners are habitually unfaithful? Why are people today choosing not to commit to a relationship but instead to become 'friends with benefits'? Why do so many find themselves 'falling' for the wrong type of people; people who take advantage of them?

Negative patterns affect far more than just our romantic relationships! Do you find yourself impatient with and unable to get along with most people? Are there some close relationships, with family members, friends or colleagues, that you find hard to not to be indifferent to? Do you find yourself holding on to bitterness and grudges, or being jealous of other peoples' success? Do you ever struggle with low self-esteem, lethargy or low self-motivation? Do you find it difficult to say 'no' or to confront people who have wronged you? Are you the addictive type; a person who easily becomes gripped by compulsive behaviors, either those celebrated or accepted by society like workaholism and media addiction or the more frowned upon ones like alcoholism, drug addiction, masturbation, pornography or risky sexual behaviors?

> Our enemy, the devil, often uses strongholds in our lives to keep us from effectively and joyfully pursuing our God-given purpose

It is not just in the realm of relationships that negative patterns impact us. Some of us have come to accept as normal things that others would not. Perhaps the men in your family never amount to much in their careers or the women have children out of wedlock. Perhaps there is a pattern of early death or certain illnesses that always affect members of your family. Perhaps you are conscious of patterns of addictions, godlesness or angry outbursts in your generation that can be traced back to your parents or even earlier in your family tree.

Many of the negative patterns that affect us, our relationships and our families are directly related to strongholds. What then are strongholds? A stronghold is exactly what it sounds like: Anything that has a strong hold on you or someone else. Biblically, it was often used as a military term, like an outpost in a foreign territory. A stronghold was a fort or strategic location that gave military advantage to the army that controlled it. It allowed them to have a foothold a superior vantage point from which to defend their position and made it difficult for an enemy to dislodge them.

Our enemy, the devil, often uses strongholds in our lives to keep us from effectively and joyfully pursuing our God-given purpose. That is why the writer of the epistle warned the church in Ephesus: *'In your anger do not sin: Do not let the sun go down while you are still angry, and do not give the devil a*

INTRODUCTION

foothold. [1] Simply put, unchecked anger can allow the enemy legal rights into your life! The apostle Peter warned the early church to watch out for the enemy's strategy: *'Be alert and of sober mind. Your enemy the devil prowls around like a roaring lion looking for someone to devour. Resist him, standing firm in the faith, because you know that the family of believers throughout the world is undergoing the same kind of sufferings.'* [2]

As a born-again follower of Jesus, the enemy cannot have any access to your life except that which has been legally granted to him. Think of it as doors, spiritual doors that have been left open in our lives that the enemy has used to gain access to us. The only way to keep him out is to stand on our authority as children of God and resist him. We close any door that he has used to gain access into our lives and to harass us and our families. We shut down his strongholds.

> Why do I do the things I do? Who am I?'

That's what this course is about. Each week of the Simama course is designed to help you become more alert and self-aware. By looking inside, starting with yourself and then moving on to your family of origin, we want to explore the potential strongholds that would keep each of us from living fulfilled and purposeful lives. In the process, we close any 'doors' that may have granted the enemy access to us. Some of the chapters contain extra prayers and assessments. You will find these in the appendices. Please pray through these as well to ensure that you close all the doors that the enemy would use to harass you and your family. After each days reading, you will find a question for further reflection. We encourage you to get a journal or notebook that you will use to write your reflections based on the question asked.

Through this course, we will explore fundamental questions like, 'Who am I?' 'Why do I do the things I do, or think the way I do?' 'What are the blind spots in my life and in my family that the enemy could use against us?' As we explore these questions, we hope that the end result will be:

Increased Self-Discovery – An understanding about the 'baggage' that we and our families have carried thus far that has limited us from experiencing life as God intended us to;

Reconciliation – A coming-to-terms within ourselves and, ultimately among our family members, with the hurts, disappointments and wounded-ness that may have limited our relationships and trapped us in negative relational patterns; and

Freedom – As the apostle John wrote, 'If the Son sets you free, you will be free indeed,' our prayer is that what the enemy intended for harm in your life will end up, with God's help, working out for your good, and that your pain will become a platform for your purpose. [3] We desire to see any present and generational oppression of the enemy ended in your life and in that of your family, so that you are all free to joyfully pursue the purpose that God created you for!

God bless as you as you begin your journey of freedom!

Muriithi and Carol Wanjau

---

1   Ephesians 4:26-27
2   1 Peter 5:8-9
3   See Genesis 50:20, Romans 8:28

GROUP COVENANT

BECOMING A SAFE PERSON

Getting the most out of this course requires us to be willing to be vulnerable with each other. However, many of us agree and resonate with the saying, 'Once bitten, twice shy.' Through being hurt by others, we have come to appreciate the value of 'keeping things to ourselves' and would rather not take the step to be vulnerable. The problem with this resolution though is that refusing to resolve issues not only makes matters worse, but also makes us into people we have vowed not to be like! We therefore need to create spaces in which we can feel safe to share. This starts with us making the commitment to, first of all, be safe people. Here then are a few commitments that you must be willing to make in order to maximize your experience in this course.

Everything shared in the group MUST be kept confidentially. The nature of this course is that people will be sharing very personal and intimate information. This information cannot be shared outside the group meeting, between prayer partners or even with a spouse!

> Discomfort is part of the healing process

Keep your sharing to what you are learning about yourself. This means that you do not give advice to other members of the group.

Do not criticize other members of the group. Allow members to share, even if you do not necessarily agree with them or feel that their contribution is not significant. Remember that everyone is sharing what they are learning about themselves!

Be willing to be real with yourself when you realize you are being judgmental of others in the course. Being judgmental will often happen. This is because as people share their experiences, they may trigger something in us that causes us to react in a judgmental way. Part of our healing will be a commitment to be real and explore the reason why we are reacting in this way. The process involves confessing to God this attitude and then asking Him to help you understand why you have reacted like you have in the first place. Pray expecting God to answer and to give you a more gracious view of the other person. Talk about this with your prayer partner and ask them to pray with you to overcome this sin.

Commit to being a trustworthy person. Do not use what someone shares in class against them. If tempted to do so, remember to confess this to God and ask Him for help to overcome the temptation. Ask your prayer partner to keep you accountable not to yield to temptation!

Understand that discomfort is part of the healing process. The course will delve into areas of your life that may cause you discomfort almost like undergoing an emotional and spiritual surgery. It might get painful enough for you to consider quitting. We encourage you to hang in there. Our hope is that the environment provided will be a safe and supportive one to help you deal with the issues that you need to.

GROUP COVENANT

Commit to your prayer partner. The journey may get rough and you will need the support of someone else. Commit to pray for your prayer partner and ask God to give you oneness and a friendship that will help you, not only as you go through this course, but even beyond. Be sure to do the activities suggested for prayer partners as these will help you become better support partners for one another.

GROUP COVENANT

Sign the statement below as a commitment that you will keep the promises above.

I, _____, commit to keeping the above

promises in order to be a safe person who others will feel free to share with.

Date: _____

WEEK
– ONE –
WHAT'S ON YOUR TREE?

WHAT'S ON YOUR TREE?

What is the one notable trait you celebrate about your family of origin? I (Muriithi) can think of many! One that my wife noticed soon after we got married is that I come from a loud family. Growing up, we all had strong opinions and we expressed them quite liberally. At the family table, it wasn't unusual to find several conversations going on at once. The rule almost seemed to be, 'If you don't say anything, then we'll assume you have nothing to say!' Carol's family was quite the opposite. At their table, they all took turns to speak and if someone was quiet, the rest would enquire to find out what they were thinking. As you can imagine, this brought some rather interesting dynamics into our marriage!

Family traits are often passed down from parents to children, and this cycle has been repeated for thousands of years. Some of these traits may be positive and beneficial—like nurturing skills, an entrepreneurial spirit, valuing hard work or a passion for education. However, negative and destructive behaviors are also passed down within families. For every one of us in this side of life, there is a pattern of character or traits in our bloodline.

Each human family has its own culture

You see, each human family has its own culture, including unique strengths and weaknesses. Some of these may be the result of genetic inheritance. For example, some families have a history of significant musical or athletic accomplishments passed down from parents to children, to grandchildren and even great-grandchildren. Even though it takes great skill development to be an excellent musician or athlete, a certain natural endowment seems to be inherited from birth by children in these families. I (Carol) remember one family that had six children in the primary school I attended. On sports days, they all won different awards. It seemed that their surname was the only one being called out for prizes!

Modern science has shown that our genetics may predispose us to certain abilities and also to certain weaknesses or diseases. This is referred to as being caused by 'nature'. Other strengths and weaknesses within an individual family culture are the result of its environment or choices. These include values, priorities and decision-making skills. When negative choices and a bad home environment become deeply entrenched within a family culture, individual members can become self-destructive and unknowingly pass on these traits. We refer to these as being caused by 'nurture'.

Every family, if they look diligently into their history, will find that there are particular patterns or events that recur in their family tree, whether due to nature or nurture. Entrepreneurial or scholastic ability, musical or athletic abilities, intuitiveness, good health and long life. The list is as varied as there are families! But it is not just the positive traits that are passed down.

Having grown up in homes where their fathers physically abused their mothers, why do some men repeat the same pattern in their marriages? Having been victims of abuse in their childhood, why do some women choose to marry men who continue the abuse? Having seen the effects of alcohol on a parent, why do some become addicted to it themselves? Why do some of us remain chained to inherited ways of thinking and acting that we know are destructive but that we seem unable to change? After an episode of pain caused by our acting out in the same old broken way, why do we say, "I'll never do that again" and then turn around and do it again over and over and over? It is the result of being chained to a recurring pattern. The baton of self-destructive behavior is passed down to each succeeding generation in an unbroken line. The abused becomes the abuser. The victim becomes the perpetrator. Warped ways of thinking and self-destructive ways of acting literally become diligently preserved and passed on to each successive branch of the family. Thus, the brokenness and pain of the family continues to flow like a river of acid down through each generation.

A famous singer and songwriter, Harry Chapin, recorded a song titled "Cat's in the Cradle." The song is about a father who is too busy to spend time with his son, instead offering vague promises to spend time with him in the future. In time, the boy grows up to become a man very much like his father, focused on his career and other personal pursuits at the expense of family relations. As the father grows old and finally has time to look back on his life, he deeply desires to get to know his adult son and have a meaningful relationship with him. Sadly, the father comes to realize that his son is absorbed with the same materialistic priorities he had, and that a close relationship will never happen. The last verse concludes with this sad line: "And as I hung up the phone, it occurred to me, he'd grown up just like me. My boy was just like me." This song reminds us of the universal influence one generation has on another.

> The primary aim of this book is self-discovery

Everybody reading this is affected by their family tree. Whether you are aware of it or not, you are dealing with the fruit of your family tree. You are dealing today with some negative stuff that you inherited from your mum, your daddy, your grandparents and your great grandparents. So, allow us to ask you a question, 'What's on your tree?' What legacy of recurring patterns exists in your family? Is it alcoholism? Is it drug abuse? Is it sexual promiscuity? Is it physical or verbal abuse? Is it a poverty mentality? What legacy of sin has impacted the generations in your family? Some of us come from family backgrounds of defeatism, divorce, pessimism, selfishness, greed, anger, addictions and laziness. Unless we break these bloodline patterns, these traits may be passed on to our children. One's dysfunctional personal behavior becomes a model or example to the next generation, and the cycle can be repeated over and over again. What's on your tree?

In the introduction, we mentioned that the primary aim of this book is self-discovery. We want to understand why we do the things we do. What are our motivations? What are the fears, blindspots or sinful patterns we have inherited from our families and are in danger of blindly passing on to the next generation? As you do this course, some of the discoveries may be uncomfortable, and you might be tempted to stop reading and to go back to 'life'. But, our prayer is that you will realize that the discomfort of rooting out the issues in your tree is much less than the discomfort of maintaining the status quo in your family. Our prayer is that someone, because of this course, will be able to say, 'It stops with me!' and that the next generation of your family will be stronger, healthier and more aligned to God's purpose than previous generations ever were.

This week, we are beginning the journey of exploring our family trees where we will celebrate the good and root out the bad. We acknowledge that 'looking inside' can be fearful and intimidating. This course, therefore, seeks to equip you with the skills and knowledge to make the experience

PERSONAL COMMITMENT

less and less intimidating. However, to gain the most from the experience, you will need to make the following commitments. Read through the list and then sign it as your commitment to fully engage in the course.

I, _____, agree to fully participate in the course.

I will:

Make this course a priority and set aside at least 45 minutes daily to both read and do the assignments.

Be as honest as possible in all things, especially with regard to what I am learning about myself – past and present.

Be on time for class.

Be fully attentive in class.

Signed: _____

Date: _____

Question For My Journal

What are some strengths that you saw in your family of origin that are worth celebrating?

Verse To Remember

Romans 3:23-24: …For all have sinned and fall short of the glory of God, and all are justified freely by his grace through the redemption that came by Christ Jesus.

Prayer For Today

Thank you Lord that You are the One who put me in the family that I was born into. Thank you for the strengths in my family. Lord, please help me to be the one who stops the negative traits from passing on to the next generation. In Jesus' name. Amen!

BIBLICAL FAMILIES

W hy is it important to have an understanding of your family tree? The Bible often reminds us that it is important to think generationally. Consider God's instruction communicated through the great leader Moses: '… *I, the Lord your God, am a jealous God, visiting the iniquity of the fathers upon the children to the third and fourth generations of those who hate Me, but showing mercy to thousands, to those who love Me and keep My commandments.* [4]

It is easy, from a surface reading of this scripture, to understand that God simply punishes those who disrespect Him and blesses those who love Him. But God is not a vengeful and angry Father who intentionally punishes great-grandchildren for the sins committed generations earlier by others! A better way to understand this scripture is to realize that the consequences of our rebellious actions against God are passed down as family dysfunctions from parents to children and from generation to generation. Our brokenness is a result of breaking God's law and many sins are perpetuated in the next generation. This is because parents have set a poor example that is emulated by the previous generation. But another reason is because our rebellion gives the enemy legal access into our lives, so that he is able to oppress us and our families. Thankfully, God in His mercy, steps in after the third or fourth generation to say 'Enough is enough!'

Rebellion gives the enemy legal access into our lives

The bible does not keep the door shut on the skeletons in the family closets of its heroes. In the bloodline of Abraham there was a trait of attraction to beautiful women and deception. Sarai, Abram's wife was beautiful and therefore Abram, fearing that the Egyptians would kill him and spare her if they learnt that she was his wife, conspired and lied to the Egyptians that Sarai was not his wife but his sister. [5] This same pattern is seen in his son, Isaac, who married an extremely beautiful woman and then lied to the people of Gerar that she was his sister. [6] There was no need for Isaac to lie since the people of Gerar had no ill intentions against him as was the case with his father, Abram, in Egypt. The sin of the father was being blindly repeated by the son!

In the following generation, Jacob was the son of Isaac and a grandson of Abraham. He too lied to his father, Isaac, that he was Esau, his elder brother in order to receive his brother's inheritance. [7] The root cause of the lie here is not with Jacob but his grandfather, Abram. It was even worse for Jacob because his mother, Rebekah, also came from a family whose bloodline was marked with deception. Her brother, Laban, was a master of deceit, as we shall see in a later chapter. The Bible records that Isaac loved Esau and Rebekah loved Jacob and when Isaac was about to die, he called Esau so that he could bless him. Rebekah overheard, schemed and caused Jacob to steal Esau's blessing from their father. Jacob's lies were not just what he observed in the family, but were actually approved of by his mother!

Another example of negative family traits in the bible is the failure of firstborns. The firstborn of Abraham, Ishmael, never succeeded him, just like Isaac's firstborn, Esau did not. Reuben, Jacob's first son also never succeeded him and was actually replaced by Judah, his fourth born son. Joseph's firstborn, Manasseh followed suit and was surbodinated in pre-eminence to his brother, Ephraim. Much later on in the same family tree, we find a man named Jesse, whose firstborn, Eliab, did not succeed him. His lastborn, David,

---

4   Exodus 20:9-10 (NKJV)
5   Genesis 12:10-13
6   Genesis 26:7
7   Genesis 27:18-19

BIBLICAL FAMILIES

is the one who carried on the family name! David's own firstborn, Amnon, also did not succeed him but, instead, it was Solomon, a much younger son, who succeeded him on the throne.

Even when tracing the ancestry of the Jesus, the bible shows us the unsavory characters in Jesus's bloodline. The list includes (and even highlights) an adulterer who murdered his lover's husband to cover up the misdeed. There are idolaters, liars and a man who committed incest with his daughter-in-law, whom he had thought was a prostitute (which says something about his lack of morals). Another woman in the list is a prostitute. And there is a notoriously wicked king who burned his sons to death as offerings to a pagan idol. It took a rather 'bad blood' crew to produce the Savior of the world. If you know much about your ancestors, it is likely that you know of a few skeletons in your family closet. What's on your tree?

> The enemy has no power over us unless it is given to him

Someone may be asking, "How does the enemy get a foothold in our families?" Once a person becomes a follower of Jesus, can the enemy still harass them? Our answer is that the enemy has no power over us unless it is given to him and, throughout this course, we shall be looking at different ways through which the enemy gains legal access to our families.

But there is hope! We are not doomed to repeat the patterns in our families. God is looking for one person to say, 'Enough is enough' on behalf of that family. Will you stand up and be counted on behalf of your family? Every negative recurring pattern that was established either willingly or unknowingly must be broken by someone who understands it and stands in the gap. It is until you personally stand and deal with your negative patterns that they can be broken. It does not matter what prayers are made on your behalf. Breaking negative patterns requires your personal action and involvement. Someone needs to realize that he or she can be the one to break the cycle and make a difference. Stop fighting with or in your family. Today I challenge you to fight for your family and we will not only become more enriched and fulfilled, but we will also benefit many others, including our own descendants. What's on your tree?

Question For My Journal

What are some negative traits that you can identify in your family of origin?

Verse To Remember

Psalm 133:1: How good and pleasant it is when God's people live together in unity!

Prayer For Today

Lord, I pray that you will help us to no longer fight with or in our family. Instead, show us how to fight for our family. Amen!

SKETCHING YOUR TREE

So far, we have talked about family traits that are passed across generations and seen from the bible how even some of the heroes of faith had family drama because of negative traits passed down through generations.

What do we need to do to dismantle these strongholds that the enemy is using so we can move forward in God's design for us? Every week we shall be talking about practical things we need to do in dismantling the negative patterns that are in our family trees. For today, the first thing to do in breaking and living free from generational issues is to know your enemy. You must know the issues you are dealing with before you confront them. We need to recognize what is happening and make a conscious decision to, with God's help, create a new, positive family heritage. You must take a critical look at your family tree and be cognizant of where you came from.

> ## With God's help, create a new, positive family heritage

So, how do we identify sin patterns in our families? How can we identify generational issues in our lives so that we can be set free from them? It is important for us to open our eyes and consider these things, rather than passively make peace with the status quo and normalize what was never meant to be normal. Allow us to share with you four specific things that can help you identify generational patterns in your family.

1. **Your Own Recollection**

   Is there a problem in your family that stubbornly resists any genuine attempts to bring a change? Nothing seems to work long-term, including prayer, counseling, medical intervention, and even intensive discipleship. You may get a bit of a reprieve from it sometimes, but it is a problem that always plagues your family. Think about any experiences you have like that, including even things you see as normal. How were your relationships as a family (warm, indifferent, angry)? What role did each child play (for example, favorite, dark sheep, neglected middle child, third parent)? What challenges did the different family members face? What were the family's defining moments? Who is close to whom in the family and who is awkward with whom?

2. **Observation and Research**

   Different members of your family will have a different perspective of the family from you, especially as you cross generations. If we are close to our relatives, it can be helpful to sit down and talk with parents, aunts and uncles, grandparents, great-grandparents, and so on to learn a little bit about our family. Sometimes we can see certain issues like addictions or other negative traits start to surface. There may be recurrent health issues or patterns like early death, unwed mothers, or sons who did not amount to much. As we understand what has gone on in our families, we begin to understand more about ourselves. Then we want to find the source. When did these issues start to happen? Why did they happen? We need to learn as much as we can through observation and research.

SKETCHING YOUR TREE

3. Pray For Discernment

Some patterns will remain hidden unless God reveals them. So engage in a time of prayer as a Simama group. Pick one day each week that you can pray and fast for your family or families. Ask God to reveal issues and their roots to you and to your family members.

4. Draw Your Family Tree

This week, draw a family tree going back at least three generations and find out what you can about each member of that tree. If you are doing the course with family members, you can each fill out what you know and then plan to connect with older generation members to fill in the blanks and also share what they know about each family member. You will find a sample family tree in the appendixes.

As you draw the tree, keep your senses alert. What particular issues do you see recurring? What are some of the open and hidden rules, roles and rituals in the family? What are the issues no one wants to talk about? Each week as we do this course, add more information on your tree about the different family members. Even if you lack the personal desire to overcome serious problems for your own sake, do it for your family. Think generationally about how your behavior will benefit or harm your descendants. What will be on your tree long after you are gone?

Question For My Journal

Draw your family tree to your best recollection, going back for at least three generations (See Appendix 1 for an example of how to do so). What do you know about each person? Do you see any patterns?

Verse To Remember

Deuteronomy 29:29: *The secret things belong to the LORD our God, but the things revealed belong to us and to our children forever, that we may follow all the words of this law.*

Prayer For Today

Thank you Lord that you bestowed such honor in me by creating me as your masterpiece! Help me Lord, live up to this truth and never allow others to tear me down. In Jesus' name. Amen!

FAMILY DESTINY

What type of legacy would you like to pass on to the next generation? As we are learning this week, we all have the responsibility to ensure that the generation that comes after us will love and serve God even better than our own generation. We must, as far as it is possible, root out the negative traits that exist in our families so that they are not passed on to the next generation.

There is a great story that demostrates the power of family traits, both positive or negative.[8] In 1900, American educator and pastor A. E. Winship studied the descendants of Jonathan Edwards, one of America's most renowned preachers and theologians, almost 150 years after his death. Edwards was born in Connecticut in 1703. He attended Yale University at the age of 13 and later went on to become the president of a school now known as Princeton University. He and his wife, Sarah had 11 children, for whom he always tried to make time. Here is what was discovered about the approximately 1,400 descendants of Jonathan and Sarah Edwards:

> **Root out the negative traits that exist in our families**

- 13 were college presidents.
- 65 were college professors.
- 100 were clergymen, missionaries or theology professors.
- 100 were attorneys.
- 32 were state judges.
- 85 were authors of classic books.
- 66 were physicians.
- 75 were army or navy officers.
- 80 held political offices, including three state governors.
- 3 were state senators.
- 2 were mayors.
- 1 became vice president of the United States. There were practically no lawbreakers!

There was another man who lived in New York around the same time as Jonathan Edwards by the name of Max Jukes. The Jukes family originally was studied by sociologist Richard L. Dugdale and described in a book he published in 1877. Dugdale decided to do his research after the family trees of 42 different men in the New York prison system were traced back to this man named Jukes. In his lifetime, Jukes was considered lazy and godless, with a reputation as the town troublemaker. He was also an alcoholic and viewed as having low moral character. To make matters worse, he married a woman who was much like himself, and together they had eight children. Here is what the report revealed about the approximately 1,200 descendants of this couple:

---

8   Disclaimer – the exact historical facts behind this case study are difficult to determine, but the point and value of the story remains nonetheless!

FAMILY DESTINY

- 280 were homeless.
- 128 were prostitutes.
- 440 engaged in drug or alcohol abuse.
- 140 were criminals who spent time in prison, including seven for murder.
- 300 died prematurely.
- 67 contracted syphilis.

The report also found that the State of New York had spent $ 1.3 million—a shockingly high number at the time—to care for this line of descendants, and not one had made a significant contribution to society.

What a startling difference! The two families show us how family traits, both negative and positive, can be passed down generations. Like Jonathan Edwards, we too can bring blessings and opportunities for generations yet to be born!

Question For My Journal

List down three things or patterns of behavior in your life or in your family that you would like God to free you from. We shall trust God with you that by the end of this course, God will have come through in unbelievable ways!

Verse To Remember

Romans 5:7-8: Very rarely will anyone die for a righteous man though for a good an someone might possibly dare to die. But God demonstrates his own love for us in this: While we were still sinners Christ died for us.

Prayer For Today

Forgive me Lord for hurting (list all who come to mind). Help me make amends with them as you continue to work on me. In Jesus' name. Amen!

STARTING OVER

The focus this week has been on showing that each of our families has positive and negative traits that affect us and that are passed on from generation to generation. Through the rest of the course, we will be identifying some of the reasons for these traits and giving you the tools to fight for victory for yourself and for your family.

The question that we asked before will have come up for some of you: If Jesus has already won the victory, why then do we have to fight? There is a great story we know that may help answer this question.

The Second World War pitted the Allied forces, led by the UK, USA and Russia against the Axis of Germany, Japan and Italy. This war technically came to an end on June 6th, 1944, officially known as D-Day. On this day, in what was known as 'Operation Overlord', some 1,000 ships—the largest armada ever to set sail—carried some 200,000 soldiers across the English Channel to the coast of Normandy in France where they made a surprise attack on the German position there.

> ## We are going to war for our families

With the victory won that day, the war was technically over as there was no way the German army was going to recover. That is why many celebrate D-Day as the end of the war.

However, despite having been struck a mortal blow and knowing that it was all over for them, many of the scattered German troops continued to fight. For this reason, the Allied armies on the ground continued to enforce the victory that was already sure. It was not until May 8th, 1945, almost a full year later, that the Axis formally surrendered. During that year, despite being on the winning side, Allied soldiers were still dodging bullets and working hard to avoid ambushes. They were still bleeding and wounded and many still lost their lives in the fight. Even though the war was won, there were some harrowing days of fighting after D-Day!

Today we are challenging you to fight for your sons and daughters, grandsons and daughters. We are going to war for our families. Remember, we are not fighting to win; that work was already done by Jesus when he died for our sins at calvary and triumphantly rose again. The battle has already been won! Our work is to enforce the victory that Christ has already given us.

This perspective is important as we go through the *Simama* experience because the enemy who has been harassing your family will not give up without a fight! As you go through the *Simama* experience, you may find yourself becoming discouraged or wanting to give up. All kinds of distractions may come up to keep you from completing the experience or taking your family through it. So, like any soldier on the battlefront, we must be prepared! How then should we prepare?

Prayer: As mentioned before, we would like to encourage you to commit to pray and fast one day each week for your family. Basically, this means you eat only one meal a day (for example, supper) and then use the other meal-times to spend some time in prayer, for example, take a prayer walk during your lunch hour on that day. This day of prayer and fasting could be on the same day that you meet as a class.

STARTING OVER

Jesus demonstrated the importance of this when he was asked why his disciples were not able to cast out a demon from a young boy who was being oppressed by the enemy. His answer? *'This kind does not go out except by prayer and fasting.'*[9]

In addition, we recommend that you set aside at least half an hour each day to do your daily reading and to pray through what you have read. Before you start reading each day, take the first 10 minutes to worship God. Select an adoration song that you can play and sing along to. Use it to prepare your heart to hear what God will say. Then, ask God to open your spiritual eyes and ears so that you will understand what God is saying to you and to your family through the reading. After you're done reading, write down your answer to the question asked each day in your prayer journal. Then spend a few minutes in conclusion, thanking God for what He has said and praying for your family.

Finally, starting from week Three, at the end of each week's chapter, you will find a 'Freedom Prayer'. Please pray this prayer aloud for yourself as a way of formally closing the doors that the enemy might have used to afflict you and your family. In the appendices, you will also find the *'Steps To Freedom'* prayers that we would encourage you to pray out aloud in a time of prayer once you have completed the course.

Self-care: With prayer, we take care of our spiritual states, but we also must care for our minds and bodies during the extent of this course. This course will be emotionally engaging. We will be exploring areas in your life that might cause you great discomfort. The important conversations you will be having and the discoveries and prayers you will be making, will require you to be at your best. How do we care for our minds and bodies? We do it through proper nutrition and exercise!

Everyone should pay attention to proper nutrition, regardless of their weight, body shape or age. Healthy nutrition will ensure your mind and body are at their best during this season. Nutrition is not the same with dieting. The problem with diets is that once you resume your regular eating habits, as long as they were unhealthy, the weight comes back, which can be quite discouraging. Proper nutrition is having a healthy eating lifestyle.

Here are a few unhealthy eating attitudes and habits. Put a tick on all or any that you have had in the past or have now:

- I can eat anything; I am still young and have a long way to go before lifestyle diseases are an issue.

- I am too thin anyway and I am trying to put on weight.

- I do not pay attention to what I eat as I am currently okya with my weight. My weight does not increase or decrease much.

- I have given up on dieting. Nothing I do seems to make a difference to my weight. I have been overweight since childhood.

- Diabetes and hypertension run in my family and there is nothing I can do about it.

---

9   Matthew 17:21 (NKJV)

- It is socially acceptable for a person of my age/stature/social position to carry the weight I do. It is a sign of prosperity and wellbeing.

- Healthy food is too expensive.

The benefits of healthy eating are many and include the following:

1. You set yourself up for a long and vibrant life, full of accomplishments, radiance, productivity and sense of wellbeing the abundant life.

2. You feel strong and clearminded enough to meet challenges and make decisions.

3. You collaborate with God, who desires you to be healthy.

(See Appendix 2 for examples of healthy eating).

Apart from eating right, proper exercise will also be extremely helpful! There are many reading this who already exercise regularly, but there are also many who do not. We can assure you that regular exercise will greatly increase your ability to get the most out of this course.

The benefits of exercise include the following:

1. It releases brain chemicals that make us feel good. It is amazing how a bad situation all over sudden feels manageable after a workout!

2. It reduces or eliminates the chemicals in the immune system that make us feel poorly. This helps us feel better.

3. It helps us 'decompress' our worries. As the body feels energized, the mind feels 'lighter' and problems are put into perspective. If you easily get anxious, tense or are an 'intense personality', working out is one way of getting rid of tension. Working out with others would especially be useful for a good laugh - a therapy to the soul!

4. It improves your memory and brain function, allowing you to be at your best in the different conversations you will have.

5. It reduces feelings of anxiety and depression and improves your quality of sleep.

6. It is a more healthy way of coping with life's challenges than drinking, eating, overworking, obsessing or using other addictive habits to soothe ourselves.

Therefore, we encourage you to make exercise a part of your routine and at least work out (for example, walk, jog, jump rope, swim, do an aerobic workout, lift weights, etc.) for at least thirty minutes three times a week. Believe me, the benefits will far outweigh the cost!

STARTING OVER

Activities

Plan to do the following activities during your next meeting with your Simama Group.

a. Share how your week has been and also what your expectations or fears are regarding this course.

b. Discuss what each person will do for exercise over the next 10 weeks so that you can hold each other accountable.

c. Agree on how you will ensure you are eating healthily over the next 10 weeks. Plan to have a meal together with only healthy foods served!

d. Go over the group promises and the personal commitment in the introductory sections of this book with your prayer partner and agree on how to keep each other accountable to fulfilling them.

Question For My Journal

Which of the three, eating right, exercising or being a safe person is the most difficult thing for you to do consistently? What will you do to succeed in your area of difficulty?

Verse To Remember

I Corinthians 9:24: Do you not know that in a race all the runners run, but only one gets the prize? Run in such a way as to get the prize.

Freedom Prayer

Dear heavenly Father, you have said that pride goes before destruction, and an arrogant spirit before stumbling. I confess that I have been thinking mainly of myself and not of others. I have sinned by believing that I could be happy and successful on my own. I confess that I have placed my will before Yours and I have centered my life around myself instead of You. As a result, I have given ground to the devil in my life.

I repent of my pride and foolishness and pray that all the ground gained by the enemy in my life because of it would be cancelled. I choose to rely on the Holy Spirit's power and guidance so that I will do nothing from selfish ambition or vain conceit. With humility of mind, I will regard others as more important than myself, and I choose to make You, Lord, the most important of all in my life.

Please show me this week all the specific ways in which I have lived my life in pride. Enable me, through love, to serve others and, in honor, to prefer others. Give me the grace to take responsibility for this life you have given me—through healthy eating and exercise. I ask all this in the gentle and humble name of Jesus, my Lord. Amen.

WEEK
– TWO –
MODERN FAMILIES

GOD'S 'IDEAL'

Growing up, I (Muriithi) had absolutely no doubt that I would grow up to become a happy man, married to a woman who would count herself very lucky to get me! We would have three or four wonderful, well-behaved children, a big dog and live happily ever in a large house in an upscale leafy suburb of our city. I maintained this dream until I was rudely awakened quite early in our marriage. By then, to my dismay, my wife had not only discovered all my character flaws (many of which I had no idea I was carrying), but it had also become quite clear to me, upon honest reflection, that my flaws were creating a very miserable spouse who was far from living happily ever after!

Well before you laugh at me to hard at me, let me pause and ask you this question: What is your ideal family? When I asked my friend this question, he shared with me something pretty similar to what I thought he would, but also had an addition. He told me that he would like to marry a woman who would be the mother of his children, but he was also quite happy to continue with the current relationship he was in! When I asked him why he would not just marry the current girl he was seeing, he said that if he did that, then, she would become boring and a nag like all wives!

What is your ideal family?

A lady friend answered by saying that most of her pals were not even contemplating marriage. Majority of them were looking to get to the age when they were materially comfortable enough to get a child whom they were happy to raise as singles. According to her, marriage was simply a disaster and it was time to look around for other options. To prove her point, she recounted tales of people she knew who, on the outside, looked happily married but were not. In one particular instance, the man was married with kids but on the side had another man as a lover.

Today it is not as straightforward as it was in the past to come to an agreement on what the ideal family should look like. Should it comprise of a man and a woman? Should it be a married couple or does any couple in a committed relationship count? And isn't single parenting or co-parenting a lot more realistic and less complicated?

With your car or a computer, whenever there is doubt about how it is operating, a good place to consult for wisdom is the owner's manual. It is the same with the family. The best place to begin is to consult the Owner's manual to help us understand how families were created to function. This week, we want to examine some of the challenges our families face and how we can begin to celebrate the good things in our families while also becoming aware of the unhealthy traits that our families carry. The first book of the bible tells the origin story of the first family.

The LORD God took the man and put him in the garden of Eden to work it and take care of it. The LORD God said, "It is not good for the man to be alone. I will make a helper suitable for him." Now the LORD God had formed out of the ground all the wild animals and all the birds in the sky. He brought them to the man to see what he would name them; and whatever the man called each living creature, that was its name. So the man gave names to all the livestock, the birds in the sky and all the wild animals.

But for Adam no suitable helper was found. So the LORD God caused the man to fall into a deep sleep; and while he was sleeping, he took one of the man's ribs and then closed up the place with flesh. Then the

LORD God made a woman from the rib he had taken out of the man, and he brought her to the man. The man said, "This is now bone of my bones and flesh of my flesh; she shall be called 'woman,' for she was taken out of man."[10]

Despite Adam being in idyllic conditions, he still had needs that neither the animals nor God could fulfill. God's solution was to create Eve. In the previous chapter, there is a powerful reason given for the creation of the first couple...

So God created mankind in his own image, in the image of God he created them; male and female he created them. God blessed them and said to them, "Be fruitful and increase in number; fill the earth and subdue it. Rule over the fish in the sea and the birds in the sky and over every living creature that moves on the ground."[11]

We learn from this passage that:

- **Marriage is God's Idea:** This was not an idea that Adam came up with. God, the Creator, is the one who actually spotted the need that Adam had. There is no indication at all that Adam was aware of his predicament, let alone a solution for it! God saw the need, that humans were not created to exist in isolation, and God created another human being of the opposite gender to fill that need.

- **Gender is God's Idea:** The image of God comprises of *both* male and female. Neither gender by itself comprises God's image; and there is a differentiation between them each plays an important role. Together, they would be co-image bearers of God. Maleness and femaleness together form the complete image of God. You cannot have one without the other; a colony of men, for example, would not in itself represent the full image of God (Adam tried it!), and neither, for that matter, would a company of women! Modern society is moving towards ascribing the matter of gender to choice, but here we clearly see that gender is an essential and integral part of how God created us.

- **Purpose is God's Idea**: God created men and women to together give stewardship over creation. God's intention for humanity was to care for His creation. The word 'rule' expresses the role of a caretaker or manager one to whom God was delegating full authority over the rest of creation. You were created for purpose, and your purpose predates you. The apostle Paul wrote in his letter to the Ephesians, *'For we are God's handiwork, created in Christ Jesus to do good works, which God prepared in advance for us to do.'* Even before you were conceived, God had already prepared specific 'good works' for you to do on His behalf on planet Earth. That is your purpose; the thing that you were uniquely created to do.

The complementarity of men and women goes beyond marriage and into society. After all, if it was God's will that every human being should be married, then Jesus would have been married! I believe the greater point of this passage is that as men and women, we need each other. There is a unique role that men play in society that cannot and should not be replaced, and this goes beyond simply fathering children. There is a unique role that women play in society that cannot and should not be replaced, and this goes beyond simply nurturing children. We need to exist together in community as men and women in

10   Genesis 2:15-23
11   Genesis 1:27-28

GOD'S 'IDEAL'

order to faithfully express our purpose, which has to do with giving care to the rest of God's creation as His appointed stewards. This is where family comes in. As we take a look through scripture, we find that the family exists to:

- **Foster Companionship.** None of the animals and not even God, could fulfil the deep need for companionship Adam had. That's why Adam's spontaneous reaction on seeing Eve was, '*This is now bone of my bones and flesh of my flesh!*'[12] He instinctively realized that he belonged to her and she belonged to him, and in a very deep way. Family was created to provide a place of belonging. Each of us belongs to our family (both nuclear and extended family) in a way that is unique from any other relationship.

- **Complement Each Other.** Eve was referred to as Adam's '*suitable helper.*'[13] This does not refer to a subordinate role! The word, 'helper', is the same word that Jesus used for the role that God's Holy Spirit plays in our lives.[14] Family is meant to be a place where each person is important, and has a useful role that blesses and helps everyone else, as they too receive blessings and help from the rest of the family.

- **Bring Up Children.** The command to Adam and Eve was to '*be fruitful and increase in number; fill the earth and subdue it.*' Family was created to be a nurturing place where children would be born and brought up in God's ways to become everything that God created them to be.[15] Through family, children should experience God's love through their parents, grandparents, siblings, uncles, aunties, cousins and so on and, in the process, learn to love other people.

- **Reveal God's Character.** The love between a husband and wife was meant to provide a glimpse into God's passionate devotion to His people.[16] In other words, people are meant to look at your marriage or your family and come away saying, 'just from experiencing those people, I now clearly have a picture for how God loves us!'

- **Bless The World!** The role of the first family was to multiply and rule the earth. Ultimately, the role of every family is to help its members fulfil their God-given purpose of being a blessing to the rest of society. As families, we are partakers of God's blessing to Abraham, '*All the families on earth will be blessed through you.*'[17]

Family is God's beautiful idea and is created to provide belonging, service to each other, nurture, a model of God's love and character and, ultimately, propel each person to their purpose!

---

12 Genesis 2:23
13 Genesis 2:20
14 John 15:26 '*But when the Helper comes, whom I shall send to you from the Father —the Spirit of truth who goes out from the Father—he will testify about me.*' (NKJV). This word can also be translated as Advocate, Comforter or Counselor.
15 Malachi 2:15: *Has not the one God made you? You belong to him in body and spirit. And what does the one God seek? Godly offspring.* Luke 2:52: '*And Jesus grew in wisdom and stature, and in favor with God and man.*'
16 Ephesians 5:32. After a discussion on how husbands and wives need to relate to each other, the writer concludes, '*This is a profound mystery—but I am talking about Christ and the church.*'
17 Genesis 12:3 (NLT)

Question For My Journal

What have you learnt about family today?

Verses To Remember

Malachi 2:15. Has not the one God made you? You belong to him in body and spirit. And what does the one God seek? Godly offspring.

Prayer For Today

Lord, I thank you that you created marriage and family. Help me, Lord to understand what it means to trust you to build my life and family. Amen.

THE SHIFTING TIDES OF THE AFRICAN FAMILY

Yesterday, we looked at God's ideal for the family. But alas, this ideal picture lasted only a short time! A few chapters later (Genesis 3), trouble came knocking on the door of this family and the idyllic existence came to an abrupt end. It began the day Adam and Eve declared their independence from God, opting instead to do things their way. Indeed, on that day, all hell literally broke loose, and this loving couple all of a sudden found themselves blam`ing and hurting each other. Sadly, it did not end with the parents. The children who later arrived on the scene took the conflict, treachery and domination for power even a notch higher when the older brother, Cain, murdered the younger one, Abel. The rest of the bible is the unedited story of human families broken by insecurity, pain, jealousy, betrayal and all manner of strife.

Families were not isolated

Families in modern times have not been spared either from drama. Since the Adamses, the forces at work to destroy families though essentially the same, have grown in complexity. Today, we want to take a journey back to the last approximately 100 years (that is, three or four generations) and chronicle some of the changes that have happened in families across Africa and in many other parts of the world.

PRE-COLONIAL AFRICA

About 100 years ago, the only model of family in Africa was the traditional one. With some generalizations, the traditional African family was characterized by:

1. **Strong Family Bonds.** Most African cultures were polygamous and homesteads were made up of a man, his wives and children. However, social interactions with the larger extended family including grandparents, aunties, uncles, cousins, nephews and nieces were prevalent. Many African cultures did not have unique words for uncle and aunty as they used the same words for them as they did parents. Cousins were likewise referred to as siblings. Functions like cultivating land, initiation ceremonies, marriage ceremonies and some religious activities involved the participation of the entire extended family. Because of these interactions, families were not isolated and received adequate support in times of need.

2. **Well-defined Marital Roles.** Roles between men and women in marriage were clearly defined. The husband was typically the undisputed leader at home and the protector of the family and tribe during war. A man was also the provider. He owned all the land and/or livestock, although the wives may have done the cultivating. The man was expected to display wisdom, kindness and consideration to his family. He was not to speak to them harshly or be cruel; he would be fined by the clan if he did, or be passed over when leaders were elected at the tribal level. The wives managed their households and it was frowned upon if a woman did not have adequate supplies for herself and her children.

3. **Strong Value System.** Traditional cultures had very strong value systems that safeguarded the wellbeing of the tribe, as well as individual members. Children were taught certain values at different stages in their lives and had distinct rites of passage to affirm their transition from one stage of life to another. There were penalties for breaking the values. Conformity to rules and

regulations was reinforced by a host of taboos. If one broke a taboo, he had to make restitution (for example, offer sacrifices) to make up for their offending actions.

4. **Spiritual Awareness.** African communities were very spiritual. They understood that material blessings came from God, often mediated through the ancestors. So, when it did not rain or when the crops failed, they attributed it to an offence against God for which an appeasement would be sought.

COLONIAL AND POST-COLONIAL CHANGES

A wave of change came that would forever revolutionize the African family; the influence of the western culture as exported by the late 19th century and early 20th century explorers and missionaries. The westerners introduced (often forcibly) European economy, education system, political system and practice of Christianity.18 The first generation that encountered missionaries had to adjust to these influences. Beginning with children, traditional informal education was substituted for the formal European one. Families also had to shift from subsistence and barter economy to a cash economy which necessitated the migration of parts of or entire families to urban centers in search of employment.

As it became normal for educated Africans to migrate to town centers from rural villages, huge shifts happened to the culture as a consequence.

1. **Diminished Extended Family Support.** The life of educated Africans in urban centers was so radically different from that in the rural areas that the social training received in the village was not always applicable. Urban families faced considerable pressure without much wisdom of how to conduct themselves. This strain affected the marital relationships and ultimately the children of that first generation. Families became nucleated with time as the parents that left the proximity of the extended family had to fend for themselves and their children. Some nuclear families were split, with fathers working in urban centers and their wives raising children in rural areas. Some men sought a second wife in the urban centers to the neglect of the first wife.

2. **Disintegration of Social Mores.** Migrating into urban centers freed one from the social mores that restrained behavior. In the absence of these mores which spelt out the roles of men and women, the place of elders, and the things that were encouraged to build up community as opposed to those that were proscribed or taboo, many were adrift, not knowing how to bring up children in a rapidly changing culture. The result was addictions, sexual experimentation without the consequences, and many other negative cultural trends in the absesnce of general disintegration of agreed definitions of morality.

3. **Blurring of Roles in Marriage.** In an agrarian setting, men, being physically stronger, were the protectors, providers and leaders in the home whereas women played a more nurturing role. In a cash economy however, both men and women often earned money in jobs outside the home

---

18   An fact unknown to many is that Christianity existed and thrived in Africa long before it was established in Europe. The history of Christianity in Africa begins right from the book of Acts when the church was founded! Read Mark 15:21, Acts 2:7-12 and Acts 8:26-28 with the knowledge that Cyrene, Egypt and Ethiopia are names of kingdoms that existed on the African continent. By the 4th Century AD, there were at least two African kingdoms in which Christianity was the official religion (Ethiopia and Aksum). This was centuries before Ireland and England received their first missionaries!

THE SHIFTING TIDES OF THE AFRICAN FAMILY

which meant that traditional roles like provider could no longer be assumed. Many men sought to exert their authority through controlling the resources in the home, sometimes resorting to violence to assert themselves. Many women, in the absence of the social mores that could protect them, found themselves in abusive relationships with no place to go.

4. **Valueless Education.** The inherited and often under-resourced western educational systems often did not teach national community values but focused more on academic achievement. Children grew up in a moral vacuum, the pursuit of academic excellence being the most celebrated goal. Also, as young men and women were no longer trained on manhood and womanhood, people were left to guess what societal roles they should play.

> Children grew up in a moral vacuum

5.**Spiritual Confusion.** The place of African spirituality was left in confusion as people began attending churches and mosques. On one hand, African spirituality was touted as superstitious and backward and therefore dismissed altogether. On the other hand, it was still called upon during important rites of passages such as birth, initiation, marriage and death. This resulted in people attending church as regular goers but, when crises arose, they consulted the local witchdoctor.

6. **Western Christianity.** Those who accepted the Christian message accepted it with the forms practiced by the missionaries. They sang hymns, acquired new names and demonized African culture. This would result in later generations seeing the church as something foreign and irrelevant to the African.

THE MODERN AFRICAN FAMILY

Since most African nations attained independence in the sixties, an entire generation has arisen in African urban centers that has no recollection of African traditional life or the struggle for independence and have very loose attachments, if any, to life in the rural areas. Characteristics of this generation include the following:

1. **Media Influence.** They are greatly influenced by western media. Societal norms are generally set by what they consume in the media which includes T.V., podcasts, social media and the internet in general. More and more, modern families take their cues from what media espouses as right or wrong. The result has been an ongoing deterioration of moral values. The younger generation is increasingly open to 'alternative sexual lifestyles' being propagated by Western media.

2. **Materialism and Self-Centeredness.** People are less spiritual and more materialistic, pursuing wealth as the ultimate goal. For those who do get married, the pursuit of personal growth and happiness marks many marriages with each partner unreservedly pursuing their career at the expense of the marriage. It is not uncommon to find spouses working apart for many years in different countries! Many live unrestrained lifestyles, having multiple sexual partners, running up debts, and having no sense of purpose except pleasure.

THE SHIFTING TIDES OF THE AFRICAN FAMILY

3. **Blurred Roles.** As part of a global trend, gender roles seem to have reversed with women being more assertive and men being more passive. An encouraging trend is the empowerment of women to access equal opportunities in education since women were considered inferior in many cultures. But the opposite trend that has taken place is the passivity of men as witnessed by the increasing numbers of irresponsible and self-absorbed young men, living only for themselves. The girl child has in many cases been left with no one to marry and raise the next generation with!

4. **Marital Stress.** People have little societal support for their marriages resulting in more marital stress and increasing divorce rates. The younger generation is increasingly wary of marriage and more prone to sexual experimentation before and outside of marriage.

5. **Unparented Children.** In the absence of involved parents or extended family members, children receive little guidance on their identity and what is acceptable social behavior. Rebellion, unruliness, early sexual experimentation and abuse of drugs and alcohol are pervasive.

Clearly, the African family, just like families in many other parts of the world, is in a season of crisis! Unanchored from tradition and yet not truly anchored to any genuine alternative, we are fast heading in the way of selfishness and moral decadence that will wipe us out faster than civil wars ever could! While the solution is not to retreat or revert to traditional marriage roles, the complete lack of roles in modern egalitarian marriages is not proving an effective solution to building effective and satisfying families and societies.

Question For My Journal

Draw a family tree and, alongside each generation, write the characteristics that are true as described in the preceding paragraphs. (See Appendix 1 for an example of a family tree).

Verse To Remember

Matthew 7:24-27 "Therefore everyone who hears these words of mine and puts them into practice is like a wise man who built his house on the rock. The rain came down, the streams rose, and the winds blew and beat against that house; yet it did not fall, because it had its foundation on the rock. But everyone who hears these words of mine and does not put them into practice is like a foolish man who built his house on sand. The rain came down, the streams rose, and the winds blew and beat against that house, and it fell with a great crash."

Prayer For Today

Lord, I recognize that through the generations my family has been hit by the storms of life and, because of this, we have experienced many troubles. Build my faith, Lord, so that I can trust your leading for, in this way, my life will be founded on You, the Solid Rock. Amen.

ANCHORING THE FAMILY IN SHIFTING TIDES

If families are to survive the storms of life or the winds of change that inevitably come in each generation, then we will have to look for truth to live by that is able to withstand these changes. This truth should anchor a family firmly enough so that, with each succeeding generation, the family becomes stronger as opposed to being left weaker. Our focus today will therefore be on the role of men and women in marriage. We firmly believe that getting a proper perspective on this is key in determining whether or not a family thrives. It is one of those pivots that when not balanced, brings much suffering on the family as a whole.

A look to nature and at the biological differences between men and women provides us helpful indicators of how God created us to live. For example, by the age of eighteen, boys have about 50% more muscle mass than girls, particularly in their upper body. Males, on average, have denser, stronger bones, tendons and ligaments which allow for heavier work. Males of most species studied, including humans, appear to be more aggressive, dominant, assertive, hierarchical in their relationships, and seekers of control. Whereas female aggression is usually in response to impending danger or harm to offspring, females generally tend to be highly intuitive, conciliatory in their relationships, more relational and nurturing, finding their fulfillment in caring for others and meeting their needs.

Husbands are called to be protectors

The bible also clearly affirms the distinct roles of men and women. On Day One, we saw that a man was not created to look after the earth alone but that he needed a helper. In this relationship, God envisioned a situation where a man and his wife would build a family together that would care for the planet and be able to withstand the enemy's onslaught. In this relationship, they would have distinct roles that they would use to support and encourage each other as together, they provide care, nurture and protection to their children and society in general. It would be a partnership where both partners would build the family with the ultimate goal of extending God's rule here on earth.

God created men and women as equals, since they are created in His image. When He says that the woman is a 'helper', this is an exalted role as it is the same word that God uses when describing the role of the Holy Spirit. But who is the Holy Spirit? The Holy Spirit is actually God! God exists in three distinct forms Father, Son, and Holy Spirit and yet, He is one! By God calling the woman the man's 'helper', it tells us that we should take our cues about gender roles in marriage, not from culture which shifts with changing tides but from God Himself.

As we read through the bible, we see several themes of godly masculinity. When it comes to the home, husbands are called to be **protectors** - we often see men being called upon as warriors to defend their families and nation. For example, if you are lying in bed with your wife, and you hear the sound of a window being opened in your kitchen at 3 a.m., would you shake her awake and say, 'The last time this occurred, I was the one who investigated to see if someone was breaking into our house. Now it's your turn, sweetheart?' No![19] But, being a protector is more than just ensuring physical safety. King Solomon talked about the role of a father as being one who

---

19   Illustration borrowed from John Piper and Wayne Grudem ed, 'Recovering Biblical Manhood and Womanhood'

ANCHORING THE FAMILY IN SHIFTING TIDES

protects his children by passing on godly wisdom that would help them build godly character and reject the temptations of the world.[20] Husbands also protect their homes by keeping their marriage pure. They protect their wife and children from the devastating cost of sexual affairs.[21]

In the home, husbands are also called to be **priests**. Right from the garden of Eden, God held Adam, and not Eve, accountable for the spiritual wellbeing of the home and, in the New Testament, men are admonished to present their wives to God without blemish but in holy and blameless states.[22] Another practical example of this is a man called Job who, after his children had had a party, would offer sacrifices for each of them, just in case they had sinned and cursed God in their hearts.[23] It is sad that, in many homes, the wives are the ones that are the spiritual leaders, leading prayer and teaching their children about God, simply because men have refused to take their rightful role!

> Husbands are called to be servant leaders

Husbands are also called to be **providers**. The apostle Paul said to one of his mentees, '*But if anyone does not provide for his own, and especially for those of his household, he has denied the faith and is worse than an unbeliever.*[24] Tough words, right? The reality is that when a man does not work and provide for his family, he feels a sense of shame. In a healthy marriage, there is no competition between men and women, even on those occasions when the woman earns more than the man, or the man may be out of work. However, a biblical man will always seek to assume responsibility for his family by ensuring that his wife never carries the load by herself. Even in those seasons when he is not able to carry a financial load, rather than being self absorbed, he ensures he is providing for the emotional and spiritual needs in the home, supporting his wife's business and training his children to become responsible adults who can successfully navigate the challenges of adulthood.

Lastly, when it comes to the home, husbands are called to be **servant leaders**. While the apostle Paul tells us that '*the husband is the head of the wife,*'[25] he quickly disabuses us of any notions of a leadership based on selfish male dominance by adding, '*as Christ also is the head of the church*'. He goes on to say that husbands should love their wives '*just as Christ also loved the church and gave Himself up for her.*'[26] Remember, Christ died for the church! This is a radically different type of leadership. The husband is called to take responsibility for his wife and children and to put their needs ahead of his own. He is to ensure that he works with his wife to call out the best in their children. Fathers have a huge role to play in helping children have positive values and follow meaningful pursuits. He is to demonstrate selfless, sacrificial love the type of love we see in God toward his children.

How about women? The bible also has much to say about godly femininity. Unlike in the surrounding cultures in which women had no voice, the bible teaches that women are an essential part of God's image. Apart from roles in the home, women played important and assorted roles such as

---

20   Proverbs 4:10-15
21   Proverbs 5:15-21
22   Ephesians 5:26-27
23   Job 1: 4-5
24   I Timothy 5:8
25   Ephesians 5:23
26   Ephesians 5:25

ANCHORING THE FAMILY IN SHIFTING TIDES

national leaders (Judges 4 & 5, Esther 9:29-31), prophets (Exodus 15, II Chronicles 34:22-28, Isaiah 8:3), rebuilders of towns (I Chronicles 7:24, Nehemiah 3:12), manual laborers (Ruth 2:7), assassins of national enemies (Judges 4:17-22, 9:53), temple musicians (Psalm 68:25), entreprenuers (Proverbs 31:10-31), wise counselors (II Samuel 20:14-24), prayer warriors (Luke 2:37-38, Acts 1:14), financiers of Jesus's ministry (Luke 8:1-3), coworkers of the apostle Paul (Philippians 4:2-3), teachers and apostles in the early church (Acts 18:26, Romans 16:7), hosts or leaders of house churches (Acts 16:40, Colossians 4:15) and so on.

Wives play a unique role as empowerers

Clearly, even though men and women are created different, they are equally gifted. Remember, both genders are necessary to complete the image of God! And when it comes to the workplace, it is clear that there are just as gifted women leaders, administrators, financiers, doctors, marketers, scientists, teachers, etc., as there are men. Societies that empower women to equally contribute their skills and perspectives will always have advantages over those that do not. The question thus begs, 'How within the family should husbands and wives relate to one another?' To answer this question, we must look again to the Godhead for our answers.

When it comes to their role in the family, wives play a unique role as **empowerers**. God said He would make a helper for Adam. This is the same word used to describe the Holy Spirit by Jesus. When we read the gospels, we see that Jesus had a very close relationship with the Holy Spirit. The Holy Spirit empowered Jesus to fulfil His earthly mission.[27] As a wife, you have unique gifts that you contribute to the home as you come alongside your husband and empower him to lead your family to its God-given vision. When you fully engage in your empowering role, there is a supernatural ability and favor that is released on your marriage and family. That's why King Solomon says, *'He who finds a wife finds what is good and receives favor from the LORD.'*[28]

In the home, wives are also called to be **nurturers**. In the creation narrative, we learn that *'Adam named his wife Eve, because she would become the mother of all the living.'*[29] Eve means 'living' and the woman is uniquely shaped to receive the male seed into her womb and to nurture the resulting human being to life. Women have an amazing body chemistry, regulated by hormones, which gives them the potential to carry new life. Hormones released in a new mother's brain cause her to want to protect and care for her child. This is what is known as the 'maternal instinct'. Incidentally, these hormones are usually released whether the woman gave birth to the child or adopted them. It is common to hear women admiring an infant and saying, 'Awww, so sweet!' When the wife plays her role as a nurturer, the home is a warm and lifegiving space, full of healthy relationships, where everyone feels cared for.

In the context of the home, wives are called to be **companions**. Despite being in God's presence, having an invigorating and satisfying job and being surrounded by the wonders of creation, something was missing in Adam's life. God's diagnosis was that he was 'alone'.[30] Clearly, no one or nothing else in creation could take away that sense of being alone, except Eve! The reality is that we were all built for companionship and friendship, whether married or single.

---

27 See Luke 4:14, for example. *'Jesus returned to Galilee in the power of the Spirit, and news about him spread through the whole countryside.'*
28 Proverbs 18:22
29 Genesis 3:20
30 Genesis 2:18

Every single man needs friends of both genders, as does every single woman. The context of marriage, however, calls for a particular companionship or friendship with your spouse. While both spouses definitely have a role to play in this, women tend to be more intuitive, relationally aware and in touch with their emotions than men their age. Men tend to catch up somewhat in their late thirties to mid-forties, when they begin to become more aware of their feelings and are able to express them! A wife, therefore, can play a great role in catalyzing friendships with her spouse and children.

> ## Submission is not letting him do all the thinking

Finally, the wives within a marriage are called to be **culture setters**. They set the relational culture of their home whether it is a warm, kind place or a competitive, uncaring space. King Solomon wrote, '*The wise woman builds her house, but with her own hands the foolish one tears hers down.*'[31] He also wrote a whole poem about the 'Proverbs 31 woman' who uses her leadership and entrepreneurial strengths to ensure that her family is cared for. This woman is quite a leader! Using her gifts, she works with diligence to create profits that feed her family and bless the poor. A wise and dignified woman, she is loved by her children and husband. She makes her husband look good! As a result, he praises her and is respected by his fellow men.[32]

One of the ways a wife sets the culture of her home is through her submission to her husband. This is clearly a taboo concept, and many will consider us patriarchal for even thinking it! The apostle Paul taught, '*wives will submit to your husbands as to the Lord.*'[33] To submit means to honor your husband and to treat him with respect as the leader of your family, and also to teach your children to do so. It has to do with letting go of the reins and supporting him as he leads, affirming him, and learning to trust him, faults and all. It means bringing your best to support the vision God has given him for your family. Submission is not letting him do all the thinking or make all the decisions, neither is it being a doormat or pretending that all is well! That clearly is not what a Proverbs 31 woman does! As the husband dies (prefers his wife over himself) and as the wife submits (honors and respects her husband), your marriage becomes a model that teaches your children, as well as a watching world about the self-sacrificing love of God for His people, and the kind of loving submission that we in turn should give to Him.

Now, these roles are not meant to put us into a rigid box! Each spouse plays a role in protecting and nurturing the marriage and family, and these roles can vary depending on season, circumstances (for example, stress, busyness or illness) and the giftings of the couple. However, understanding our God-created strengths and roles goes a long way towards eliminating the frustration, competition, conflict and confusion that has broken many homes. We are called to play our roles, not based on our spouses' response, but based on our own response to God.[34]

---

31 Proverbs 14:1
32 Proverbs 31:10-31
33 Ephesians 5:21
34 For more on this topic, our book '*Ndoa*' has a chapter on self-sacrificing love and submission entitled, 'The "S" Word'.

ANCHORING THE FAMILY IN SHIFTING TIDES

Let me (Carol) end by sharing what I witnessed at home between my mother and father. My parents were among the first in their families to be educated and among the first generation of Africans who moved into the city. Their marriage was formed in a time of great confusion, when the traditional roles of husbands and wives had greatly been disrupted. Of key consideration was the question of authority. How was the husband to continue being the head of the home if his wife could be as educated and potentially earn the same as he could?

> ## "Be all you can be to build the family!"

Many in their generation solved this problem by taking several options. One was by men marrying women of lower educational standards so that the question of earning more would never be an issue. In other families, women were required to stay at home and not to engage in income-generating activities. In others yet, the husbands tightly controlled the family assets without input from their wife.

Given this context, I can only describe what I witnessed at home as exemplary. Somehow my dad was secure enough to encourage my mum to advance in her education to the level she wanted to attain. They also worked out a way of complementing each other in their areas of strength. My dad was quick to confess that, whereas he could easily conceptualize new businesses or projects, my mother was far better at implementing them! They agreed on the projects they wanted to pursue together and because of this, they achieved a lot together. My dad's vulnerability did not in any way diminish his headship. If anything, we held him in high esteem as the visionary of the home. We saw our parents taking turns to pursue their education and supporting and encouraging each other as they both worked to build our family. Their motto was not, 'Be all you can be for yourself' but rather, 'Be all you can be to build the family!'

Sadly, not all their peers had their relationships worked out in this way. The struggle to rule and dominate each other resulted in abusive marriages with one spouse suffering great injustice at the hands of the other. I remember growing up hearing stories of families with violence and brutality; families that fought and quarreled; stories of husbands and wives dominating one another, with the result that one of them was denied the opportunity to advance in their career. There were many stories of families in distress and in difficult situations, and a large part of the struggle was the failure to understand how God structured the husband and wife relationship.

Question For My Journal

Growing up, what kind of relationship did your parents have? How did it affect how you function in relationships?

Verse To Remember

Ephesians 5:21–28. Submit to one another out of reverence for Christ. Wives, submit yourselves to your own husbands as you do to the Lord. For the husband is the head of the wife as Christ is the head of the church, his body, of which he is the Savior. Now as the church submits to Christ, so also wives should submit to their husbands in everything. Husbands, love your wives, just as Christ loved the church and gave himself up for her to make her holy, cleansing her by the washing with water through the word, and to present her to himself as a radiant church, without stain or wrinkle or any other blemish, but holy and blameless. In this same way, husbands ought to love their wives as their own bodies.

Prayer For Today

Lord, I confess that my parents did not always act consistently with your will regarding how they treated each other. I ask that you forgive them (if still alive) and I cancel the ground gained by satan in my family as a result of their actions, conscious or unconscious. Please bring healing and reconciliation to my family. In Jesus' name. Amen.

FAMILY VALUES

Yesterday, we looked at the first pillar a family needs to thrive: We determined this as a godly view of roles within the family. Today, we are going to look at the second pillar which is godly values. Successful families are usually backed by godly family values. Family members who carry out these values as adults go on to become successful because they are living according to their Maker's instructions.

To give a definition, values are the intrinsic beliefs we hold as truths and which largely determine the way we live. If you were asked the values your family holds dear, you are only likely to mention the few that were overtly stated. These would be the ones that your parents clearly stated to you. But it goes deeper than that! So, to get to the values your family really holds, we will give a few moral dilemmas and give you an opportunity to gauge your family on their/your likely response. Please be as real and honest, as no one else gets to see your answers!

THE FAMILY VALUES QUIZ

i. **Finances have really been low and as you cross the street, you notice a well-padded envelope. On opening it, you discover wads of notes, sufficient to get you out of your current debt. Your family would:**

   a. Thank God! He has answered your prayer and would urge you to keep the money.

   b. Look around and, failing to notice anyone who might lay claim on the money, decide that lady luck has smiled on you and so would encourage you to keep the money.

   c. Look around, and failing to notice anyone who might lay claim on the money, encourage you to give it to a charitable organization.

ii. **Your best friend is engaged to get married but you know he has an ongoing relationship with his former girlfriend. You have urged your friend to stop but he is not willing. Your family would:**

   a. Tell you to mind your own business, help out your friend with his wedding plans and hope for the best in their marriage.

   b. Tell you that you probably need to talk to your friend about it but after that is done, there is nothing more you can do.

   c. Urge you to tell his fiancé about the ongoing relationship with the former girlfriend.

iii. **Your workmate is about to be fired under false allegations of misappropriation of company funds. Your family would:**

   a. Empathize with them and hope or pray they get another job.

   b. Tell you that it is best to keep out of the situation lest you jeopardize your own position.

   c. Encourage you to find ways of digging out the truth with the intention of talking to your boss to rectify the situation.

iv. Your friend's boyfriend is pressuring her to have sex with him because they are now engaged. Your family would:

a. Ignore the issue and look the other way as the couple have almost tied the knot.

b. Advise your friend that the relationship can easily break up if she refuses to comply.

c. Advise your friend to say 'no' until the relationship is formalized through marriage.

v. Your sibling is in dire need of money. Your family would:

a. Lecture him/her on the need to be frugal with money but they give it to them anyway.

b. Avoid them, hoping that they get the money from another source.

c. Loan them the money but with deadlines of when they need to pay it back.

vi. You've finally got some extra cash for a badly-needed upgrade of your phone, but you remember that you promised your workmate that you would repay him for money you have owed him for the last three months. Your family would:

a. Tell you to pay your workmate and request you to be patient for another six months or so before buying another phone.

b. Help you plan on how to 'sweet talk' your workmate into giving you another month to clear your debt.

c. Tell you to conveniently 'forget' the promise you made to your workmate with the hope that he will not bring up the matter.

How we manage moral dilemmas often comes from the family values that were shaped as we grew up. However, each of us has a choice to celebrate and hold on to the good values we gained from our parents' family and to put aside and reject the ones that were not healthy, in order that we will not pass them on our our children. For such values we must say, 'it ends with me!'. But what do healthy family values look like? Let us now examine at some values that even though not exhaustive, capture the essence of the second pillar that keeps families strong.

1. **Integrity:** Being trustworthy, objective, fair and sincere. Families of integrity must embrace the following attitudes:

   a. **Humility:** Being open about their strengths and weaknesses, including acknowledging areas where they are susceptible to being tempted.

   b. **Consistency:** Having the same character in the private and public sphere.

   c. **Trustworthiness:** Keeping confidences and being reliable.

   d. **Honesty:** Truth telling, even when it is inconvenient.

FAMILY VALUES

2. **A Teachable Spirit:** A teachable spirit begins as family members come to the humble realization that they do not know it all—intellectually, morally or spiritually. Such members want to grow and are open to learning from anyone and any situation and thus, do not justify mistakes or resent it when errors and shortcomings are revealed. Families with a teachable spirit exhibit the following:

   a. **Value for others:** Taking time to be good listeners with the aim of learning from other people.

   b. **Utilizes discernment:** Taking the time to discern good and evil.

   c. **Appreciate perspective:** Being open to learning from others.

   d. **Hunger to grow:** Reading widely and taking every opportunity to grow, not only in their skills professionally but also on their character.

3. **Self-Discipline:** This is the ability to be a master rather than a slave to one's passions and desires. In order to express this value, family members must be able to do the following:

   a. **Communicate principles.** Understand their convictions and be able to communicate these, not as rules, but as the principles they live by.

   b. **Be responsible:** Be able to carry out their responsibilities as adults, including participating in caring for ageing parents.

   c. **Encourage resilience:** Appreciate the value of difficult experiences, encourage family members to delay gratification and be willing to learn, even from difficult experiences.

4. **Compassion:** Compassion is 'concern that acts.' Compassion is family members having pity towards each other or sympathy for another and doing something about it. Five components are essential for having a compassionate heart:

   a. **Humility:** Understanding that we all have issues and need God's compassion. None of us is close to perfect! It is recognizing that whatever issues anyone else in the family is going through, that could have been me, given a different set of circumstances.

   b. **Patience:** Be willing to allow the other person time to act and be willing to forgive, knowing that we fail one another as families all the time.

   c. **A sense of justice:** This says, 'It is not right that this should be happening. As a family, we've got to do something.'

   d. **Care for the less fortunate:** This is a family where members are passionate to help the poor and those who have less than we do.

5. **Selfless Love:** This is the kind of love that seeks the best in the other person by being:

   a. **Kind:** Family members speaking kindly and courteously to each other.

   b. **Appreciative or thankful:** Our natural tendency is to take family members for granted rather than appreciating them. Thank one another for simple, small and big things, as well as just for being in the family.

c. **Respect and honor:** It is showing honor, consideration or esteem for one another. As with all other values, respect is a habit that is developed in little ways.

d. **Generosity:** Money, time, materials, talents and relationships are resources that families must be willing to share. The natural tendency is to hold onto things tightly, but true joy comes out of sharing.

e. **Reciprocity:** Taking turns or doing for family members what one would like done for them.

Question For My Journal

Go over the list of moral dilemmas again. In light of the values you have just read, which are some of the ones you would want your children to respond to differently from how you or your family would have responded?

Which of the values has struck you the most and why?

Verse To Remember

Psalm 24:3-6 Who may ascend the mountain of the Lord? Who may stand in his holy place? The one who has clean hands and a pure heart, who does not trust in an idol or swear by a false god. They will receive blessing from the Lord and vindication from God their Savior. Such is the generation of those who seek him, who seek your face, God of Jacob.

Prayer

Lord, I thank you for the positive values I received from my family growing up. Please help me to be aware and conscious of the unhealthy values that I may have picked up in the process. Lord, help me to break away from such values so that I will not pass them on to the next generation! Amen.

FAMILY TALK

Communication is the final pillar, important for families, that we want to look at. How well a family is able to communicate determines the extent to which family members feel cared for and can grow together.

Have you ever felt misunderstood? There is a time when I (Carol) organized a surprise anniversary trip for my husband. I lovingly took hours to plan the treat to ensure that he would enjoy it. I even bought a couple of new dresses for the occasion. I wanted it to be an unforgettable event! But alas! I discovered in the middle of the trip that it was not what my husband would have preferred. In fact, I felt he was quite critical about it! I was obviously very hurt that he did not at least recognize how much I had slaved to make it happen. How frustrating!

> You influence by listening and not by downplaying someone's problems

How frustrating it is to share openly and vulnerably only to have a family member downplay the problem or offer simplistic advice, without giving careful thought to what you are saying. How about when someone completes your sentence or, worse still, picks up their cell phone in the middle of your conversation or get this, continues watching T.V. or working on their computer! Have you wanted desperately to say something to a family member but felt they would not really hear you and would probably react negatively without really listening to what you had to say? Have you heard the story you shared in confidence doing its rounds in the family grapevine? Now this one gets me the most: You are busy sharing an animated story and your relative snatches the thunder from your story by either changing the topic or diverting the story to themselves! How frustrating!

Communication is very important because it is the way God has provided for us to share with others our joys, ideas, victories, concerns and needs. As we share or communicate with others and especially our family members, we receive validation for our existence. For example, when an idea or a concern you shared is acknowledged by someone you value (whether or not they agree with you), you feel validated as a worthwhile and valuable member of the society; someone who has something useful to contribute! On the contrary, when our contribution is not acknowledged, it is like a part of us is denied existence and we feel like an insignificant person who has nothing worthwhile to contribute to society. After a while, such a person is likely to be filled with self-doubt and may also begin invalidating their own ideas.

The problem of invalidating each other in communication is that relationships do get adversely affected. People lose trust in each other, misunderstanding is rife and the walls that develop between family members could lead to divorce or rivalry that goes down through several family generations. Listening to each other and giving opportunity for everyone to be heard is, therefore, very important.

How then should we grow to become better at communicating with other people? There are several things we need to realize about listening to other people.

Listening is foundational for developing and growing friendship. The way we listen to others communicates our love for them. When we honestly take time to listen, a person feels appreciated, loved and worthwhile.

Often, we take for granted our closest relationships, including our families, thinking that we do not have to work as hard as we might do with others to retain our friendships. Nothing could be further from the truth! A history of invalidating someone as they speak will whittle down any friendship, irrespective of how close it has been in the past.

Actively listening to others is hard work! Some people are naturally skilled at listening but a good majority of us have to learn to listen. It takes effort and self-sacrifice to learn a new skill, but, without this skill, one is likely to suffer when building and maintaining friendships.

TIPS FOR GOOD LISTENING

Do not assume you know what someone is going to say and therefore complete their sentence for them. Even if you think you know, allow them to speak. It shows your respect for them. A sign that you have really listened is that you should be able to repeat back to them what they have said and have them agree that that is exactly what they are saying.

Some people assume that when someone is sharing a problem they are being asked for a solution and, therefore, enter into a problem-solution mode. This is not necessarily the case. Many times, listening and entering the other person's shoes is all that is required at that moment. As a person shares, solutions may become obvious to them, all without your help!

Even if you think the other person is making a big deal of a situation, do not dismiss them. Listen anyway. Invite them to explore solutions to the situation they are presenting and then, if they are open to listening to your opinion, go ahead and share it. Remember, you influence by listening and not by downplaying someone's problems.

Set aside distractions like computers, phones, T.V., newspapers or people walking by and give attention to the person talking. If it is not a good time to speak, then ask if you can speak at a specific time in the very near future and commit to be fully available then.

If needed, go with the person to a more private place than you ordinarily meet in. Turn to face them and maintain appropriate eye contact. Stay alert and engaged, using encouraging facial expressions and nodding to draw the person out.

Connect with the person at the level they are at. If they are sharing ideas, then respond at idea level. If they are speaking about heart issues, then respond at heart level as opposed to idea or head level.

FAMILY TALK

QUIZ: HOW GOOD AM I AT LISTENING?

Consider how you are at listening to family, friends, and others who are close to you, and use this scale to indicate your responses.

1 = Hardly Ever;   2 = Occasionally;   3 = Sometimes;   4 = Often;   5 = Nearly Always

1. I am patient with those who have difficulty putting their feelings into words.

2. When someone wants to talk with me, I make sure he is physically comfortable.

3. I am concerned and empathetic when someone expresses very deep feelings.

4. When others share with me, I encourage them to continue as long as they need to, without changing the subject.

5. I give appropriate eye contact, looking at the person enough, but not too much as to make them uncomfortable.

6. My body posture and other nonverbal behavior communicate interest in the person.

7. I hold in strict confidence what is shared with me, unless I have permission to share.

8. I respect others' privacy by encouraging them, without force or manipulation, to share from the heart.

9. I withhold making judgments until I have heard the whole story.

10. My facial expressions show that I am feeling with the person.

11. If someone comes to talk about a serious matter, I let them know upfront if my time is limited by another commitment.

12. When I am listening, I keep interruptions such as telephone calls, to a minimum.

13. I gladly stop what I am doing when someone comes to talk with me.

WEEK
- THREE -
DEBUNKING THE LIES

THE LIES WE BELIEVE

In high school, I (Muriithi) loved to play competitive sports, both team sports like rugby, soccer and hockey, and individual sports like tennis, squash or table tennis. One thing that I learnt in competitive sports is that if you could psyche out your opponent, you could throw them out of stride. By taunting them, laughing at them or making them angry, you could mess around with their thinking. So, for example, I would serve the ball and if they would hit it out, I would laugh and say, 'Ha! You're in such trouble!' And I would serve again and laugh again, doing the same thing. Or, if it was in team sports, we would celebrate our goals and really make the other side feel bad. The intention was to intimidate and demoralize our opponents, causing them to lose their focus and lose heart. If this was done properly, then, no matter how good they were, their thinking would shrink, panic would set in and confusion would reign. From that point on, they would commit errors that would deny them any chance of winning!

In the same way, one of the most effective ways that the evil one keeps us from being what we were created to be is by causing us to have a distorted view of our reality. And so, this week, we want to look at

> 'Where are all his wonders that our fathers told us about?'

what the bible says about our identity. The biblical book of Judges[35] talks about a terrible time when the Israelites had been under enemy occupation for seven years. They had been forced out of their homes and now lived in caves in their own country, hiding for fear of enemy militia. Whenever they planted crops, the enemies would come with their livestock and turn them loose on their farms, ruining the harvest. The enemy's strategy was not just to defeat them but to completely demoralize them so that they would become helpless and hopeless, so intimidated so that they could not think or resist.

The Israelites tried to manage their situation until, eventually, things were really bad. After seven years, they finally gave in. Like many of us at that point, it was, when all else fails, pray! Here's the thing people, God will not force His solutions on us. He respects our freewill. As long as we are committed to managing ourselves, He will let us do exactly that. For many of us, we go through a lot of unnecessary pain because we rely on our own strength and wisdom and only call on God when things have gone out of control.

At that point in the story, we are introduced to a man named Gideon, son of Joash, who was threshing wheat in a winepress. Now, just in case you did not know this, a winepress is used for making wine and not threshing wheat. If you are threshing wheat, you would rather do it outside where there is wind to blow away the chaff. But Gideon was a demoralized man whose life was ruled by fear. Not only had he grown his wheat in secret, but he had to thresh it in secret as well. He was used to a life of fear and hiding. This had become a part of his psyche.

As he was busy at work, an angel appeared and greeted Gideon in an unexpected greeting: 'The Lord is with you, mighty warrior.' Gideon's next few sentences reveal his distorted picture of himself and of God. '*If the Lord is with us, why has all this happened to us?* The painful circumstances of the past had left him feeling unfairly treated and asking, 'Why us?' For some who are reading this, like Gideon

---

35   Judges 6:1-16

have gone through extremely hard circumstances growing up and have asked yourself this question, 'Why me?' 'Why our family?' 'What did we do to deserve this?'

Gideon's next question was, '*Where are all his wonders that our fathers told us about?'* Gideon felt that God's blessings were reserved for other people and not for him. Have you ever looked at other people's families and wondered why God blessed them so much? Maybe those people are your classmates. Things seem so much easier for them, and you are asking why God's blessings are reserved for others and not for you or your family.

Gideon's final statement was, '*The Lord has abandoned us and put us into the hand of Midian.'* He felt completely abandoned by God. Have you ever felt that you have been deserted by God and that you have to fend for yourself? This is how Gideon felt and it affected how he viewed himself. I believe this is one of the most effective ways that the devil uses to keep many people from living effective lives. He knows that if he can get you to believe a lie about your true situation, he can demoralize you so that you give in without a fight!

The reason many of us live weak and ineffective lives is because of the lies we have come to believe: These are lies about ourselves, lies about God and lies about the way we should interact with one another. Lies about ourselves cause us to think poorly about ourselves; lies about God cause us not to put our trust fully in Him, thereby cutting off God's ability to intervene in our situations; lies about the way we should relate with others cause us to mistrust each other and, in the process, we end up isolated, not being able to receive help from our friends. These lies often come at us in attractive and convincing ways that make them very easy to believe. The problem though is that when we choose to believe these lies, we rob ourselves of the joy and abundance we were created to enjoy.

Question For My Journal

What do you fear most about God getting into your business?

Verse To Remember

Matthew 11:28-29. "Come to me, all you who are weary and burdened, and I will give you rest. Take my yoke upon you and learn from me, for I am gentle and humble in heart, and you will find rest for your souls."

Prayer For Today

Dear Lord, please reveal to me all the ways that my family and I have believed the enemy's lies. Amen.

OUR DADDY IN HEAVEN

Growing up, neither of us (Carol or Muriithi) was particularly close to our fathers. Both our dads grew up in contexts in which the man showed his love for his family by providing for and taking care of them. We are grateful that both our dads did a phenomenal job with this! But, as with many men of their generation, they were often busy at work and did not know how to connect emotionally with their children. It was only when they grew older that it became easier to relate with them and form friendships with their adult children. As a result, I (Muriithi) did not find it natural or easy to express affection to our children as they grew up. I found it much easier to be a disciplinarian! I am grateful for friends who had a different experience, and on whom I leaned as mentors in choosing the kind of relationship that I wanted to have with our kids. I pray that they will, in turn, find it much easier than I did to have an intimate and expressive relationship with their own children.

Humans have struggled with trusting God

Now some of you reading this had extremely affectionate relationships with your dads. We bless God because a healthy relationship with your earthly father makes it far much easier to engage in a healthy and undistorted relationship with your heavenly Father. But of course for many others, dad was not in the picture or was not someone you could relate to without fear or insecurity. Our own negative view of our fathers can easily distort the picture of who God truly is. We need a fresh picture of God to help us overcome our past. So, why not learn from Jesus? One of Jesus's biographers, a doctor named Luke, wrote about an occasion in which Jesus's disciples were watching him praying. Jesus lived his life authentically and transparently in front of his disciples, desiring that they would learn from his example. And, sure enough, after he was done praying, the disciples told him, 'Lord, teach us how to pray.' The very first thing Jesus taught the disciples in his model prayer was that they should address God as Father.[36]

For centuries, the Jews had maintained that God's name was too holy to utter or even write. From their reading of scripture, they felt He could only be related with from a proper distance, through the appointed representatives, using the correct protocols, and that not just anyone could approach Him. The spiritual leaders of the day demonstrated prayer as something to be done with great show and eloquence. So, you can imagine the disciples' surprise when the first thing Jesus taught them about how to pray was to refer to God not as their Lord or their King (all appropriate titles, by the way), but as their Father!

Jesus used an endearing term for God one that we should all be able to relate to because every single one of us has a father. The problem, however, is that our earthly fathers are often a very poor representation of our heavenly Father! Fathers are supposed to take care of us, love us, nurture us, protect us and guide us. But for many reading this, our experience of a father was someone who was either absent, distant, harsh, irresponsible, selfish, violent or many other attributes that are far from what God intended a father to be!

---

36 Luke 11:2

Right from the garden of Eden, the enemy has worked hard to distort the view of humans towards the intentions of their heavenly Father. The devil's first question to Eve was, *'Did God really say, You must not eat from any tree in the garden?'*[37] We will look at this question in a little more detail in a later chapter but the thing to note here is that the enemy's intent was to make Eve and her husband doubt that God had their best interests at heart, and to encourage them to take charge of their own lives. Since then, humans have struggled with trusting God. We see this over and over in the Old Testament story of the Israelites. Despite God doing great miracles for them, protecting them, providing for them and regularly declaring His love for them, they still found it difficult to trust Him or accept this love. They constantly turned away from God's ways and copied the ways of the cultures around them, often even choosing to worship their gods as a self-protective plan B, just in case God did not come through for them!

But Jesus taught us to affirm, every time that we pray, that God is our Father. Jesus's relationship with his heavenly Father was one of trust and affection. He referred to him as 'Abba', which is an Aramaic informal or pet name used by little Jewish children towards their fathers, closer even to 'daddy' or 'papa' than the more formal 'father'.

> God forgives us completely! He does not harbor bitterness against us.

Here are some pictures of God the father from the bible...

1. **Our Daddy does not easily get angry.** Unlike some of our parents who were quick tempered, He understands that we are prone to fail and, therefore, shows us compassion and patience. King David wrote about Him thus, *'The Lord is compassionate and gracious, slow to anger, abounding in love; for He knows how we are formed, He remembers that we are dust.'*[38]

2. **Our Daddy is merciful.** In some of our family backgrounds, hurts were nursed for so long and the punishments meted so severe that we imagine that this is how God is. But no, God forgives us completely! He does not harbor bitterness against us and neither does He treat us as our sins deserve. Listen to King David again, *'He will not always accuse, nor will He harbor His anger forever; He does not treat us as our sins deserve or repay us according to our iniquities.*[39]

3. **Our Daddy's discipline is always restorative.** In His dealings with Israel, God many times had to show 'tough love' by allowing them to face the consequences of their rebellion against Him. But even then, unlike the 'discipline' of many earthly parents, His intention was not to make them suffer but to lead them back to life through repentance. As the writer of the book of Hebrews said, talking about God, *'It's the child he loves that he disciplines; the child he embraces, he also corrects.*[40]

---

37 Genesis 3:1
38 Psalm 103:8,14
39 Psalm 103:9-10
40 Hebrews 12:6

OUR DADDY IN HEAVEN

4. **Our Daddy's love is unconditional and not dependent on our performance!** Unlike many spiritual parents, God's love is not dependent on what we do but on who He is. Thus, these words by the writer of the book of Lamentations: '*The faithful love of the Lord never ends! His mercies never cease. Great is his faithfulness; his mercies begin afresh each morning.*'[41]

5. **Our Daddy doesn't just love us but He likes us!** He enjoys and desires our presence and interaction as His children. Listen, you are not an interruption to Him. He loves your company! Here's another incredible picture of our Daddy from the prophet Zephaniah: '*For the LORD your God is living among you. He is a mighty savior. He will take delight in you with gladness. With his love, he will calm all your fears. He will rejoice over you with joyful songs.*'[42]

6. **Our Daddy works out all things for our good.** Many times, things will go badly in life, either because of our own sin or rebellion or because of that of others. Or sometimes, life simply just happens and we are affected by situations that had nothing to do with us and that we did not deserve. But, even then, God uniquely promises to work all things out so that the end result will be for our good. Read again these famous words by the apostle Paul: '*And we know that in all things God works for the good of those who love him, who have been called according to his purpose.*'[43]

> The enemy's intent is to cause you to distrust God's intentions for you.

As one preacher said, 'Father - that single word sums up what the Christian faith is all about. It answers the philosopher's question "Is the universe friendly?" For when we say 'Father' we are affirming that at the heart of the universe there is not only an ultimate power but there is an ultimate love.'[44]

We realize that many reading this did not grow up with affectionate and intimate memories of their earthly father. We thank God for those of you that did! But regardless of what your background was, God wants to redeem this term for you so that you will know Him as your father the One who loves you so much He would do anything for you.

Gideon felt that God had treated his people unfairly. He felt that God's blessings were reserved for others and not for him. He felt abandoned by God. But here is what the truth of the matter was...

Truth #1: The reason for their situation not God's unfairness; instead, it was because when the Israelites had chosen to worship the gods of the people of the land, God had simply allowed them to live with the consequences of their choices.

Truth #2: God's power was still available to them to fight their enemies. He was not God only of previous generations, but their God as well, and he had never abandoned them. Despite their walking away from Him, he still loved them very much and longed to save them from their enemies.

---

41 Lamentations 3:22-23 (NLT)
42 Zephaniah 3:17 (NLT)
43 Romans 8:28
44 C. John Steer

Now, while Gideon's feelings may have been legitimate, they came from a place of deception! And that is where many of us are. We have been deceived by the enemy's lies. The enemy's intent is to cause you to distrust God's intentions for you. He wants you to feel that you cannot trust God with your life; that you have to remain in control, 'just in case'. But that is the oldest lie in the world! Your Daddy is a good father. It is His nature! His love for you never fails and never runs out! He rejoices over you and wants you to succeed. And He is able to work out all things, not just the good things, but all things, for your good so that you will accomplish the great purpose that He created you for!

Questions For Your Journal

What truth has struck you about God today?

What would you do differently if you truly believed God totally and unconditionally loved you and enjoyed your presence?

Verse To Remember

Romans 5:8. But God demonstrates his own love for us in this: While we were still sinners, Christ died for us.

Prayer For Today

Lord, I often struggle to relate with You as a loving father. Please rescue me from the deception of the enemy and help me to see you as you truly are!

SEEING ME RIGHT

We began this week by learning that the reason many of us live weak and ineffective lives as Christians is because of the lies we have come to believe: These are lies about ourselves, lies about God and lies about the way we should interact with one another. Because Gideon and the Israelites had believed these lies, they had been demoralized by the enemy to give up without a fight! They blamed God for their predicament and felt that He had abandoned them. As for Gideon, his own view of himself was severely distorted. When God invited him to deliver his people, he gave this classic reply…

"Pardon me, my lord," Gideon replied, "but how can I save Israel? My clan is the weakest in Manasseh, and I am the least in my family."[45] In other words, I am the last person God can use in Israel! I'm the least qualified to serve God! I've got too many issues of my own to solve my nation's problems! Ever felt that way? I'm too young! Or too poor! Or too unspiritual! Or too unqualified! Surely God can use someone else to do His work!

But once more, the truth was completely different!

When Gideon finally agreed to obey God, we are told, *'So Gideon took ten of his servants and did as the Lord told him.'*[46] So, now tell me, how does the least person in Israel have ten personal servants? Gideon's view of himself was clearly far from accurate!

> Just like Gideon, we are held in captivity by our wrong thinking about ourselves

Just like the Israelites, our enemy also tries to lie to us about our true situation. He does this for many of us by attacking us at our most vulnerable times. Through things said about us and actions done to us by people in authority over us, we come to believe certain things about ourselves that are lies; lies meant to demoralize us and discourage us. Some of us grew up listening to negative messages: 'You're just like your mother!' 'You will never amount to much.' 'You're not as pretty as your sister.' 'You're stupid or ugly or fat or thin.' 'God is angry at you.' 'It's your fault your parents fought.' Some of us were shown conditional love where we were only appreciated when we performed in certain ways. 'Wow, you got an A! That's my son!' These may have been statements meant to encourage us to perform better, but the way they were framed only made us feel that we would only be worthy of life or praise when we performed. Just like Gideon, we are held in captivity by our wrong thinking about ourselves.

Here are the **four** main lies about ourselves that the enemy uses to keep us in captivity…

1. **The Performance Trap:** The lie here is, 'I must meet certain standards in order to feel good about myself.' The person may look good on the outside but on the inside is driven by the fear of failure. I (Muriithi) have known several friends who are extremely driven at their workplace because of the unrealistic standards they have set for themselves. Fear of failure means that everything needs to be done perfectly. In the process, they become workaholics who can only feel

---

45   Judges 6:15
46   Judges 6:27

good about themselves if they are sacrificing everything in order to get their work done. The sad thing is that we even cheer them on (It's an acceptable 'weakness' at an interview). Now don't get me wrong; I am not advocating for mediocrity, but perfectionism and fear of failure means that even while they are a 'performer', their inner life is driven by fear and anxiety. This can lead to psychological and physical illnesses. It is also a very unhappy way to live!

2. **Approval Addiction:** The lie is, 'I must be approved by certain 'others' to feel good about myself'. When I (Muriithi) was very young in primary school, I did extremely well in my exams and was third in my class, a great improvement from fifteenth the previous term. My dad was delighted, and gave me a small transistor radio as a gift (It was quite the gadget back then)! I learnt from this that I could get the approval of adults in my life through performing academically! And I did that throughout my school life, projecting the picture of a perfect student, even though I was a completely different person in my personal life. People with an approval addiction are driven by the fear of rejection and try and please significant others at any cost. They are extremely sensitive to criticism and react defensively because when you critique work they have done, they feel that you are attacking them personally. They also are needy, constantly demanding compliments and awards from others to feel good about themselves. Some of you know this hunger for approval in your work and in your relationships.

> People with an approval addiction are driven by the fear of rejection

3. **The Blame Game:** Here the enemy's lie is, 'Those who fail are unworthy of love and deserve to be punished.' A person who believes this lie lives in fear of punishment. For them, punishment for wrongdoing while growing up was probably very severe and involved withdrawal of parental love. The result is that the person feels unworthy of love when they do wrong. They are so afraid of being 'caught' that they will blame others for personal failure and are afraid of trying out new things to avoid failure. They may even inflict pain on themselves as a means of punishing themselves when they feel they have acted badly. The enemy truly works overtime to mess us up!

4. **The Shame Game:** Here the lie is, 'I am what I am; I cannot change.' This happens when someone has been told over and over that they will not amount to much or perhaps they messed up big time in the past and felt that they had let important people around them down. They feel worthless at the core of their being, resulting in feelings of hopelessness and inferiority. They lose confidence in themselves and do not think that their ideas or contributions are worthwhile. That is why Gideon says when God sends him, *'How can I save Israel? My clan is the weakest in Manasseh, and I am the least in my family.'*

You see, your self-image is like a speed governor that controls your life. It does not matter if the car was manufactured to drive at speeds of up to 240 kilometers per hour. If the speed governor is set to 70 kilometers per hour, then the car will move at 70 kilometers per hour! Your self-image may be because of what others said about you, how your parents or peers regarded you, or some traumatic or shameful experience you had growing up. But the question is, 'Does your image of who you are line up correctly with who God says you are?'

SEEING ME RIGHT

God sees you as a strong, courageous, successful and overcoming person

There is only one way to break out of the enemy's lies and live the life that God created you to live. You need to **see yourself as God sees you**. See how God greets Gideon: '*The Lord is with you, mighty warrior.*'[47] The Amplified Version of the bible says it even more dramatically, '*The Lord is with you, you mighty man of fearless courage.*' Believe it or not, that is how God sees you too! He sees you as a strong, courageous, successful and overcoming person. While Gideon felt unqualified; God saw him as mighty man of fearless courage. Gideon felt weak; God saw him as strong. Gideon felt insecure; God saw him as a champion with everything that was needed to lead an army into victory. Similarly, you may not think much of yourself but God sees you as His word describes you. You may feel insecure, unqualified, overwhelmed by life, fearful, weak, or insignificant but that does not change God's view of you one bit! He sees you as His champion.

Question For My Journal

In what ways do you think that you have had a distorted view of yourself?

Verse To Remember

Psalm 139:14. I praise you because I am fearfully and wonderfully made; your works are wonderful, I know that full well.

Prayer For Today

Lord, please reveal to me all the ways that I have had a distorted veiw of myself. Help me to see you as you see me! Amen.

---

47   Judges 16:12

SEEING OTHERS RIGHT

The key reason many Christians live weak and ineffective lives is because we have come to believe lies about ourselves, lies about God and lies about others. The story of Gideon demonstrates this truth powerfully to us today.

Here was a man who had been created to be a mighty warrior. Here was a man whose destiny was to lead an army, to deliver millions of people from oppression and to inspire generations to come by helping them see that God is able to save, whether you have many or few resources. And yet where do we find him? We find him demoralized and in hiding, surviving and ekeing out a living, working in secret. We find him doubting God, feeling abandoned, wondering why God cares for others and not for his people. We observe him express serious self doubt, seeing himself as among the least of the least.

Gideon already had what it took he just didn't know it!

Gideon had so allowed the enemy to distort his view of himself that he had lost his sense of agency. What do we mean by that? In social science, agency is defined as the capacity of individuals to act independently and to make their own free choices.[48] Many people in Africa feel helpless to do anything about the huge challenges the continent faces. When they look at things like poverty or corruption or poor leadership or poor education systems, they feel overwhelmed. When they encounter injustice at work or in society, they figure that this must be someone else's problem. The government or a donor (read someone or some institution from the West) needs to deal with this issue!

But I love what God proceeds to tell Gideon: '*Go in the strength you have and save Israel out of Midian's hand.*'[49] Gideon already had what it took he just didn't know it! In the same way, if you have accepted Christ, God has already given you all that you need to be a blessing to your family and your society, regardless of your past or what others have said about you! As the apostle Peter put it, '*His divine power has given us everything we need for life and godliness.*'[50]

Some of us may be reading this and God stirs in you some hope, only for you to face your normal life and doubt if this message was really meant for you. It is interesting to note that God called Gideon a 'mighty warrior', not when he was leading an army, but when he was hiding in fear. What is God calling you in the situation you are in? God calls you 'fearless influencer of society'. You are his agent! You are the one He will use to end the oppression in that very messed up family tree of yours. You are the one He will use to change your workplace and to bring change to your city and nation!

So, start by agreeing with God. Start seeing yourself as God sees you. Do not let your feelings of inadequacy stop you from being the blessing to those around you that you were created to be. Do not make excuses not to take up a new leadership position or get involved in a ministry or serve the community. Do not focus on your weakness or your past or on yourself. Focus on God. If God chose to use perfect people only, He would have no one to use. He loves to use ordinary people like you and me, faults and all, to do extraordinary things. When we are weak, He is strong. Do not allow

48   https://en.wikipedia.org/wiki/Agency_(sociology)
49   Judges 6:14
50   II Peter 1:3 (ISV)

SEEING OTHERS RIGHT

yourself to be shaped by non-biblical concepts that are contrary to God's opinion of you.

If lies about ourselves is what the devil has used on us, then the way to correct this is by acquiring the truth about ourselves. We do this by reprogramming our minds with God's word. We change the negative, defeated self-image and start seeing ourselves as God's fearless champions. As the apostle Paul said to the church in Rome, '*Do not conform any longer to the pattern of this world, but be transformed by the renewing of your mind. Then you will be able to test and approve what God's will is — his good, pleasing and perfect will.*'[51] And as John, one of Jesus's followers wrote, '*You will know the truth and the truth and the truth will set you free.*'[52] Our journey to transformation begins when we reject the lies we have come to believe about ourselves, and replace them with the truth of who God says we are.

> God can completely reformat our minds and turn us from hiding in the winepresses of fear to leading a movement of godly and loving change across our society!

How do we do this? By knowing what God's word says about us!

- If the enemy tells you that are a nobody, tell him, 'I am a child of God.' '*Yet to all who received him, to those who believed in His name, He gave the right to become children of God.*[53]

- If the enemy tells you that God cannot like someone like you, tell him, 'I am Christ's friend.'[54]

- If the enemy reminds you of all the bad things you have done, remind him that you are completely forgiven: '*Therefore, there is now no condemnation for those who are in Christ Jesus.*[55]

- If the enemy points to the bad things that have happened in your past, point out that God will work all things out in the end. '*… and we know that in <u>all</u> things God works for the good of those who love Him, who have been called according to His purpose.*[56]

- If he says you will never change; you will always repeat your mistakes, remind him that nothing is impossible for you! '*I can do all things through Christ who strengthens me.*[57]

- And if he tells you that God has abandoned you, enlighten him with the fact that God can never do that! '*For I am convinced that neither death nor life, neither angels nor demons neither the present nor the future, nor any powers, neither height nor depth, nor anything else in all creation, will be able to separate us from the love of God that is in Christ Jesus our Lord.*[58]

---

51 Romans 12:2

52 John 8:32

53 John 1:12

54 John 15:15. '*I no longer call you servants... instead I have called you friends...*'

55 Romans 8:1

56 Romans 8:28

57 Philippians 4:13

58 Romans 8:38-39

SEEING OTHERS RIGHT

Are we together? God can completely reformat our minds and turn us from hiding in the winepresses of fear to leading a movement of godly and loving change across our society! But, it takes more than making a declaration. It takes making a conscious effort to allow God's truth to wash over us, soak in and replace the old scripts. It takes believing that God has called you to be a mighty warrior and given you everything you need to be a blessing to those around you!

Question For My Journal

What are some of the strengths, gifts or passions God has given you that you could use to bless those around you?

Verse To Remember

Ephesians 2:10 (NLT). For we are God's masterpiece. He has created us anew in Christ Jesus, so we can do the good things he planned for us long ago.

Prayer For Today

Lord, open my eyes and help me to see myself as your masterpiece! Give me a clear vision of myself, not one inflated by pride or one that is deflated by false humility and low self-esteem. Help me instead to see myself as you see me and, in the process, show me how You uniquely created me to be a blessing to those around me. Amen.

REFORMATTING MY MIND

Clearly, if you have been used to thinking about God and about yourself a certain way all your life, it is going to take supernatural assistance to start to see yourself differently! If your sense of value has been based on your achievements, on how well you perform, on how others treat you, or on how popular or successful you are, it will take a huge shift for your sense of value to be based solely on the fact that you are a child of the Most High God! If you have lived a self-protective life, it will take a change of paradigm to begin to live a life that is intentionally pointed towards being a blessing to others.

The good news is this: God knows everything about you, both good and bad, and He still loves you and values you unconditionally. He may not always approve of your choices or be pleased when you go against His will. The reality is that even knowing the things you know, you will find yourself messing up

> Nothing you have done can cause God to love or value you less!

again in the future. Gideon certainly did! But here's a startling truth that you might not know: Nothing you have done can cause God to love or value you less! Here's the way I like to think about it: Imagine that someone gave you a new, crisp, 100 dollar note. Would you want it? Probably! What if they crumbled it up so that it was not quite as good looking, would you still want it? Sure! But wait, what if they took it out to the parking lot, threw it on the ground and stomped on it until it was dirty, stained and soiled. Would you value it less? Of course not! Why? Because it is still valuable; it is still 100 dollars, despite the rough treatment it has experienced! It does not lose its value simply because it has aged, is not as pretty as it once was or has taken some bumps or bruises in life.[59]

And so, as part of our mental reformatting, here are a few things to help us apply what we have learnt this week:

Identify The Lie: Ask God to show you lies that you have believed about yourself or about Him that have kept you from being the person He created you to be. Pray the prayer of King David: *'Search me, O God, and know my heart; test me and know my anxious thoughts. See if there is any offensive way in me, and lead me in the way everlasting.*[60] This is a prayer I pray often for myself.

Replace The Lie: Each morning this week, defeat the lie by declaring aloud what the word of God says you are. This is how we defeat the enemy's lies![61] At the end of today's reading, you will find a list of scriptural affirmations that you can use to reformat your mind with God's truth. I challenge you to pray them out aloud every day this week. Take a moment each day to look up some of the scripture references. Ask God to help His word soak into your inner self. Whenever the old lie comes up, declare the truth in Jesus's name and ask the lie to flee instead. I have also found it useful to listen to worship music in the car or on my phone as I work out or when I drive or take public transport. I specifically enjoy music that is uplifting and that helps reinforce the truth of God's word.

---

59   Thoughts quoted from a message by Pst. Joel Osteen.

60   Psalm 139:23-24

61   Ephesians 6:17 says that the word of God is our spiritual sword, our weapon for defeating the enemy's lies.

Expose The Lie: The third important thing to do is to talk about the lies you have discovered in yourself with your prayer partner, your class members or with a trusted friend. James, one of Jesus's followers wrote, '*Therefore confess your sins to each other and pray for each other so that you may be healed. The prayer of a righteous man is powerful and effective.*'[62]

> Defeat the lie by declaring aloud what the word of God says you are.

As you intentionally replace the lies about God, yourself and others with the truth, we believe that you will be amazed to find your mind being completely transformed. As Jesus said, '*You will know the truth and the truth shall set you free!*'[63]

We end this week's reflections with an affirmation of biblical truth. Read aloud the following affirmation of faith, and do so again as often as necessary to renew your mind and take your stand according to the truth. I recommend that you read it daily for several weeks, especially if you are just resolving a personal spiritual conflict.

AFFIRMING THE TRUTH

In Jesus, I Am Accepted:

- I am God's child (John 1:12)
- I am Christ's friend (John 15:15)
- I have been bought with a price. I belong to God (I Corinthians 6:19-20)
- I am a member of Christ's body (I Corinthians 12:27)
- I am a saint (Ephesians 1:1)
- I have direct access to God through the Holy Spirit (Ephesians 2:18)
- I have been redeemed and forgiven of *all* my sins (Colossians 1:14)

In Jesus, I Am Secure:

- I am free from any condemning charges against me (Romans 8:1-2, 31f)
- I am assured that all things work together for good (Romans 8:28)
- I cannot be separated from the love of God (Romans 8:35)
- I am confident that the good work Christ began in me will be perfected (Philippians 1:6)
- I am a citizen of heaven (Philippians 3:20)
- I will always find enough grace and mercy in my time of need (Hebrews 4:16)
- I am born of God and the evil one cannot touch me (I John 5:18)

---

62   James 5:16
63   John 8:32

REFORMATTING MY MIND

In Jesus, I Am Significant:

- I am seated with Christ in the heavenly realm (Ephesians 2:6)

- I am the salt and light of the earth (Matthew 5:13, 14)

- I am a branch of the true vine; a channel of His life (John 15:1, 5)

- I have been chosen and appointed to bear fruit (John 15:16)

- I am God's temple (I Corinthians 3:16)

- I am a minister of reconciliation for God (II Corinthians 5:17f)

- I am God's coworker (I Corinthians 3:9)

- I am God's masterpiece (Ephesians 2:10)

- I am God's ambassador on earth (II Corinthians 5:20)

- I can do all things through Christ who strengthens me (Philippians 4:13)

Question For My Journal

What is your main takeout from this week's chapter? How do you sense God wants you to respond to what you have learnt?

Freedom Prayer

Dear heavenly Father, I know that You desire truth in my inmost self and that facing this truth will set me free (John 8:32). I acknowledge that I have been deceived by the father of lies (John 8:44). I pray in the name of the Lord Jesus Christ that You, dear Father, will rebuke all deceiving spirits that have distorted my view of myself and of You. And since by faith I have received You into my life and I'm now seated with Christ in the heavenly places (Ephesians 2:6), I command all deceiving spirits to depart from me. I now ask the Holy Spirit to guide me into all truth (John 16:3). I ask You this week to "search me, O God , and know my heart; try me and know my anxious thoughts; and see if there be any hurtful way in me, and lead me in the everlasting way" (Psalm 139:23, 24). In Jesus' name I pray. Amen.[64]

---

64   Adapted from Neil Anderson, 'The Bondage Breaker'.

WEEK
- FOUR -
IT'S MY LIFE!

MY LIFE, MY WAY

Let me (Muriithi) begin by making a confession. It is not one I am proud of. I sometimes have a real problem following instructions, especially when they do not make sense to me. For example, in Kenya, most office buildings have a security guard at the reception. When you come in to see someone, they ask you to surrender your national ID to them until your visit is done. My temptation is usually to say I don't have one! First of all, there's no legal requirement that I should carry an ID with me. Secondly, something in me pushes back against being asked to do something I don't want to do by someone that I don't think should have a right to do so! But you know, when I'm really honest with myself, the issue is not the ID or even the security guard's manner. It's the fact that he or she has authority that I do not want to submit myself to! What I'm really wondering is, 'Why do I have to do it *your* way?'

I suspect this is a very Kenyan illustration, but I also suspect that it is not just Kenyans like me who like to do things their way! As a generation, we are suspicious of authority and push back against being told what to do. Some of us are active rebels we pride ourselves on being nonconformists. Others are passive-aggressive rebels. We are not the activist type, but we quietly and stubbornly do our own thing.

> Men and women pursue their career ambitions at the expense of the family

Whether it is national or spiritual or civic authorities, it is far more acceptable and admired today to stand out as a rebel against the 'status quo' than to be someone who accepts or follows established norms. We want to do it our way at work: We pride ourselves on being nonconformists; those who disagree with everything that others say. We want to do it our way at home: Many husbands or wives today believe they are entitled to their own happiness, regardless of the effect it will have on their spouse or children. So, men and women pursue their career ambitions at the expense of the family or cheat on their spouses because they feel it is their right to pursue what they desire. The media greatly reinforces this message, whether it is music videos, podcasts, talk radio or the latest T.V., series. The more non-conventional and 'push against established norms' they are, the more popular they tend to be!

No wonder then that our children, who are constantly watching us, also want to do things their way. Today, overworked and absent parents guiltily compensate by allowing their kids to get away with everything and anything. We feel like bad parents if our kids do not have whatever we can afford. None of us want to see our kids on a talk show one day saying that their parents repressed them! And so, we give them whatever they want, resulting in a rebellious generation that has little respect for authority.

Why are we so insistent on doing things our way? Why do we rebel? There are many reasons for this:

1. It could be that our parents were really hard on us and, in the process, they exasperated us. This may have made us feel unfairly treated and our reaction to every authority therefore became defensive and rebellious.

2. Some of us could have grown up in families where parents did not enforce discipline. Either they were too busy at work, or they were reacting to the mistakes of their parents, or perhaps they

simply did not know how to discipline in a modern context. Whatever the case, children were left to do what they felt was right in their eyes.

3. It could be that we grew up in families where we felt neglected and, to attract attention, we decided to rebel against our parents and authority figures in general.

4. Lastly, we could have been in a setting where abuse was the order of the day, or we faced some trauma growing up, for example, our parents' divorce. As our reaction, we decided to rebel.

Whatever the presenting reason, the truth is that the underlying problem is that within our hearts, each one of us has a sense of rebellion¾we don't like being told what to do! There is an old song by Bon Jovi called, 'It's My Life', whose title could easily be our generational slogan. The lyrics go like this:

> *It's my life | It's now or never | I ain't gonna live*
> *forever | I just want to live while I'm alive (It's my life)*
> *My heart is like an open highway |Like Frankie said, "I did*
> *it my way" | I just want to live while I'm alive |Cause*
> *IT'S MY LIFE!*

And yet doing things your way is one of the things that could greatly hinder you from ever achieving your God-given purpose! We have seen already that right from the garden of Eden, satan's lie to Adam and Eve was that they should do not trust God's authority, and that they should instead do things their way. And ever since then, our natural instinct has been to be suspicious of those in authority over us, and to not to submit to them.

This week, we want to understand why rebellion is such a huge doorway for the enemy to have legal rights over our life. In so doing, we want to also demonstrate the benefits and value of following God-ordained authority in our lives, whether at home, at work or elsewhere in society!

Question For My Journal

In what areas do you struggle to follow or obey rightful authority? Why?

Verse To Remember

Romans 13:1 (NLT). Everyone must submit to governing authorities. For all authority comes from God, and those in positions of authority have been placed there by God.

Prayer For Today

Lord, open my eyes and help me to see the ways in which I rebel against God-ordained authority in my life.

IT'S ABOUT ME

We learnt yesterday that at the heart, each one of us has a sense of rebellion we don't like being told what to do! And yet doing things your way is one of the things that could greatly hinder your ever achieving your God-given purpose.

This truth is well-illustrated by an interesting incident that happened in the life of Moses, one of the greatest leaders who ever lived. God had dramatically used him to free the people of Israel from being enslaved by the most powerful nation on earth at the time and to set them on their journey towards becoming an independent nation. Over the following years, Moses had faithfully led the Israelites, performing miracles with God's help, including helping them find food and water in a barren wasteland. He had helped them win a battle when they were attacked by an enemy nation. He had also effectively created a system of law and government so that everyone knew their national rights and responsibilities. He had done all this while remaining morally upright and selfless, never using his position to enrich himself. Because of Moses, the Israelites had moved from being a mass of slaves to a nation that was able to defend itself. Many agree that Moses is one of the greatest national leaders the world has ever known!

> The Lord had also spoken to them, so why should Moses get all the credit?

In light of all this, it must have been a huge surprise when Moses's only siblings decide to lead an active rebellion against him. Miriam, his older sister, was a songwriter and poet and Aaron, his older brother, was the high priest. We would have expected they would be Moses's greatest support, but, instead, they complained publicly against their younger brother. They said that he should not have married a woman from a different race.[65] But the real issue became apparent the more they spoke. '*Has the Lord only spoken through Moses?*' '*Hasn't he also spoken through us?*[66]' This was a challenge to Moses' spiritual authority by leaders from his own family. And they were accusing him of being proud; of going around acting as if he was the only one God could speak through. Maybe they didn't see why their baby brother should be getting all the attention. And after all, the Lord had also spoken to them, so why should Moses get all the credit?

Now we've seen that Moses was an incredible leader who had accomplished things no one else before him had. You'd expect a man like that to be extremely cocky and self-confident. But no, the same account says, '*Now Moses was a very humble man, more humble than anyone else on the face of the earth.*[67] This shows that the problem was not with Moses but with his siblings. Basically, it did not matter who their leader was, they would have found a reason to cut him down anyway.

Now contrast this with the story of David, the young shepherd boy who later became Israel's greatest king. His boss was King Saul, an insecure and violent man. Saul was so angry at David's success and popularity that he tried to assassinate him two times. He even tried to enlist the help of his own daughter and son, who were David's wife and best friend respectively. David eventually had

---

65   Numbers 12:1 '*Miriam and Aaron began to talk against Moses because of his Cushite wife*'

66   Numbers 12:2

67   Numbers 12:3

to flee for his life.[68] Saul gathered his army together in hot pursuit. On two distinct occasions, David had an opportunity to kill Saul. His men urged him to strike the blow and end their suffering. But on both occasions, David refused their advice. His reason? As he explained to his men, *'The LORD forbid that I should do such a thing to my master, the LORD's anointed, or lay my hand on him; for he is the anointed of the LORD.*[69]

I hope you catch the contrast between the two stories! Aaron and Miriam dishonored their leader even though he was a humble and honorable leader. David honored Saul, despite the fact that his king was not an honorable leader. You see, being a person of honor does not depend on who your leader is; it depends on who you are! Failure to honor says much more about you than it does about your leaders.

> ## Since Adam and Eve did it their way in the garden of Eden, rebellion is our natural instinct.

Since Adam and Eve did it their way in the garden of Eden, rebellion is our natural instinct. Many people only obey law and authorities when it is convenient for them. There is a general lack of respect for those in authority, whether it is government leaders, spiritual leaders, societal leaders, workplace leaders or family leaders. And we Christians are often as guilty as the rest of society in fostering a critical, rebellious spirit. Now we want to say this clearly: We are not saying we must agree with all our leader's policies. We certainly believe that it is important to refuse to obey any directives by those in authority that are morally wrong. However, many times, our disobedience comes not from a place of moral authority but from a place of rebellion.

Question For My Journal

What do you sense you need to do differently based on what you learnt today?

Verse To Remember

Leviticus 19:32. Stand up in the presence of the aged, show respect for the elderly and revere your God. I am the LORD.

Prayer For Today

Lord, teach me to be a person of honor; one whose honor is not dependent on who my leader is. Amen.

---

68   In some cases, the only way to show honor is to leave, rather than to stay and cause trouble for the authority God has placed you under

69   I Samuel 24:6; I Samuel 26 details the second time that David spared King Saul's life.

WHO TO HONOR

Who are the God appointed authorities in our lives that we must show honor to? The scriptures clearly define several layers of authority:

- **Divine.** Jesus taught his disciples to begin their prayers with the words, '*Our Father in heaven, may your name be honored.*'[70] In Hebrew thought, there was no difference between the name and the person. The bible teaches us that God is the primary authority to be honored. There is no one above Him. No one is as worthy of honor as He is. All other authorities derive their authority from him and honoring them teaches us to honor Him.

- **Spiritual.** The apostle Paul wrote the following words to a young leader he was mentoring, '*The elders who direct the affairs of the church are well worthy of double honor, especially those whose work is preaching and teaching.*'[71] He wrote to Christians in a church that he had started, '*For even if you had ten thousand others to teach you about Christ, you have only one spiritual father. For I became your father in Christ Jesus when I preached the Good News to you.*'[72] As a generation, we have lost the concept of honoring our spiritual authority. We do not know how to relate to spiritual fathers and mothers and, as a result of that, we have become spiritual orphans, adrift, and without spiritual cover. And just like orphans are vulnerable without the protection of parents, we have allowed ourselves to become spiritually vulnerable to the enemy's attack.

> We do not know how to relate to spiritual fathers and mothers and, as a result of that, we have become spiritual orphans,

- **Family.** The writer of the book of Ephesians urges, '*Children, obey your parents in the Lord, for this is right. Honor your father and mother*' – which is the first commandment with a promise – '*that it may go well with you and that you may enjoy long life on earth.*'[73] The apostle Peter also wrote, '*Wives, in the same way be submissive to your husbands so that, if any of them do not believe the word, they may be won over without words by the behavior of their wives, when they see the purity and reverence of your lives.*'[74] Peter was not endorsing child abuse or partriarchy! What he was saying is that within the family, there are God-ordained authorities that we need to learn to honor.

- **National or Civic.** The apostle Paul wrote to one of his mentees, Titus, '*Remind the people to be subject to rulers and authorities, to be obedient, to be ready to do whatever is good.*'[75] In other words, God is the ultimate authority, and all human governments practice delegated authority. Whenever you honor delegated authority, you are honoring the source of that delegated authority. Even if the occasion arose when we must disagree with our governments (for example, when they demand that we do

---

70   Matthew 6:9
71   I Timothy 5:17
72   I Corinthians 4:15
73   Ephesians 6:1
74   I Peter 3:1-2
75   Titus 3:1

something immoral or that violates our conscience), we must always show honor in disagreeing, as opposed to disrespect or insults.[76]

- **Institutional.** In the early church, several of the new followers of Jesus were slaves. And yet the counsel given to them was, '*Slaves, obey your earthly masters with respect and fear, and with sincerity of heart, just as you would obey Christ. Obey them not only to win their favor when their eye is on you, but like slaves of Christ, doing the will of God from your heart.*'[77] Paul was not endorsing slavery, but he was teaching those unfortunate enough to be in that situation to treat their masters with honor and to carry out their duties to the best of their abilities.[78] In today's world where we do not practice slavery, the principle remains true that we should give those who lead us in our workplaces our full respect, and that we slander God's name when we serve sullenly or half-heartedly.

> Some of us struggle with this topic of honor because we have been let down by leaders before

- **Societal.** Finally, there are many admonitions to treat older people with honor. The apostle Paul wrote, '*Do not rebuke an older man harshly, but exhort him as if he were your father. Treat younger men as brothers, older women as mothers, and younger women as sisters, with absolute purity.*'[79] The apostle Peter also wrote, '*Young men, in the same way be submissive to those who are older.*'[80] And Moses, that great liberator wrote, *You shall rise before the aged, and defer to the old; and you shall fear your God: I am the Lord.*[81] I remember growing up that as young people, we were expected to give up our seat on a bus to an older person. Modern society has lost this value; instead we honor the young and disregard the aged. Yet God says we don't honor those older than us because they are better or smarter than us, we do it because He is the Lord.

Some of us struggle with this topic of honor because we have been let down by leaders before. Someone in authority took advantage of you, or hurt or harmed you greatly. Often, that could be a parental figure, but it could also be a spiritual leader or a teacher who, instead of leading you well, brought harm to you. And as they say, 'once bitten, twice shy!' If this is you, we are really sorry for all that you went through. The pain of betrayal by those who should know better is a deep pain. Our prayer for you is that God will give you the grace to process all you went through and that your pain will not trap you in bitterness but will instead become a platform that you will use to bless others, sort of like the biblical Joseph who, when he finally had an opportunity to take revenge on his older brothers who had

---

76   A great example is when the authorities forbade Jesus' disciples from sharing the faith. Their respectful answer was, '"We must obey God rather than human beings!' (Acts 5:29). The bible is full of stories of people who stood up against unjust leaders who were violating God's laws. For example, Moses before Pharaoh (Exodus 10:24-29), Elijah before King Ahab (1Kings 21:20-24), Shadrack, Meshack and Abednego before King Nebuchadnezzar (Daniel 3:16-18) and the disciples before the Sanhedrin (Acts 4:18-20). More recent are Dr. Martin Luther King Jr. before President Lyndon B. Johnson, Dietrich Boenhoffer before Adolph Hitler, Archbishop Desmond Tutu before the Afrikaner government and Rev. Timothy Njoya before President Moi. All these spoke out against injustice *because* of their faith! And in their civil disobedience, they demonstrated that divine authority was higher than any human authority. In the process however, they did not insult, disrespect or dishonor their national or spiritual leaders. We can politely and yet firmly refuse to accept injustice while still respecting the office of our appointed leaders!

77   Ephesians 6:5

78   Some argue that this shows the bible's support for slavery but this is reading the bible out of context. Most of those who tirelessly worked for the abolition of slavery were Christians whose convictions came from scripture, for example, the bible story of Exodus, where God in His compassion, raises a leader to free His people from oppression and slavery.

79   1 Timothy 5:1-2

80   1 Peter 5:5

81   Leviticus 19:32

WHO TO HONOR

sold him into slavery and destroyed his childhood, he instead said (granted after sobbing many tears), *'You intended to harm me, but God intended it for good to accomplish what is now being done, the saving of many lives.* [82] May that also be your testimony!

Question For My Journal

Which of the above authorities have you honored well in your life? Which have you struggled most to show honor to?

Verse To Remember

Leviticus 19:32. You shall rise before the aged, and defer to the old; and you shall fear your God: I am the Lord.

Prayer For Today

Lord, forgive me for places I have dishonored God-appointed authorities in my life, either out of ignorance, pain or active rebellion. Please show me how to actively honor my leaders. Amen.

---

82   Genesis 50:12

LEGAL ACCESS

Yesterday, we learnt about the God-given authorities in our lives. One of the ways that the enemy uses to gain legal entry into our lives is through our rebellion against those that God has put in authority over us. When we rebel against them, several things happen:

We Rebel Against God (Numbers 12:4-8)

When you are driving and a policeman or woman puts up their hand, what do you do? You stop! You don't stop because she is stronger than you or better educated. You do not stop because he is tall, dark or handsome. You do not stop because you trust the police. You do not even stop because you are in the wrong. You stop because that lone policeman represents the power of the state. His or her authority is a derived authority and if you defy their orders to stop, you can expect the full force of the state to be marshaled against you. You have now become an enemy, not of that policeman, but of the government that they represent!

As we learnt earlier, Moses may have been Aaron and Miriam's baby brother but God had also appointed him to be their spiritual leader. By rebelling against him, they were rebelling against God. And God did not take long to respond. His response was rather dramatic. '*At once the Lord said to Moses, Aaron and Miriam, "Come out to the Tent of Meeting, all three of you."*'[83] Once they got there, God strongly rebuked Aaron and Miriam. He let them know that because it was *His* servant that they were speaking against, that meant they were rebelling against him!'

When we rebel against the authority God has instituted, we put ourselves on a collision course with God. We need to understand that God takes rebellion seriously. In the words of the prohet Samuel, '*Rebellion is as bad as the sin of witchcraft, and stubbornness is as bad as worshiping idols.*[84] We need to understand that choosing to submit to the people God puts in authority over us teaches us to submit to God's authority. It helps to tame our naturally rebellious hearts.

For a long time, I (Muriithi) was a very difficult person to lead, and I brought a lot of grief to those who were in authority over me. Many times I acted as if I was God's agent to keep my leaders humble. I had a critical and contrarian spirit. At other times, my rebellion was on the inside. On the outside, I looked like I was going along with what my parents, teachers or boss said, but on the inside, it was another picture! I listened politely to what they said and then I did what I had planned to do anyway! I remember my mentor, Pst. Oscar one day pulling me aside and saying something that really struck me. He said, 'Muriithi, you will never be a good leader unless you first learn to be a good follower.' Somehow God used that conversation to point out some of the rot in me. I began to realize that I would pass my rebelliousness and issues with authority on to all the people that I led, including my kids. From that day, I began to change in my response to authority so much so that some of my colleagues wondered what had happened! But for me, it had finally become clear that when we rebel against our human authorities, we rebel against God!

---

83   Numbers 12:4
84   I Samuel 15:23

LEGAL ACCESS

We Open the Door To the Enemy (Numbers 12:9-12)

After God rebuked Aaron and Miriam, He abruptly left them.[85] Here's something we have come to understand, God will never force himself on us. This is one of the amazing things about Him. When we resist earthly authorities, they fight back. If you write a hostile letter to your national revenue authority and tell them that you have decided not to pay taxes, a process begins at the end of which your head will be spinning! Or imagine when you were a teenager telling your parents or guardians, 'I'm sick of all the rules. So, let me tell you what's going to happen around here. I'm going to come and go whenever I feel like it and I'm going to keep my room however I please, and I'll dress however I want.' For some of us, those would have been famous last words! When we resist human authorities, they tend to act quickly to squelch our rebellion.

But when we reject God, He simply leaves us to our own devises, as the apostle Paul explained to Christians in Rome about what happens when people rebelled against God, '*therefore God gave them over to their sinful desires.*'[86] Without God, we are left to deal with life on our own, and that is the definition of hell. When we push God out, evil comes in. We have removed ourselves from God's cover and protection and given the enemy a right to operate in our lives. Sickness becomes our portion. Frustration becomes our daily bread. We have opened up a door in our lives and given legal access to the enemy to harass us.

This is a difficult chapter for us to write simply because it is so 'politically incorrect.' Submission to authority is one of the things we instinctively rebel against as humans., but it is also possible that some of us might be suffering because of the consequences of rebellion. It does not matter how hard we try, things never seem to work out, or even if they do, they bring us no joy. Some of us have emotional, psychological and even physical illnesses that are the result of our rebellion. You have prayed and gone for deliverance sessions and nothing has worked.

The only one of the Ten Commandments that comes with a promise says, '*Honor your father and your mother, so that your days may be long in the land that the Lord your God is giving you.*'[87] You see, it is possible to have blessings (land) and yet not enjoy those blessings (live long in the land the Lord has given) because of your rebellion against those in authority over you (in this case parents). And yet the opposite is also true; honor opens the door to enjoying God's blessings in our lives.

---

85 Numbers 12:9
86 Romans 1:24
87 Exodus 20:12

Question For My Journal

Which of the above authorities have you honored well in your life?

Which have you struggled most to show honor to?

Plan to do the prayer exercise in Appendix 3, 'The Spirit Of Rebellion'.

Verse To Remember

Proverbs 14:12 (NRSV). *There is a way that seems right to a man but in the end it leads to death.*

Prayer For Today

Lord, forgive me for places I have dishonored God-appointed authorities in my life, either out of ignorance or rebellion. Please show me how to actively honor my leaders! Amen.

TEMPTATIONS

This entire week, we have been learning that rebellion is one of the things that could greatly hinder us from ever achieving our God-given purpose. We have seen that failure to honor says much more about us than it does about our leaders, and that there are several God-appointed authorities in our lives that God wants and expects us to show honor to. We have also seen the consequences that come about when we choose the way of rebellion and dishonor, including the fact that we give the enemy legal access to harass and frustrate us.

To conclude our chapter, we want to talk about how to close the doors in our lives that may have been left open for the enemy because of our rebellion. How can you respond to this chapter in a way that helps you begin a completely new chapter in your life? There are three steps you need to take.

1. **Identify The Rebellion:** The first step is to ask God to show you specific authorities you have been rebellious against. A prayer that you will find useful throughout this course is one prayed by King David in the book of Psalms, '*Search me, O God, and know my heart; test me and know my anxious thoughts. See if there is any offensive way in me, and lead me in the way everlasting.*'[88] Make a list of all authorities that God shows you that you may have dishonored, whether it is government authority (this could be national leaders, traffic police, tax authorities, etc.), parents, teachers, employers, your spouse, spiritual leaders or even God. For each one, write out how you feel you may have dishonored them.

2. **Confess The Rebellion:** For each authority that God shows you, pray a prayer of confession. Confession is basically acknowledging your rebellion and apologizing for it. Remember, this does not have to be a complex or elaborate prayer! A simple prayer could be, 'Lord, I confess I have rebelled against (name the authority) by (name the rebellious action or attitude). Please forgive me for the sin of rebellion.' Go through your list until you have confessed every rebellion that God brings to your attention.

3. **Replace The Rebellion:** The third step is to choose, going forward, with God's help, to actively honor those in authority over your life. We do this by praying for our leaders, affirming them (do not let your leaders be affirmed everywhere else except at home) and, where possible, actively seeking to go an extra mile to help them in their task. Leaders are neither perfect nor all-knowing. So, rather than criticize or rebel, pray in those qualities you desire to see in your leader and then stand back and see how God answers those prayers. In some situations, God may choose to change you, while in others, He may choose to change your leader.

Rather than disrespectfully exposing your leaders' 'lack' or 'nakedness', seek to build them in the areas they are deficient. Seek to serve them by humbling offering your solution in their area of lack. As you pray and serve your authority in this way, you will be surprised that the initial disconnect and conflict you had with them may very well turn to be the partnership that opens doors for you! God promises to help you in all this. Philippians 2:13 says, '*It is God who works in you to will and to act according to his good purpose*'

---

88   Psalm 139:23

One of the greatest areas of rebellion today is when we choose to live life on our own terms. All across the world, in every single cutlure, humans do all kinds of elaborate religious activities in order to connect with the Divine in the way they think best. But Jesus said about himself, '*I am the way and the truth and the life. No one comes to the Father except through me.*[89] Through Jesus, God has created the only way that we can be reconciled with God. This is through confessing our rebellion and accepting Jesus as our leader. As the apostle Paul put it, '*If you declare with your mouth, "Jesus is Lord," and believe in your heart that God raised him from the dead, you will be saved.*[90] Perhaps you have heard the message of salvation before but felt it wasn't for you, or that the time wasn't right. But, my hope is that through this week, you have learnt how choosing God's way, as opposed to your own, is critical towards ever living for the things that God created you for. As you seek to break the strongholds that have held sway in your life and in your family, one of the most important things you must do is to surrender your life to your Creator, so that He can show you the reason why He created you. Our prayer is that you will not delay that decision any longer, but that you will give or recommit your life to God by inviting Jesus into your life as your leader and Lord. Here is a prayer that you could pray to do so:

Dear Lord,

I admit that I am a sinner. I have rebelled against you by thinking and doing many things that do not please you. Knowingly and unknowingly, I have lived my life on my own terms. I am sorry and I ask you to forgive me.

I believe that you came to earth and took up the consequences of my sin by dying on the cross for me, to save me. You did what I could not do for myself. And so, from today, I give you my life and ask you to take full control of it. Help me to live every day of my life for you and in a way that pleases you. Through me, may your kingdom come and may your will be done on earth as it is in heaven.

Thank you for saving me Lord. I love you, and I thank you that I will spend all eternity with you.

I pray this in Jesus' name. Amen.

If you have prayed this prayer, kindly talk about it with your *Simama* group leader or with one of your pastors so that they can pray for you and help you take the first steps towards living a life of purpose. May you truly experience the blessings of being a man or woman of honor!

---

89   John 14:6
90   Romans 10:9

TEMPTATIONS

Question For My Journal

Which God-appointed authorities have you been in rebellion against and how will you choose to honor them going forward?

Verse To Remember

Hebrews 3:12. *See to it, brothers and sisters, that none of you has a sinful, unbelieving heart that turns away from the living God.*

Freedom Prayer

Dear heavenly Father, You have said that rebellion is as the sin of witchcraft and insubordination is as iniquity and idolatry (I Samuel 15:23). I know that in action and attitude, I have sinned against You with a rebellious heart. I ask Your forgiveness for my rebellion and pray that by the shed blood of the Lord Jesus Christ, all ground gained by evil spirits because of my rebelliousness would be cancelled. I pray that You will shed light on all my ways that I may know the full extent of my rebelliousness and choose to adopt a submissive spirit and a servant's heart. In the name of Christ Jesus, my Lord. Amen.[91]

---

91   Adapted from Neil Anderson, 'The Bondage Breaker'.

WEEK
— FIVE —
LET IT GO!

WHEN FAMILY MEMBERS WRONG EACH OTHER

I (Carol) remember swapping war stories about our families as we grew up. Some were downright hilarious and harmless, like stealing sugar and then blaming a younger sibling! Others were a lot more deadly, with lifelong consequences. I remember a classmate sharing how their parents used to come home and proceed to beat all six of them as a matter of routine. Asked why they were being beaten, my classmate replied that their parents figured that they must have done wrong in the course of the day and so, without finding out exactly what, if anything at all, the parents proceeded to mete out 'discipline'! Now I wish that it was one or two smacks on the buttocks, but no! It was all out war, complete with bodies being flung on the wall with accompanying kicks and punches! For this classmate, childhood memories are dark, foreboding and quite traumatic.

What was going on here? I believe that it was abuse. Simply put, abuse occurs when parents reject their God-given mandate to nurture and provide care for their children by, either being too forceful, or being negligent altogether. If you remember, we said that parents play a hugely important role on behalf of God in the lives of their children. They are to provide protection, provision, nurture and discipline, not as they think best, but within the guidelines that God has provided. They are to carry out their mandate by being merciful, just, kind and considerate of their children.

> Abuse occurs when parents reject their God-given mandate to nurture and provide care

When these guidelines are rejected, abuse occurs. Abuse is normally classified as: physical, verbal, sexual and emotional abuse. With these kinds of abuse, direct harm is inflicted on a child. But there is another kind of abuse that is less direct; neglect. With neglect, a child is not adequately supervised or provided for. Short-term neglect occurs when parents are going through a temporary stressor whereas mid-term to long-term neglect can happen when families are exposed to prolonged periods of stress like chronic severe disease, ongoing severe conflict between parents, families with drug or alcohol abuse or mental illnesses, divorce, death in the family, demanding work schedules and severe poverty. Parents who experienced neglect in their own families due to these conditions did not acquire the skills or emotional capacity to care for their children adequately and will, therefore, also tend to neglect their own children, although in varying degrees. Cases of abandonment happen in situations of extreme poverty where a family feels inadequate to care for another child. In some cases, a single mother, even if coming from a family that could help take care of child, might be forced to abandon the baby if the family feels they do not have the emotional resources to withstand the social stigma that comes with an 'illegitimate' child.

Let's examine the types of abuse in some detail.

Emotional and verbal abuse normally occur together and involve:
- Constant belittling and humiliation of a child.
- Insults, name-calling and making negative comparisons of them to others.
- Using shaming language, including telling a child that he or she is 'no good', 'worthless', 'bad', or 'a mistake'.
- Yelling, threatening, or bullying.

WHEN FAMILY MEMBERS WRONG EACH OTHER

- Conditional love – a child is made to feel that they need to perform certain acts so that they can be good enough to be loved.
- Ignoring or rejecting a child as punishment, giving him or her the silent treatment.
- Limited display of affection for the child.
- Failing to protect the child from or ignoring the claims of the abuse by others, whether it be a parent or close relative.

Physical abuse is said to occur when a child is mistreated physically, often resulting in physical injuries. These may result from a deliberate attempt to hurt a child or through the use of excessive force in the name of making a child 'behave'. The difference between physical abuse and discipline is that with God-ordained discipline, excessive force is never used, it is not done in anger and neither is it is done to manipulate a child. Godly discipline involves the sparing use of the consequences, only administered in love, in conjunction with teaching values and then training and coaching a child on how to apply these values in their lives.

One of the worst forms of physical abuse is sexual abuse

One of the worst forms of physical abuse is sexual abuse. Sexual abuse can be divided into three: Verbal sexual abuse includes sexual threats, sexual comments about the child's body, harassment or suggestive comments. Visual sexual abuse includes the introduction to viewing of pornographic material while physical sexual abuse includes fondling of breasts or genitals, intercourse, sodomy or masturbation in front of the child or masturbation of the adult by the child. Research shows that sexual abuse occurs in one in every four families all over the world with girls being the majority of victims. Abuse usually starts between the ages of six to twelve years and is usually perpetuated by a trusted care-giving adult, for example, the father, stepfather, grandparents, cousins and uncles. Sexual abuse with children often happens when parents fail to or are unable, for some reason, to play their roles in the home of protecting and nurturing their children.

Meeka is a survivor of childhood sexual abuse. Her abuse started when she was four years old and continued until she left home at the age of seventeen. Her father would tell her that she was bad and that was the reason for the treatment she was receiving from him. But he would also threaten her and tell her not to tell anyone about what was going on. Once, she found a way of telling her mum that her dad was hurting her, but her mother dismissed her story and told her never to talk about her father in that way. Meeka was confused. Even when she tried to be good so that her father would leave her alone, it was to no avail. She would pray and ask God to stop daddy but even God did not seem to care. In the process, she aborted four babies and came to believe in what her father said of her: she was of no use to anyone, except sexually. As a result, most of her relationships in college were always sexual, without any meaningful intimacy, and as one relationship after another failed, she came to view herself as a total failure.

The net result of abuse is trauma. Trauma is experienced as pain seated deep down in one's soul that cannot seem to be easily shaken off. Such a person may often experience some of the following symptoms:

WHEN FAMILY MEMBERS WRONG EACH OTHER

1. **Shame** – a person grew up so used to being labeled bad, selfish, lazy, etc. that they have come to believe that this is who they are.

   Sadness – a deep sense of pain, sorrow or gloom, loss and general disatisfaction with life.

2. **Bitterness** – an ongoing sense of anger against the perpetrators of the abuse. Such a person may become known as an angry person who easily lashes out at others. They may have a propensity to become abusers or to, on the other extreme, become over dependent on others and, thus, open to further abuse.

3. **Emptiness** – a void due to deprivation of love and care. Such a person grows up feeling hollow and unloved. They may also experience emotional paralysis or numbness. They have this great void within themselves that is looking for 'someone' or 'something' to fill it up. When they turn to their friends to fill that void, they tend to be clingy and needy and therefore prone to be taken advantage of. This is how you find intelligent men and women remaining in abusive relationships and not being able to pull themselves out! If one does not turn to friends, the other options are addictive behaviors such as alcohol drinking or drug taking or even work.

4. **Blame and helplessness** – victims of abuse end up either blaming themselves, their parents or even God for the abuse committed against them, and the negative consequences they experienced then and may continue to experience in their lives. This is accompanied by a distorted image of God, which prevents one from experiencing God's love and grace.

5. **Relational awkwardness** – that is, an inability to form and grow relationships or to trust people in relationships. This could also create a fear of intimacy and commitment, although there is ironically a simultaneous longing for closeness.

6. **Addictions as alcohol, food, spending, work, drugs, sex, etc.** These behaviors are often used to comfort and self-soothe whenever one is overwhelmed by anxiety or other painful feelings.

7. **Self-harm** – thoughts of suicide or actual self-mutilation behaviors as burning, self-bruising, biting, sticking oneself with pins, scratching and beating oneself over the head. These behaviors again serve to relieve tension and anxiety or sometimes serve as punishment for overwhelming feelings of self-loathing.

8. **Sexual dysfunctions** – an aversion to sex, coupled with an inability to be sexually aroused or, on the other extreme, a compulsive need for sex which is expressed in the pursuit of multiple partners, compulsive masturbation, a desire for sadomasochistic sex and prostitution. This compulsion is driven in a similar way to self-mutilation. It normally comes after feelings of anxiety and agitation, similar to the feelings one used to get before the abuse. Sex, therefore, comes in as an antidote to the anxiety.

9. **Inability to trust and love God.** The utmost question is, "Why would a loving God allow this to happen to me?"

WHEN FAMILY MEMBERS WRONG EACH OTHER

Question For My Journal

As you have gone through today's reading, you may have identified yourself in some of these situations and therefore felt a return of some of the pain of the past. Restoration begins, not by burying the truth, but by acknowledging the evil done to us and directing our pain to God. So, for your journal today, write out, in full, how abuse happened in your family (if that was the case) and also how it has affected you. If it didn't, then write out the things you are grateful for in your environment that protected you from it and that you would like to have for your own children.

Next, turn to God for healing and comfort. God is the only one who can comfort us and soothe us deep down where we have been hurt. Only He can wipe away the pain and give us a new lease of life. Yes, this may seem like a miracle because of how hurt you feel, but God is a God of miracles! God is able to comfort us and soothe us from emotional pain. It takes being totally honest with Him and bringing Him all the pain. Bring to mind all the hurt and pain and, yes, it is okay. Even if it gets emotional and messy, God your Father is able to handle it. Cry before God, if necessary, and then ask Him for comfort and healing. You will be surprised at how much God is able to take away your pain!

Alternatively, if you have harmed others through abuse, confess and write in your journal exactly how that happened. Repent and ask God to forgive and deliver you from this evil. God is gracious and merciful to forgive and is more than willing to give us a second chance.

Verse To Remember

Isaiah 61:1-3. The Spirit of the Sovereign LORD is on me, because the LORD has anointed me to proclaim good news to the poor. He has sent me to bind up the brokenhearted, to comfort all who mourn, and provide for those who grieve in Zion—to bestow on them a crown of beauty instead of ashes, the oil of joy instead of mourning, and a garment of praise instead of a spirit of despair.

Prayer For Today

Lord, please heal me from all the pain I have experienced because of abuse in my family. In Jesus' name. Amen.

Lord, forgive me and cleanse me from all the pain I have caused my family through my acts of abuse. In Jesus' name. Amen.

GETTING UNSTUCK

Yesterday, we talked about the pain that results when family members wrong each other. There is nothing more devastating than the betrayal of those that God has placed in your life to lead and protect you. Many people find that the pain of the past keeps them tied up in bitterness towards those who hurt them. You may not think about them often, and you may even have moved on and succeeded in life despite the hurt, but whenever you meet that person or think about what they did to you, you realize that you are still bitter. How do you even begin to deal with this bitterness?

Fortunately, the bible has an amazing story of a man who had every reason to be bitter and yet, by God's grace, was able to move beyond surviving to thriving. Joseph was a man who had lived a harsh life, harsher than most. He had experienced disloyalty, betrayal and even brutality at the hands of close family members. Abducted and sold into slavery by his jealous brothers when only 17, he was bought by a senior government official whom he served so faithfully that he had been promoted to chief slave. Just when it had seemed that things were becoming bearable again, the man's wife had tried to seduce him and when he resisted, she had framed him and he was thrown into maximum security prison. Approximately thirteen years of his life were stolen from him the prime of his youth while he languished in slavery and prison. By an amazing miracle, God had delivered him from prison and had given him an opportunity to solve a problem for the king, who was so impressed with him that he had made him prime minister in-charge of the ministries of finance, agriculture and national planning. For nine years, he had been second in power only to the king. What a great story if it had ended there!

Joseph's brothers' betrayal really makes no sense...

But it hadn't. One day, in walked his brothers. The same ones who had betrayed him and sold him into slavery. Their arrival threw everything into turmoil! They did not recognize him, probably because it had been so many years. Also, he was dressed as an Egyptian and, of course, they had probably thought he was dead by now. His immediate emotional reaction was to accuse them of being spies and throw them into prison for three days. Then, he insisted on keeping one of them as a hostage while the rest were sent to fetch their youngest brother. All the time, they were speaking in their mother-tongue to each other, unaware that he could understand their every word!

The brothers went back home as directed and even though initially their father refused to risk his lastborn's life, in the end he was forced to because they desperately need more food from Egypt. They returned to Egypt. Joseph released their brother and fed them, and then set them up by putting his silver cup in the lastborn's food sack as they left, sending his guards to arrest him while his brothers were on their way back home! Of course the brothers were distraught because they knew it would kill their father if they returned home without his lastborn. So, they came and threw themselves at Joseph's feet, begging for mercy.

Joseph's brothers' betrayal really makes no sense. How do you plot to kill your own brother just because you are jealous of him? How do you strip him of his clothes and throw him into a well, and then cold-heartedly sell him to strangers for 200 grams of silver? And how do you then lie to your father that he was killed by an animal? Because of their brutal betrayal, Joseph had undergone the agony of slavery and the indignity of prison – two of the most dehumanizing situations anyone could be subjected to. All those wasted years! And the worst thing was all this time, *their* own lives had continued on as if nothing had happened! Joseph's story clearly demonstrates how painful and difficult it can be to forgive the deep pain that family members can cause to each other![92] What would you have done if you were Joseph?

Most of us would do anything except forgive. How many of you would have ordered them dead on the spot! I (Muriithi) personally like the fact that he threw them in jail for three days – I only wish it was a little longer and only after they knew who he was and could stew in terror for a while, wondering what would happen next! Of course it would not be revenge... nah, it would just be an opportunity to share with them a small taste of what I had gone through. After all, it is not good to encourage irresponsible behavior! How many are like me? Some of you are a little holier so you would have said, 'I forgive you, now get out of here and never return. But before you go, look... all this could have been ours!' How on earth could any in Joseph's position forgive someone who has hurt you so badly? There are many reasons why forgiveness is essential for us. Here are three important ones...

> There are many reasons why forgiveness is essential for us

- **God Asks Us to Do It.** When we forgive, we are recognizing that we too are sinners, in need of forgiveness. Our own sins reduce the gap between us and whoever did us wrong. Please note that this is in no way to excuse the evil that they have done against us, but it is to say that, given the right circumstances, we too are capable of great evil. We may not be murderers or rapists or adulterers or child abusers, but we too are rebels against God. The apostle John said, *'If we claim to be without sin, we deceive ourselves and the truth is not in us.'*[93] I may be a victim now, but under similar conditions, I'm also capable of being a perpetrator. It may be my abusive parent who destroyed my life, or it may be my unfaithful and reckless spouse who destroyed my marriage. By forgiving them, I am saying, 'But for God's help, there go I!'

- We do not forgive because it is 'the higher way' or 'the stronger thing to do' – that's pride! We forgive because we recognize our own capacity for sinfulness. Jesus once told a story about a servant who was forgiven for a huge debt but assaulted someone else who owed him much less. His conclusion was, *'If you forgive those who sin against you, your heavenly Father will forgive you. But if you refuse to forgive others, your Father will not forgive your sins'*[94]. Forgiveness is for faulty people and we are all faulty. This explains why Jesus was so tough on sinners who refused to forgive others. He saw the irony of people who need to be forgiven a lot by God turning their backs on people who need much less forgiving from them. God asks us to forgive because He wants us to recognize our own need of forgiveness.

The second reason we must forgive is...

- **We Leave Room for God.** When we forgive, we are saying that it is God's job to deal with the perpetrator. In the words of the apostle Paul, *'Do not take revenge, my friends, but leave room for God's wrath, for it is written, "it is mine to avenge; I will repay."'*[95] There is only one God. The last time I checked, His name was not Muriithi! When we don't forgive, we prevent God from

---

92   Genesis 45:1-15
93   I John 1:8
94   Matthew 6:14-15
95   Romans 12:19

GETTING UNSTUCK

intervening in our situation and carrying out his purposes. We try to take His job of punishing sinners. I know you are ambitious, but you are not qualified to take God's job! Step aside! Let God be God in your situation! Also, when we forgive, the pain caused to us loses its grip on us and is taken over by God. We must trust that God will deal with the person justly and fairly, something that we cannot do.

A third reason why we must forgive is...

- **We Close the Door.** By forgiving, we ensure that satan does not outwit or take advantage of us.[96] We have discovered over the years that bitterness is one of the biggest doors that the enemy uses to gain access to our lives and to keep us from being all that we were created to be. As someone once said, bitterness is drinking poison and hoping the other person dies! By holding on to your hatred, that person is still hurting you. Many families have been destroyed, even across generations, because of unforgiveness.

Here's something else we've discovered: Hurting people hurt others! It is possible that the person who hurt you is also a victim of hurt by others, and it is easy for the vicious cycle to continue. Your bitterness can lead you to treat others the same way you were treated, and this is exactly what the enemy wants! So long as I can focus on hating my spouse or my parents or my relative or my friend and not recognize that he is the true cause of my suffering, he wins. And the pain continues, passed unwittingly by me to the generations that follow. That is why we are admonished with these words by Paul, '*Do not be overcome by evil but overcome evil with good.*'[97] Bitterness is a chain that binds us to our past. You cannot turn back the clock and change the past but you can choose to be free from it.

Question For My Journal

Are there people that you have struggled to forgive? Make a list of anyone that you can think of – it could be a family member, a friend, a collegue, a neighbor, etc. Also write down why it is so difficult to forgive them.

Can you think of any ways that the enemy might take or has taken advantage of your pain?

Verse To Remember

Romans 8:28. And we know that in all things God works for the good of those who love him, who have been called according to his purpose.

Prayer For Today

Lord, please reveal to me any way the enemy may have taken advantage of me because of pain and bitterness.

---

96   II Corinthians 2:11

97   Romans 12:21

WHAT FORGIVENESS IS NOT

Yesterday, we saw Joseph's struggle to come to terms with his brothers' betrayal. The story is a real as it gets – including the prime minister of the most powerful nation of the world breaking down and crying so loudly that all his staff heard him![98] For many people, coming to terms with the pain and betrayal of those closest to us would be no less emotional, and so, we often choose to gloss over the past, stuff it and ignore it anything we can do to avoid getting into those murky, emotional waters that threaten to drown us!

Yet as we learnt yesterday, the only way to get ourselves truly unstuck from the pain of the past is through forgiveness. Ignoring it only drives it underground, where it can cause huge continuing harm to us, including psychological and physical illness. Also, what we fail to deal with in our generation will often come back to bite future generations, and so we owe it to those who come after us to ensure that it ends with us!

> You do not forgive after you've healed; you forgive so that you can heal

Perhaps it would be helpful today to deal with what forgiveness is not. There are at least three things that forgiveness is not…

1. Forgiving is Not Forgetting

Some of us are waiting for the pain to go away before you can forgive the person who caused it. The problem is that you do not forgive *after* you've healed; you forgive *so that* you can heal. Forgiveness is a choice, not a feeling. Joseph had to get to a point where he consciously chose to forgive his brothers, despite the fact that his feelings about their betrayal were obviously still quite raw so many years later. When it comes to the serious pain of betrayal by those you trust, time is not the great healer, forgiveness is.

It is important to know that you do not have to forget after you forgive, and sometimes you can't because the consequences stay with you for life. But your forgiveness can still be sincere, even if you do remember. God can heal your memories and give new meaning to them. As Joseph was able to tell his brothers, '*You intended to harm me, but God intended it for good to accomplish what is now being done, the saving of many lives.*'[99] He could acknowledge the evil intended while still understanding how God had rescued the situation and made something good out of the evil his brothers intended.

2. Forgiving is Not Excusing

Forgiving is not pretending that the person did not really hurt us. To forgive is not to accept or say what happened is okay. It isn't! It is not right that any person should have to go through the pain of betrayal by those who should have been in a position to protect them. So, what is forgiveness? It is to accept that, while you do not have the power to change what happened in the past, you do have the power to choose how to respond and to positively influence the future.

---

98   Genesis 45:2
99   Genesis 50:20

WHAT FORGIVENESS IS NOT

3. Forgiving is Not Tolerance

We do not have to tolerate what people do just because we forgave them for doing it! Forgiving heals us personally. But we need to take responsibility to remove ourselves from a place of danger or to confront the perpetrator, especially if they insist on continuing in their action. For example, if your spouse remains abusive or continues sleeping around and endangering your life, forgiveness needs to be followed by seeking help to ensure your safety.

These then are the things that forgiveness is not. It is not forgetting; it is not excusing and it is not tolerating. Knowing this, how do we deal with the pain and mess of forgiveness? That's what we will look at next!

Question For My Journal

What new thing have you learnt today about forgiveness? How could it apply in your life?

Verse To Remember

Ephesians 4:32. Be kind and compassionate to one another, forgiving each other, just as in Christ God forgave you.

Prayer For Today

Lord, I surrender any pain that may be in my life, felt and hidden, to you. Please unearth it and heal me. Please give me the courage and strength to forgive. Heal my memories and cause me to see You at work, even in the broken places of my life. I ask this in the precious name of Jesus. Amen.

BREAKING THE CYCLE OF PAIN

The 2011 Hollywood movie, 'Warrior', demonstrates in a very powerful way the pain and brokenness in families. The film is a sports action drama that evolves around a family that was torn apart by alcoholism. The background to the plot was that the father was a professional fighter and also a violent alcoholic who terrorized his family through brutal acts of aggression. When the wife could no longer take in the beatings, she decided to leave with her two sons who were teenagers at the time. However, the older brother (who was 16 at the time) chose not to go with the mother and younger brother and, unbeknown to his family, decided to elope with his high school sweetheart. Unfortunately, at that time, the family was unaware that the mum was sick and so the burden of caring for the mum until her death, was left to the younger brother.

Will mistrust of each other win the day?

The movie starts years later with the brothers all grown up; the older, a physics teacher and the younger, an ex-marine and their father a reformed, recovering alcoholic. It begins with the younger brother's visit to his father and, right from the onset, it is quite clear that he is still very bitter and angry at what his father had done to them. As the story unfolds, it emerges that the whole family is estranged from each other. The older brother does not talk to his father and the younger brother also does not talk to his older brother because he feels that he betrayed both him and their mother. The father, on the other hand, is in great pain and anguish over his actions in the past and seeks forgiveness and reconciliation from his two sons. They, however, do not trust him and hold on instead to their anger and bitterness.

This story unfolds in the midst of a greater drama, in which the two brothers, motivated by the 'winner take all' prize money of $5 million, independently of each other decide to enter professional fighting. The older brother needs the money to save his home from foreclosure as he has remortgaged it to pay medical bills for his older daughter, while the younger brother needs the money to help out the widow of his best friend who died in battle. Through sheer natural talent, they both outfight their opponents and the climax of the movie is when the two brothers face off. Will their mistrust of each other win the day or can they patch things up?

This movie was a deeply moving one for me (Carol) and the question that I kept wanting to shout into the screen was, 'Can't you see?' To especially the younger brother, "Can't you see that your anger and bitterness is poisoning you?" To the two brothers, "Can't you see that your father is genuinely repentant and that continuing in your anger will make you like your father was?"

As the two brothers fight it out, the younger quickly gets first advantage and from the way he pounds his older brother, it becomes evident that it is no longer about the money. It is about the pain and anger and betrayal he has felt towards him for failing to accompany him and his mother. He possibly is also expressing grief at what the father had done to them and the way the family had turned out.

The older brother, in the next round, manages to get the upper hand by dislocating his brother's arm, and he is seen in tears pleading with his younger brother to stop fighting, to no avail. By this time, the emotions are high and it is 'no holds barred' as the two bloodied brothers continue their fight. How will the fight end and who will be the winner? As the two lie struggling on the mat, the older brother

BREAKING THE CYCLE OF PAIN

tearfully asks the younger one for forgiveness, telling him that he loves him. After a moment of brief hesitation, the younger one concedes and the movie ends with the two of them exiting the ring, with the older brother's arms around the younger brother as their father watches them and smiles. It struck me as I watched this movie that these two brothers had taken the incredibly difficult and painful first steps towards breaking the cycle of pain.

As a result of abuse in the family, the two brothers in the movie experienced deep anger and sadness and they were caught in a pattern of blame and bitterness that was sad to watch. Forgiveness was almost inconceivable for them, based on the way they had been hurt. But what if they had not forgiven each other? It is almost certain that as painful as forgiveness was, had they failed to forgive each other, their pain would have continued indefinitely.

Close the door of bitterness

Facing the past is never easy and I know this week has opened wounds that we would rather forget about. Our pain too is likely to continue indefinitely if we do not forgive, for in as much as in the past few days we have acknowledged our pain to God, His antidote to breaking the cycle of bitterness is forgiveness. It took Joseph forgiving his brothers to break the cycle of suspicion and hatred towards each other. The family was able to have a fresh start because forgiveness broke the enemy's hold over their lives, thus freeing them to begin afresh.

So, how do we close the door of bitterness? There are four steps to this process.

1. Acknowledge The Pain

One thing I notice about Joseph is that he allowed himself to experience the pain. On two other occasions before, he had wept but managed to hide it from others. But at the end, he could not hold back any more. In his loud weeping, he was expressing the pain of a young boy betrayed and brutalized by those he trusted. To truly forgive, we must have the guts to remember the pain and wickedness of what was done to us and to say it was wrong. When you forgive, you do not ignore the sin but you make a deliberate choice to live with the consequences of what was done to us. For true healing to occur, we must allow God to bring to the surface all the painful emotions so that He can heal them.

2. Reframe The Pain

Sometimes in our pain, all we can see is what was done to us. In the process, after he had met his brothers again, Joseph had come to see that despite the fact that they had intended evil for him, God had worked it out for all their good. He was able to say to them, *'so then it was not you who sent me here, but God.'*[100] Sometimes all we can see is what was done to us. But the bible says in Romans 8:28, *'in all things God works for the good of those who love him, who have been called according to his purpose'.*

---

100   Genesis 45:8

3. Choose To Let Go

Even as you come to terms with your pain and acknowledge what happened and how it made you feel, the reality is that you may never truly understand exactly why it had to happen in the first place. But, you need to make the choice to let go and to release the other person. Like Joseph, we can forgive even a person who has not yet asked for our forgiveness. This is because we know that we are not doing it for them but for ourselves. Choosing to let go means making a decision not to hold their sin against them any more. We will not bring it up in conversations or make them feel bad for it. This is important because many people say they have forgiven but then the minute something goes wrong, they quickly get historical, bringing up the issue as a way to either keep the other person in their place or to protect themselves against further hurt.

4. Seek Reconciliation (Where Possible)

This is the final step of forgiveness. It is not always possible because, although forgiveness needs only one party, reconciliation requires both. The person you are forgiving may still be hostile or in denial, or perhaps is not accessible to us. They may have moved away or even passed on. In that case, you need to commit them to prayer and ask the Holy Spirit to give you resolution on the matter. However, wherever it is possible, we, like Joseph, need to offer an olive branch to those who harmed us.

When I (Muriithi) was in senior high school, I had a maths teacher who for some reason really disliked me. He made it his mission to cut me down to size, making scathing remarks about me and my work, whenever he could. Although I had been a top math student in my O-levels, his remarks so cut down my confidence that I did terribly in maths, and was not able to qualify for the degree I had wanted to do in university. This was an extremely humiliating time and I was depressed at my results, feeling I had let myself and my parents down. It took me years before I was able to understand what God had done despite of the evil done to me.

Because this man cut down my confidence, I did not do well enough to get the marks I wanted. Because of not having sufficient marks, I ended up doing a different degree in university. As I was in the line registering for this degree, I met my classmate, Carol, who became my girlfriend and later my wife. Because of being at the university, I met the man who would become an extremely influential mentor for me, and whom God used to call me into my purpose. Today, my family, my ministry and all the impact I have had exists because that man did what no teacher should ever do to a student. That's why the apostle Paul says, in all things, God words for the good of those who love Him![101]

So, ask God for his perspective. Remember, we are sinful people, born in sinful families who live in a sinful world. The truth about those who hurt us is that they are weak, needy, and fallible human beings. What they did to you was grievous, but God is able to turn it around for your good.

---

101   Romans 8:28

BREAKING THE CYCLE OF PAIN

So, today will be spent in confession. Confess and let go of all the anger, bitterness and unforgiveness that you have towards your family members and even God. This may sound counterintuitive, given all the pain you have undergone, but remember you are extricating yourself from satan's hold and giving God back control over the situation. When God is not in control, you will only continue to suffer more pain.

We are convinced that there are many lives that will change, many families that will be reconciled and many marriages that will be saved as we apply this week's lesson.

Question For My Journal

Do the exercise in Appendix 4, 'Responding To Pain And Hurt'.

Verse To Remember

Isaiah 61:1-3. The Spirit of the Sovereign LORD is on me, Because the LORD has anointed me to proclaim good news to the poor. He has sent me to bind up the brokenhearted, to comfort all who mourn, and provide for those who grieve in Zion—to bestow on them a crown of beauty instead of ashes, the oil of joy instead of mourning, and a garment of praise instead of a spirit of despair.

Freedom Prayer

Lord, I confess that as a family we have sinned against one another by _____ (identify the type of abuse that occurred in your family). I ask that you will forgive us for participating in these schemes as they have brought jealousy, disunity, hatred and mistrust for one another. I ask that You will destroy these works and instead give us love, unity and patience for one another. I give over my family to You and humbly request that You begin a new work of healing and reconciliation amongst us.

Lord, I also confess that I have harbored bitterness and unforgiveness towards _____ (list down all the family members you have grievances against). I now choose to forgive (list each one individually) and release them from the blame I have been casting on them. I recognize that blame, bitterness and un-forgiveness are schemes of the devil and I ask You to release my family and I from this bondage. In Jesus' name. Amen

STARTING OVER

The last few days have been spent examining the challenges our families experienced and the ways in which we hurt each other as a result. All families have been infected and affected by the effects of sin. The fall, Adam and Eve's rebellion, affected every one of us and so there is evil lurking in our individual lives and also collectively in the lives of our family members. But, the good news is that we do not have to remain stuck. God has created a way through which our families can be permanently healed, so that we pass on only blessings and not dysfunctions to the next generation!

Many times, we long for the ideal that we were created for. We long to communicate and be understood fully, without the angst of not being heard or being misunderstood. We all long to belong to families where we are loved unconditionally, even with our imperfections. We all long to belong to a family where there is peace, joy and love. However, the truth is that there is no perfect family anywhere in the world.

Our longings for the ideal are indicative of the fact that we were created for something better than we are experiencing right now God's ideal family. When God created mankind, He did so without sicknesses or diseases or the conflicts that are so prevalent in our families. His was a perfect world where there would be peace, joy and harmony among mankind, animals and even the environment, but all changed because of God's and our enemy. The work of the enemy is to steal, kill and destroy God's works thus, bringing death and frustration to humankind. God's work however, since the fall, is to destroy the enemy's work and to bring about reconciliation in families where there has been enmity.

The work of healing and reconciliation in our families is only made possible by the death of God's Son, Jesus Christ.[102] As the apostle Peter wrote, *'He himself bore our sins in his body on the tree, so that we might die to sins and live for righteousness; by his wounds you have been healed.'* Through Jesus' death, the enemy's grip and power over us is broken, making it possible for our families to be restored. Without His death then, we remain powerless to change. Without His death, there can be no hope or chance of our families being restored we remain under satan's power.

The only way of accessing God's power to heal you and your family is by first of all acknowledging Jesus's death on your behalf. You see, while under the enemy's influence, we sin and do all manner of evil deeds, incurring God's wrath and punishment. In effect, while under satan's rule, we are God's enemies and if we continue under that rule until death, then satan continues to rule over us into eternity with his tortuous and evil ways which can only be described as hell!

Unfortunately as human beings, we do not naturally seek God. Indeed we naturally rebel against God. But rather than punish us, God came in the form of a human being, the man Jesus, and took up the punishment that was justly ours. This was a very costly thing to do, but God knew that this is what it would take to reach out to us and restore us to wholeness and thus, reconcile us to Himself. This act of reconciliation is, however, not forced on us by God. It is only given to those who admit their sinfulness, chose to ask for God's forgiveness and acknowledge Christ's death on their behalf. To these is given eternal life and the power to break satan's power over their lives.[103]

Today therefore, we encourage you (even if you have done so before) to be reconciled to God. Reconciliation opens doors to your healing and to the restoration of your family. From our experience,

---

102   I Peter 2:24
103   John 1:12

STARTING OVER

we have seen and can testify that just one person reconciled to God in your family is a great enough catalyst for the transformation of the entire family and beyond!

Please pray as follows:

Dear God, I acknowledge that I am a sinner and have offended you in my sinful ways. I rightfully deserve your wrath and punishment but I ask for your mercy and forgiveness. I thank you for Jesus's death on my behalf that makes my forgiveness possible. I now denounce Satan's works in my life and ask that you move me from the kingdom of darkness and into your kingdom of light. I choose to surrender my life to your leadership from this day on and ask that you adopt me as your child and write my name in your Book of Life. I humbly ask that you fill me with your Spirit and sensitize me to your presence, leading and guidance. Thank you Lord that I am a child of God! Fill me with Your Holy Spirit and use me to bring Your love and freedom to everyone around me, including my family. Amen!

Congratulations! Through your confession and according to God's promise, you are a child of God, and you now have the right and power to destroy the enemy's works in your life and also in your family. In the remaining weeks, you will be more actively involved in renouncing the works of satan in your family so that they (and you) can be free from any strongholds that the enemy would bring against you!

Question For My Journal

How would you like the next generation to look (different) because of the prayers you have prayed this week?

Verse For Today

Romans 8:1-4. Therefore, there is now no condemnation for those who are in Christ Jesus, because through Christ Jesus, the law of the Spirit who gives life has set you free from the law of sin and death. For what the law was powerless to do because it was weakened by the flesh, God did by sending his own Son in the likeness of sinful flesh to be a sin offering. And so he condemned sin in the flesh, in order that the righteous requirement of the law might be fully met in us, who do not live according to the flesh but according to the Spirit.

Freedom Prayer

Dear heavenly Father, I thank You for the riches of Your kindness, forbearance, and patience, knowing that Your kindness has led me to repentance (Romans 2:4). I confess that I have not extended that same patience and kindness toward others who have offended me, but instead I have harbored bitterness and resentment. I pray that during this time of self-examination You would bring to mind all those people that I have not forgiven in order that I may do so (Matthew 18:35). I also pray that if I have offended others, You would bring to mind all those people from whom I need to seek forgiveness and the extent to which I need to seek it (Matthew 5:23-24). I ask this in the precious name of Jesus. Amen [104]

---

104   Adapted from Neil Anderson, 'The Bondage Breaker'.

WEEK
– SIX –

WRESTLING WITH
THE FATHER
(WWF)

FAMILY TRAITS

In high school, I (Muriithi) had three physical features that I did not like and that I blamed on my dad. They were my dental formula, my big nose and my receding hairline! Of course I hope that you're not laughing at me but with me! And now that we are talking about you, what features did you have growing up that you wished were different?

Many of the features that we like or do not like about ourselves have been with us since childhood. One of the things you always hear when people visit new mums in the maternity ward is, 'He looks just like his father!' Or 'She looks just like her mum!' It is obvious from observation that many different characteristics are passed on from parents to their children. These include looks, behavior and personality. What is the cause of these inherited traits or behaviors?

Sociologists differentiate between nature and nurture. Nature has to do with genetically inherited traits. Physical features like height or size of nose are usually a result of nature. Propensity to some illnesses can also come about because of inherited genes. Nurture refers to learned behavior. Children will always emulate their parents; this is how they learn! If you laugh a lot in your home, chances are that your children will laugh a lot in the own homes. If you are very intense and structured on the other hand, chances are their own homes will be the same. Right from an early age, we learn by imitating.

However, not all things we inherit have to do with nature or nurture. One of our friends, Sophie, shared a fascinating story about her large family. Her mother had eleven siblings while her father had five from his mum, with many others from the rest of his other three stepmothers. Her great-grandfather was a famous witchdoctor. As she grew older, she realized an interesting thing about her mother's family. None of the siblings got along! It was only as an adult that she began to bump into some of her first cousins. The strife was so intense that some of the brothers had even ganged up and paid some thugs to kill two of their own brothers because of a land dispute!

> Not all things we inherit have to do with nature or nurture

Our friend was very suprised when she finally realized this about her mum's family because she could see the exact same pattern among her own siblings. None of them got along with each other! She also began to notice other disturbing similarity of traits in the two families. For example, one of her sisters had sons from different fathers, exactly the same as the auntie she was named after. Her other sister had huge problems with her in-laws, similar to what her mum had gone through. Her oldest brother had once disappeared from home for many years, exactly like her uncle had in his generation. Another brother did drugs and was a Rastafarian, just like one of her uncles. Another interesting trait was that none of her uncles on either side of the family had intact marriages. In fact, on her father's side, her grandfather had actually cursed any one of his children who would marry someone from a particular tribe, which all of them proceeded to do!

Now, the interesting thing about our friend is that both her parents were born-again Christians. They were both involved in ministry. Their children grew up in church and their father really tried to protect them from the evil that he saw growing up. Unfortunately, he never dealt with the issues in his family, perhaps because it was very painful to him. He completely avoided the past, but, by not dealing with it, he actually opened himself up to deeper pain, not just for him, but for his family. The last time our friend saw her dad alive, he seemed in despair. He asked what he had done wrong. Our friend believes that he died from a broken heart.

Not all that we inherit from our parents can be attributed simply to nature or nurture! Some of it seems go a little beyond that, into what we want to refer to today as spiritual strongholds and generational curses. What in the world are those? Generally, spiritual strongholds and generational curses are misfortunes that are passed on in a family line as a result of sinful actions of people in prior generations. Simply put, they are the consequences that a family line can bear as a result of ancestors breaking God's law.[105]

More specifically, **spiritual strongholds** result from sinful actions performed by an ancestor that open a door and gives the enemy the legal right to frustrate future generations. For example, many African politicians engage in witchcraft in an attempt to gain spiritual protection from their enemies and to stay in power. Many of their children have memories of being involved in rituals that were meant to protect them. The bible lists at least five sins that attract curses from God. They are occultism, for example, witchcraft, divination, New Age practices, etc. (Deuteronomy 18:10-13), sexual perversion (Leviticus 20), idolatry (Exodus 20:1-5), oppression of the poor and helpless (Exodus 22:25, 23:6-9) and shedding of innocent blood (Genesis 4).

> Spiritual strongholds result from sinful actions performed by an ancestor

On the other hand, when it comes to **generational curses**, God has given humans, who are created in His image, the power to create with their words. If you recall back to the creation narrative, God created the world by speaking it into being. We too have been endowed with a semblance of that awesome power. King Solomon said, *'Death and life are in the power of the tongue.*[106] The apostle James added, 'With the tongue we praise the Lord and Father and with it we curse men, who have been made in his image.'[107] God has given a huge responsibility to people in spiritual authority; a responsibility which they are meant to use for the good of those they lead. But they can also use it for evil or death. Fortunately, there are limits to this power as we are reminded by Solomon that a curse without a cause is ineffective.[108]

Can strongholds and curses affect Christians? Yes! They do not have eternal effect on us but they can greatly frustrate us and reduce our quality of life, just like in our friend Sophie's family. There are many righteous kings in the bible who followed God and had great success but then, because they did not deal with their family and national issues, their sons were wicked and brought great problems to their nation. The truth is everyone, before receiving God's gift of salvation, is under a curse, since are all breakers of God's law, and deserve His wrath or punishment.[109] But when we accept Christ in our

---

105   Deuteronomy 5:8-10 *You shall not make for yourself an image in the form of anything in heaven above or on the earth beneath or in the waters below. You shall not bow down to them or worship them; for I, the LORD your God, am a jealous God, punishing the children for the sin of the parents to the third and fourth generation of those who hate me, but showing love to a thousand generations of those who love me and keep my commandments.*

106   Proverbs 18:21

107   James 3:9

108   Proverbs 26:2

109   Romans 3:23. *For all have sinned and fall short of the glory of God'*

FAMILY TRAITS

hearts, God forgives us of all our sins and rescues us from the curse of the law.[110] We have now regained the spiritual authority that Adam and Eve lost in the garden of Eden.[111] But if we do not know how to use our authority, it is possible to belong to God and be assured of your eternal salvation, and yet still experience frustration and difficulty, especially if there were particular areas in which the enemy has gained legal access into your family line. God has given us victory through the cross but we still need to apply that victory into our realities!

One of the ways of identifying the presence of strongholds and curses in your family is by observing patterns of negative behaviors or a series of misfortunes in your family tree that could include the following:

- **Patterns of failure.** For example, you may come from a family where none of the men ever make it through school or find useful work and perhaps, most become alcoholics or families where all the girls have children before marriage.

- **Family illnesses.** These are illnesses that visit family members in each generation, for example, depression, dementia, schizophrenia, bipolar disorder, alcoholism, asthma, rheumatism, diabetes, high blood pressure, barrenness, miscarriages and life-threatening diseases like cancer. If these diseases are present in prior generations, then prayer, in addition to conventional treatment, is recommended.

- **Failed marriages or failed relationships.** Some families have patterns of broken engagements or failed marriages. In this case, prayer, in addition to relationship counseling, is recommended.

- **Poverty or continual financial difficulties or roadblocks to financial success.** There are some families where, no matter how hard one works, there is little to show for it. Often times family members may have great potential but then never amount to much because nothing they do seems to prosper and, as a result, they remain poor.

- **Unbelief.** Have you ever found yourself struggling to believe in God or prayed for family members for years, without much success? Is there a pattern of unbelief in your family? The condition of unbelief may need to be tackled at a generational level.

- **Strife and conflict.** This is the situation where patterns of conflicts, say between siblings or parents or even in-laws, are present in both the older and younger generation. In some families, conflict over property has left family members poor despite great wealth being left as an inheritance.[112]

- **Futility or lack of fruitfulness.** This is a situation in which effort does not result in success or even the enjoyment of that success. As Moses wrote of people cursed by God, he said, *'You will be pledged to be married to a woman but another will take her and ravish her. You will build a house, but you will not live in it. You will plant a vineyard but you will not even begin to enjoy its fruit.'*[113]

---

110 Galatians 3:13
111 Matthew 18:18. *Truly I tell you, whatever you bind on earth will be bound in heaven, and whatever you loose on earth will be loosed in heaven.*
112 1 John 2:11 *But anyone who hates a brother or sister is in the darkness and walks around in the darkness. They do not know where they are going, because the darkness has blinded them'.*
113 Deuteronomy 28:30

- **Sudden ruin.** This is when carefully built wealth, power or position all of a sudden, without warning, is destroyed. It could happen that disease completely wipes out family wealth or like Job in the bible, it could be the work of enemies. Whatever the cause, this sudden loss often impacts the family deeply as the people concerned are usually not able to regain their former status, unless, of course, an intervention in prayer is made.

- **Confusion and general lack of ability to make wise decisions.** Sometimes people make decisions that do not make sense at all and, in the process, they end up harming themselves and hurting others around them. When such patterns are observed generationally, this too is a call to prayer.

- **Being accident prone, suicide and unnatural or untimely deaths.** Some families have accidents or early death occurs so regularly that they take them for granted as normal! These two can be signs of strongholds and curses.

Question For My Journal

Look at your family tree and try and identify from the list above, negative behaviors or misfortunes that have been handed down at least two generations (though three would be the ideal).

Who in the family is most affected?

Do you personally identity with any of the traits listed? Or can you identify others that are missing in this list?

Verse To Remember

Galatians 3:13. Christ has redeemed us from the curse of the law, being made a curse for us: for it is written: 'Cursed is every one that hangs on a tree'.

Prayer For Today

Lord, give me discernment and insight to see if there are any strongholds or curses that the enemy has used to attack me and my family.

SECONDS AWAY, ROUND ONE!

How can we overcome spiritual strongholds and generational curses? Does the bible have anything at all to say about this? Fortunately for us, the answer is yes. The bible is full of stories of extremely messy families that show the limiting effects of sin, strongholds and curses. But a really good example would have to be the family of Jacob (Genesis 32:22-30).

Jacob's family was riven with issues: strife, favoritism, jealousy and fear, among others, and it seems that their root sin was deceit. Jacob's own name meant 'he grasps the heel' or 'he deceives,'[114] This character trait was not something that had begun in his generation. We first notice the pattern first with his grandpa, Abraham, who had a very beautiful wife. He was fearful that the powerful king of the Egyptians would be jealous because of his beautiful woman, so he told her to lie that she was his sister, leaving her open to being taken advantage of by others.[115] What kind of man does that? But a generation later, after Abraham had died, you see a strange thing. His son, Isaac, lied to another powerful king that his beautiful sister was his wife.[116] As they say, 'Like father, like son!'

So, that's dad's side. Now mum's side was even worse. Rebekah came from a family of expert liars. She loved her younger son Jacob because he stayed indoors and loved to cook like her, unlike his older brother Esau who was an outdoorsman like his father.[117] So she conspired with Jacob to con her own husband into leaving his brother's inheritance to him! It worked, but it resulted in great strife between the brothers. When their mum heard that Esau was plotting to kill his younger brother, she manipulated her husband into sending Jacob off to her relatives, on the pretext that he needed to find a wife.

That is how he fled from the chaos caused by his deceit and went to live with his mother's family. But he found her brother, uncle Laban, to be an even greater deceiver than his mother! Jacob labored for him for seven years to marry beautiful Rachel, only for his uncle to con him at the last minute and switch her under the cover of darkness with her rather plain older sister, Leah. He was forced to sign a contract for another seven years if he wanted to get the girl of his dreams. After he was done, he worked another seven years, which proved to be a battle of wits between him and his uncle. Uncle Laban was the boss from hell, changing his contract and cutting his fees ten different times!

Meanwhile, the strife had split over into his own family. His two wives, who were sisters, were competing in having babies to win his affection. They did everything, including bringing their maids for him to have children with and, on one occasion, Leah even had to bribe her younger sister so that she could sleep with her husband! What a messed-up competition! The negative effects of the sin of deceit were being passed on as a stronghold to the next generation.

In the midst of all this, Jacob's financial success caused his cousins to despise him and give him dangerous glances. So after twenty years of exile away from his family, Jacob had to flee with his two wives, after deciding that it was less risky to meet his brother who had hated him many years back, than it was to stay with his cousins whose hatred was a lot more fresh.

---

114   Genesis 25:26
115   Genesis 12:11-13
116   Genesis 26:7
117   Genesis 25:28

SECONDS AWAY, ROUND ONE!

It seemed everything was finally crashing down on Jacob. He had missed his father's funeral and he had not seen his mum for twenty years. His wives were constantly fighting and his uncle and cousins thought he was a crook. His own brother had put out a 'wanted dead or alive' sign for him and yet he had nowhere else to run to except home. It was at this point that a mysterious man appeared to him in the night and challenged him to a wrestling match. The fight lasted all night. Then after the man spoke for the first time, Jacob realized his opponent was not a man but a supernatural being!

The interesting thing is that this being, whether it was an angel or God Himself, could have disabled Jacob at any time, yet he allowed him to wrestle until he was exhausted. If he could have won whenever he so desired, why didn't he? It seems that the struggle was necessary for Jacob's deliverance. Through it, Jacob needed to come to the place where he realized that his hustling could not save him. His smooth tongue could not bail him out! It was at that point that his opponent asked him to let him go. The supernatural being that could have snuffed him out, but was instead asking whether they could stop! Jacob, although exhausted, refused and asked for a blessing. The prophet Hosea, puts it this way, *'In the womb he grasped his brother's heel, as a man he struggled with God. He struggled with the angel and overcame him; he wept and begged for his favor.*[118] Jacob did not just ask; he pleaded and begged for a blessing! Again, this being, the same one who could dislocate a hip with his finger,[119] agreed. And then he asked Jacob for his name.

> He would no longer be one who deceived men, but one who prevailed with God.

Do you find this question at all odd? I do. If this was God or an angel, why would he bother asking Jacob's name – he should have known who he was wrestling with! God asked Jacob his name, not because He did not know it. He wanted to know if Jacob knew it. He wanted to know if Jacob was ready to come to grips with who he really was. By answering, 'Jacob', Jacob was doing an uncomfortable thing. He was admitting the truth about himself and his family. "It's me, Jacob, the master schemer, the manipulator, the deceiver. The grandson and son of liars." It was only after he confessed this that God now blessed him: *'Your name will no longer be Jacob, but Israel, because you have struggled with God and men and have overcome.*[120]

Jacob means 'deceiver'. Israel means 'he struggles with God'. He would no longer be one who deceived men, but one who prevailed with God. No longer would he be the deceiver, but the overcomer. Even the nation that had been promised to his grandfather, Abraham, would from then on bear his name. You see, God can turn the enemy's strongholds into our strong points. He can turn your curses into resources and make you a blessing for the next generation!

The first step towards overcoming the strongholds in your family is becoming aware of them and calling them out as they are. Overcoming the strongholds is through prayer, wrestling with God, for the sake of your family until He blesses you and gives you a new identity. It is saying to God, 'it stops with me!'

---

118 Hosea 12:3-4
119 Genesis 32:25
120 Genesis 32:28

SECONDS AWAY, ROUND ONE!

My (Muriithi's) own parents were the first in their own families to come to Christ. My mum came from an extremely poor family, where the men never amount to much. Yet as she has dealt with the issues, those strongholds have not passed on to her own children, although we still see them in parts of the extended family. We have no expectation of failure, but we fully expect to succeed. My dad was the only surviving brother on his side of the family. Again, he stands out in his own family, despite being the lastborn. Because of my parents, we have not had to deal with many of the issues that they did in their generation. All my siblings are believers and I am truly grateful for my parents' investment in our lives. Carol and I are determined to root out any remaining strongholds and to close any remaining doors in our generation so that our children will work in even greater freedom than ourselves.

This is what happens when spiritual bondages and generational curses are broken. There is freedom in the next generation.

How then do we break bondages and curses?

> It is still important that you keep praying about any trends you notice; you must maintain the freedom!

1. **We Confess Ancestral Sin.** Twice in the book of Nehemiah,[121] we see people making a prayer of confession for the sin of the forefathers that brought about their exile. Some of you are first generation believers. You are the first ones in your family line to come to Christ. God wants you to deal with the curses and bondages so that they stop with you, and you leave a godly heritage with the next generation. Some are second generation believers like me. Someone else dealt with most of the issues and you are enjoying the blessing. It is still important that you keep praying about any trends you notice you must maintain the freedom! Often, it takes more than one generation to deal with the multiple issues in our families. For example, we noticed that my (Muriithi's) mum and her only sister had had a strained relationship for many years and so had my two sisters. Then we noticed our daughters were beginning to have some intense sibling rivalry. We decided to deal with it in prayer but also to prioritize teaching our girls to enjoy each other so that this stops in their generation!

2. **We Wrestle With The Father For Our Relatives.** Jacob wept with tears and clung to God until God changed his destiny. We must pray that God will open the eyes of our other family members so that they too will break the power of the curse over themselves and their own progeny. We must pray for our family members because their sin affects us. It is a big job to close the doors that have plagued our families. In my (Carol's) family, I was the first believer. I felt responsible to wrestle in prayer for my family, and by God's grace, many of my own siblings are now believers. Some of you, like Jacob are the lastborns and nobody thinks much of you, but as you deal with your own issues, God is saying He is willing to bless your family because of you. We can tell you from experience that a huge change comes to your family when every member knows Christ. Is it possible? Absolutely yes!

---

121   Nehemiah 1:5-10, Nehemiah 9:1-38

3. We Grow Spiritually. We must prioritize growing spiritually as individuals and also as families. Family growth comes through a habit of prayer and devotions together. As the saying goes, 'the family that prays together, stays together!'

One of the most astounding things to note as we conclude is that as we break the power of the curse, we learn that we have the power to do the opposite; which is to bless ourselves and our children! In fact you can learn to speak blessing over all the areas where God has given you spiritual authority. I (Muriithi) verbally bless my wife and my children, and often in their hearing. I also bless my staff team and congregation often. Why? Because I believe God honors the authority He has given me to bless them and because I want to model to them that they can bless their your own families!

Question For My Journal

Look at your family tree and try and identify from the list above, negative behaviors or misfortunes that have been handed down at least two generations (though three would be the ideal).

Who in the family is most affected?

Do you personally identity with any of the traits listed? Or can you identify others that are missing in this list?

Verse To Remember

Galatians 3:13 *'Christ has redeemed us from the curse of the law, being made a curse for us: for it is written: 'Cursed is every one that hangs on a tree.'*

Prayer For Today

Lord, give me discernment and insight to see if there are any strongholds or curses that the enemy has used to attack me and my family.

THE CURSE OF INJUSTICE

Yesterday, we began to see how to break the spiritual strongholds and generational curses that affect our families through wrestling with God in prayer. We ended by trying to identify these in our families and, naturally, the question that arises is how these generational curses come about in the first place. Later in a different chapter, we'll look at the place of a spiritual door-opener called idolatry. Today though, we want to learn how injustice opens the door to curses.

Moses, that great law-giver, defined injustice as including the following actions:

1. Moving a neighbor's boundary marker. This refers to dishonesty and corruption;[122]

2. Misleading a blind person on the road. This refers to lying and malice;[123]

3. Depriving the alien, the orphan and the widow of justice. This is taking advantage of weak and vulnerable members of the society[124]; or

4. Taking a bribe to kill. This refers to murder.[125]

A friend of mine (Carol's) grew up witnessing family drama that could only have been caused by the effect of a curse of injustice. Back in the 1960s, her grandfather's sister worked hard and painstakingly saved up enough money to buy a piece of land. She had been widowed when quite young and so acquiring land was not just a huge accomplishment for her, but was also the primary means through which she would raise her children.

Being illiterate however, it was agreed that her older brother, my friend's grandfather, would help her with the legal process of land transfer and acquisition of the title deed and, in exchange for this service, he would be entitled to cultivate on a portion of the land for an agreed upon time. Despite having already received an inheritance of land from his father, this older brother, in a coldly calculated fashion, worked out a plan to defraud his widowed sister. He worked it out so that the land was registered in his name and his sister could not lay claim to any part of it! Their father on hearing of this was very aggrieved. He tried numerous times to intervene so as to reverse the injustice between his children but to no avail – the son was adamant that the land was his. Finally, on his dying bed, their father proclaimed a curse on the land: He declared that it would never be productive!

My friend shared with me that their family land, despite being surrounded by other fertile land, is today very unproductive! Growing up, she recalls that no matter what food crop was planted, it did not thrive. Moreover there were numerous accidents that happened on the land. People would injure themselves in unusual ways while tiling the land and this family could not keep cows without them dying. As a result of this, many times the family would go without a harvest and had to buy food from their neighbors. Moreover, even on those occasions when they did get a harvest from a different piece of land, the money would be wasted in drinking, wild living and financially unwise decisions. This meant that the family did not progress despite the great potential wealth they could have made

---

122   Deuteronomy 27:17
123   Deuteronomy 27:18
124   Deuteronomy 27:19
125   Deuteronomy 27:25

from their several tracts of land. By the time she was sharing this story, it was three generations later, and none of her grandfather's children or grandchildren had had a successful life. There was a pattern of failure among the men, and incidences of barrenness and stagnation on all of them. The family had never been able to multiply the assets the grandfather had acquired.

Messing with injustice is messing with God Himself!

Why does injustice brings about a curse? In the bible, we learn that God is especially attentive to the weak and vulnerable members of the society. When they call out to him, He hears them and moves to their defence. Here's how several bible writers put it...

'You shall not afflict any widow or orphan. If you afflict them in any way, and they cry at all to me, I will surely hear their cry.[126] Moses

'Do not move the ancient boundary or go into the fields of the fatherless, for their Redeemer is strong; He will plead their case against you.[127] King Solomon

'Now listen, you rich people, weep and wail because of the misery that is coming upon you... Look! The wages you failed to pay the workmen who mowed your fields are crying out against you. The cries of the harvesters have reached the ears of the Lord Almighty... you have fattened yourself in the day of slaughter.[128] The apostle James

'Woe to him who builds his house without righteousness and his upper rooms without justice.[129] The prophet Jeremiah

From these verses it is pretty clear: Messing with injustice is messing with God Himself! How do we break curses brought about by injustice?

Breaking such a curse involves repentance and showing the evidence of your repentance through restoring what was taken through injustice. Whoever has stolen should restore what he has stolen. The story of Jesus and Zacchaeus the tax collector is a good example. As a tax collector, Zacchaeus had become rich by cheating people. When he met Jesus, however, he repented. His true repentance was shown in his willingness to repay everything he had ever taken from people.[130]

In our family settings, historical injustices can be corrected through this same process of repentance and restoration. Here is how this happened one day in a village in Fiji.

God showed this village the need to repent for the generational sin of killing and cannibalizing the first Methodist missionary to Fiji. In a ceremony filmed by CNN, tearful Fijian warriors in grass skirts and armed with clubs, begged forgiveness from the descendants of the English missionary their ancestors had killed more than a century ago. In this ceremony, villagers presented woven mats, a dozen

---

126   Exodus 22:22-24
127   Proverbs 23:10-11 (NASB)
128   James 5:1-5
129   Jeremiah 22:13 (NASB 1995)
130   Luke 19:8

THE CURSE OF INJUSTICE

highly prized whale's teeth and a slaughtered cow as they implored his descendants to forgive them for his murder and help them lift a curse which they believed had blighted their lives.

As believers in this village and other surrounding villages sought forgiveness for the sins committed in earlier generations, they experienced the healing of their land. In some cases, the process of deliverance took as long as 18 months, but as God revealed sin, they were quick to confess it and to seek forgiveness from the people they had wronged. As they obeyed God, they watched Him miraculously heal sicknesses and disease, heal broken relationships and bring reconciliation among enemies. But even more astonishing was the healing of the land.

> As far as is possible, commit to seek forgiveness from the people wronged by your family

For example, in the village of Nuku, a toxic stream that had flowed with poisonous water for 40 years suddenly healed as a result of intentional prayers for generational sins. Whereas once people developed brain lesions from the water, the people are now able to freely drink from the stream. What is even more amazing is that the stream is still polluted above and below the village, but clear and healed as it flows through the community!131

From this story, we can apply several lessons as we seek to break curses brought on through the practice of injustice in our families.

1. **Prayer:** Through a process of prayer and fasting (even a one day fast) ask God to reveal to you instances of injustice committed by your family. Ask the Lord to bring to mind past stories. Also, discuss as a family if there are any known instances of injustice that were done by members of your family.

2. **Confession:** If any such cases come to mind, here is a prayer you can pray.

   Dear heavenly Father, I confess that my family acted wrongfully by being unjust in these ways (list everything God has so far brought to mind). We have sinned against You by violating the command to be just and considerate of others. I renounce these actions in my life and also in that of my family. I choose to honor your word to love others. I cancel any ground satan may have gained in our lives through our acts of injustice and renounce all satanic assignments for my life. Bring healing and deliverance to our family as the stronghold of satan is released through this act of confession. Amen.

3. **Repentance:** As far as is possible, commit to seek forgiveness from the people wronged by your family. This may involve paying them a visit individually or with other family members. As this is a potentially very difficult thing to do, take time to prepare well through prayer and fasting. Keep each other accountable with your prayer partner to complete this process.

4. **Restoration:** Sometimes the process of correcting an injustice involves compensation. Do not, therefore, be surprised if, as you wait upon God, you sense Him asking your family to compensate for wrongs done.

---

131   Adapted from www.prayertransformation.com and www.sentinel.com

However, He alone is wise and He will not lead you through a process that you cannot manage to do.

As you obey God, ask Him to bring healing for family members who are sick, deliverance from addictions that have plagued your family, and restoration of fruitfulness so that the labors of every member of your family will be prosperous, and yes, pray healing for any unproductive land or assets.

Be patient and understand that this is a process. As the Lord over time brings to mind other circumstances of injustice, also confess these to God. Seek forgiveness from the people concerned and then, ask God for healing as you faithfully obey Him.

As we read in the Fiji story, in some cases it took 18 months of ongoing prayer before they experienced complete victory. Even if it is two days in a month, commit to prayer and fasting over your family and you will be amazed at the victories you will experience!

Question For My Journal

What have you learnt from today's reading? Are there any instances of injustice that you have identified in your family? Who do you plan to speak with to explore your family history further?

Verse To Remember

II Chronicles 7:14. *If my people who are called by my name will humble themselves and pray and seek my face and turn from their wicked way, then I will hear from heaven, (my dwelling place), and will forgive their sin, and heal their land.*

Prayer For Today

Lord, please bring to my mind any instances of injustice in my family tree that may have given the enemy legal access to affect us.

INJUSTICE AND ME

Yesterday we looked at the circumstances under which injustice was perpetuated in our families. But what about ourselves? Sometimes we unknowingly continue this pattern of injustice because we are ignorant of the practice or even if aware, nevertheless choose to continue with it. It is our hope that by now, the seriousness of this matter should have persuaded you the contrary. The gains gotten through illegitimate means are only short lived and in the long run bring much sorrow in your life and that of your children and their children's children.

Consider these sayings by King Solomon:

'A fortune made by a lying tongue is a fleeting vapor and a deadly snare.' ***Proverbs 21:6***

'Dishonest money dwindles away, but whoever gathers money little by little makes it grow.' ***Proverbs 13:11***

The only way of *being* just is by *doing* it.

Consider the actions below and evaluate what you need to stop or start doing. Put a tick on all that apply.

IN YOUR PERSONAL LIFE

1. Start sharing what you have with those in need. Use a portion of your monthly income to cater for the needs of the poor. King Solomon said that when we give to the poor we are lending to God Himself![132]

2. In family settings, do not take sides with oppressive family practices. For example, ensure that family resources are shared equitably and that special care is given to the weak and more vulnerable family members.

3. In personal relationships, do not take advantage of others. Do not take advantage of someone sexually through coercion or by leading them on, while all the time you are not really interested in them.

4. Budget for your family members in need. Do not consume all your resources on yourself but realize that we have a responsibility to help out needy family members. Give regularly, but only what you can and have predetermined to, and communicate this to family members as some have also been known to take advantage of situations in which they are being assisted.

5. Take your share of responsibility in the family. Do not watch one family member take on the full load of, for example, caring for ageing parents.

6. Take responsibility for caring for children in your extended family that are born out of wedlock or are in a situation of either divorce or separation.

7. If you are a parent, do not show favoritism to one child as this is unfair on the others. Also, do not vex your children by overloading them with too much work or responsibility. In other

words, do not 'dump' on them or abdicate your responsibility to them. Be sure that the workload is shared equally among the children, according to their age, and that you too are doing your share of the work or carrying your share of the load.

8. Do not mistreat your workers in your home by giving them substandard food to eat, or a substandard space to sleep in, by shouting at them or calling them names. Manage their workload so that they too get enough time to rest on a daily basis. Honor their leave and off-days and pay them fairly. Dignify your workers in the eyes of your children by having them use a respectful title such as 'Ms.' or 'Mister' or auntie when addressing them. As your children grow older, have them take up more responsibilities in the home. Remember, ultimately, responsibility for the workload rests with the family; the worker is only there to assist the family fulfill its role.

IN BUSINESS OR WORK SETTINGS

1. Completely cease from engaging in or profiting from fraudulent or corrupt deals. Do not enrich yourself at the expense of others.

2. If employed, do not steal from your employer by doing substandard work, using office equipment or resources for personal gain or using office time for personal errands.

3. If you are a supervisor, head of a unit or an organization, ensure that the working conditions of your employees are just and fair. For example, ensure that work is planned ahead of time and that workloads are managed efficiently so that employees are not overextended by long working hours. Lack of proper rest on a daily basis, plus inability to take leave, not only is a health hazard to the employee, but is a major contributor to the breakdown of families. Ensure then that working conditions do not endanger the health or family wellbeing of your employees.

> Do not 'kiss' up to your superiors to gain favor from them while 'kicking' down at your colleagues

4. Cease from engaging in business practices that either oppress or destroy the lives of others. For example, as far as you are able, lobby for fair policies that do not mislead or take advantage your clients. Also ensure that the products or services you offer uplift lives as opposed to destroying them.

5. If not doing so, pay your workers fair wages and take steps to attend to their welfare. For example, enroll them in savings schemes, health insurance schemes and in pension schemes (this applies to casual laborers in your home as well).

6. In the workplace, do not 'dump' on your colleagues or abdicate your responsibilities. Take full responsibility for your work.

INJUSTICE AND ME

7. Do not steal your colleagues' 'ideas' and then present them as your own. This is theft. Work hard instead and generate your own ideas as this is where your blessing will come from.

8. Do not 'kiss' up to your superiors to gain favor from them while 'kicking' down at your colleagues or those subordinate to you. This is unfair. The only way to gauge if you have treated others fairly is by asking yourself if you have treated them as you would like them to treat you. With this the Lord is pleased!

Question For My Journal

Which of these practices have you done really well? Which ones do you need to put work into? Which three can you prioritize and immediately begin doing?

Verse To Remember

Micah 6:8. What does the Lord require of you but to do justice, to love mercy and to walk humbly with your God?

Freedom Prayer

Dear heavenly Father, I confess that I have acted wrongfully by being unjust in these ways (mention all the actions you ticked). I have sinned against You by violating the command to be just and considerate of others. I renounce these actions in my life and instead choose to honor your word to love others as I love myself. I cancel any ground satan may have gained in my life through my acts of injustice and renounce all satanic assignments for my life. Bring healing and deliverance in my life as the stronghold of satan is released by faith through this act of confession. Amen.

DOORS TO CURSES - DISHONORING PARENTS

King Solomon once declared, *'there is a generation that curses its father, and does not bless its mother.*[133] He might as well have been talking about our culture today! This truth dawned on me (Muriithi) painfully one day while volunteering as a Sunday school teacher. While bending low to address a certain child, I was completely unprepared for what happened next; a blinding blow to my eye! For one dizzy moment, I could not fathom what might have happened. I could not imagine, for instance, that a child could pull such a move on an adult, but my swollen eye testified otherwise! This little boy of no more than five years old, had had no qualms punching me, and I am not sure that if I had talked to his parents, things would have been any different. My concern was, if this child does not honor and respect teachers at this age, what will make him honor and respect work, national and God's authority when he get older?

> ## Children honor their parents through obedience

The responsibility of teaching children to honor and respect authority lies squarely with parents and cannot be relegated to other institutions such as churches or schools. Honoring parents is so important to God that it is the first command He gives with a promise. The fourth commandment states, *'Honor your father and your mother, that your days may be prolonged in the land which the LORD your God gives your God gives you.*[134] The implication here is that honoring parents is directly related to God's blessing of long life and wellbeing. God took this so seriously that in ancient Israel, failure to honor parents was actually punishable by death. 'And he who curses his father or his mother shall surely be put to death,'[135] Moses relayed to the Israelites. Talk about this thing being serious!

Perhaps one of the reasons why God emphasized parental honor was because as one learnt how to honor their parents, they would instinctively know how to honor God. I (Carol) know that this has certainly been true in my life. The way my mother taught us to honor and respect my father helped me realize that I need to honor my heavenly Father in the same way. When I look to scripture, I see Jesus revering and deferring to His Father as well.

The apostle Paul admonished, *'Children, obey your parents in the Lord, for this is right.*[136] One thing we note in scripture is that the command to obey parents was given to children and not to adults! Children honor their parents through obedience. However, the command to honor our parents is true for all of us, regardless of how old we are. As an adult, I do not relate to my parents on the basis of obedience but of honor. If my father, for example, told me to stop spending time with my wife, I am not under such an obligation as I am now responsible before God for my own home! However, it is important that both my wife and I intentionally set out to honor our parents.

HOW SHOULD CHILDREN BE TAUGHT TO HONOR?

- You must teach your children to obey parental instructions at the first command without the parent having to repeat or cajole the child.

---

133 Proverbs 30:11 *He who curses his father or his mother shall surely be put to death.*
134 Exodus 20:12
135 Exodus 21:17
136 Ephesians 6:1

DOORS TO CURSES - DISHONORING PARENTS

- You must teach children not to talk back to their parents but to find respectful ways of voicing their opinions or concerns.

- You must teach your children to give preference to the parents, for example, by giving up a seat in favor of the parent.

- You must teach your children to serve their parents joyfully, as opposed to the situation today where parents are held hostage by their kids' demands.

- You must teach your children to help out with chores at home, willingly and joyfully, as part of being a responsible member of the family.

- You must teach your children delayed gratification so that they are not constantly whining and demanding from their parents!

King Solomon taught that disciplining a child was equivalent to saving their life! *'Don't hesitate to discipline children. A good spanking won't kill them. As a matter of fact, it may save their lives.'* [137] This is in stark contrast to today's psychology-driven parenting that teaches that loving parents could never spank their children. Solomon has this to say, *'Whoever spares the rod hates their children, but the one who loves their children is careful to discipline them.'* [138] It is important to say that discipline is always reasoned, limited, never meted out in anger, and is aimed at lovingly correcting your child, not cutting them down for their mistakes.

Children of all ages should honor their parents

After children mature, the obedience that they learnt as children will serve them well in honoring other authorities such as government, police, and employers. Honoring your parents evolves as you grow toward adulthood. As a teenager, honor evolves into respect for authority over us. As an adult child, honor evolves into kindness, thoughtfulness, care, provision and protection. Children of all ages should honor their parents, regardless of whether or not their parents "deserve" honor. God did not qualify the commandment to honor our parents as something they must first earn or deserve. At no time are you expected to "relieve" them of their God-sanctioned position as parent. Instead, you are to continue to respect their position while caring for them.

HOW ADULTS CAN HONOR PARENTS

- Calling and visiting your parents regularly.

- Blessing them, for example, when you visit always carry gifts as food items as an act of courtesy.

- Praying for them regularly.

- As far as is possible, plan a visit to seek your parents' forgiveness for any lack of obedience or honor that comes to mind. Ask your prayer partner to keep you accountable to this.

---

137   Proverbs 23:13-14
138   Proverbs 13:24

DOORS TO CURSES - DISHONORING PARENTS

- Attending to parental needs which may include financial and moral support, especially if they are going through a difficult time. As a family, we rallied our siblings on both sides (Carol's and I) and engaged in building projects that ensured our parents' financial stability. We wanted to ensure that as they grew older, all their basic needs for housing, food and health were covered. What do you do when your parents' needs are beyond what your budget can allow? It's important to bear in mind that we also have an obligation before God to provide for[139] and leave an inheritance to our children.[140] And so we give only what we can afford to, and then see how we can help rally whatever help we can from our siblings as well as support through prayer and ideas.

- Blessing your parents materially, even when they do not have needs. As a couple, we regularly give a monthly gift to both sets of parents that we have put in our budget. It is our way of blessing them!

- Forgiving parents for hurts committed earlier in your life, even if your parents are no longer alive.

I (Carol) felt moved one day by God to go and repent to my parents and ask for their forgiveness for the times I rebelled against them as a teenager. I believe the reason why God asked me to do this was because in my rebellion I had given satan legal reasons to have an influence in my life. The only way I could break this bondage was through repentance. I obeyed, despite my fears, and was pleasantly surprised when my parents received me so graciously and forgave my teenage foolishness.

Question For My Journal

If you are a parent, in which ways have you taught your children to respect you? In what ways have you failed to do so?

Growing up, in which ways did you fail to honor your parents? How about now? How do you honor your parents? What do you specifically need to do in order to grow in honoring your parents?

Plan to do the exercise in Appendix 5, 'Identifying Generational Patterns'.

Freedom Prayers

For Yourself

Dear heavenly Father, I confess that I dishonored my parents by (list everything God has so far brought to mind). I have sinned against You by violating the command to honor my father and mother. I renounce these actions in my life and now choose to honor my parents. I cancel any ground satan may have gained in my life through my act of rebellion and renounce all satanic assignments for my life. Bring healing and deliverance to me as the stronghold of satan is released by faith through this act of confession. Amen.

---

139 I Timothy 5:8 *Anyone who does not provide for their relatives, and especially for their own household, has denied the faith and is worse than an unbeliever.*
140 Proverbs 13:22 *A good person leaves an inheritance for their children's children, but a sinner's wealth is stored up for the righteous.*

DOORS TO CURSES - DISHONORING PARENTS

For Those With Children

Dear heavenly Father, I confess that I have failed to raise my children to honor me/us as their parent(s) by (list everything God has so far brought to mind). I have sinned against You by violating the command to raise my children in godly ways. I renounce these actions in my life and choose to honor your word regarding how I raise my children. I cancel any ground satan may have gained in the life of my child/ren and renounce all satanic assignments for their lives. Bring healing and deliverance to my child/ren as the stronghold of satan is released by faith through this act of confession. Amen.

For Your Family Tree

Dear heavenly Father, I come to You as Your child, purchased by the blood of the Lord Jesus Christ. I here and now reject and disown all the sins of my ancestors. As one who has been delivered from the power of darkness and translated into the kingdom of God's dear Son, I cancel out all demonic working that has been passed on to me from my ancestors. As one who has been crucified and raised with Christ and who sits with Him in heavenly places, I reject any and every way in which satan may claim ownership of me. I declare myself to be eternally and completely signed over and committed to the Lord Jesus Christ. I now command every familiar spirit and every enemy of the Lord Jesus Christ that is in or around me to flee my presence and never to return. I now ask You, heavenly Father, to fill me with Your Holy Spirit. I submit my body as an instrument of righteousness, a living sacrifice, that I may glorify You in my body. All this I do in the name and authority of the Lord Jesus Christ. Amen.[141]

---

141   Adapted from Neil Anderson, 'The Bondage Breaker'.

WEEK
– SEVEN –
LIVING IN A BUFFET WORLD

BUFFET SPIRITUALITY

We live in a cosmopolitan world. Unlike our parents' generation who may have grown up in one village and most likely talked only to people of their ethnic group until they were older, many today grew up and went to school with friends from different ethnic groups. We work with people from all over the world, and we have a much more exciting diet than our ancestors did. They may have been limited to food just from one region, but we regularly eat dishes that are typical not just from all over our country, but from all over the world! I still remember one of my (Muriithi's) grandmas who would not eat spaghetti because, for the longest time, thought it was snails! In this sense, our generation really has it good. Why would you want to eat one kind of food when you can have it all? Why would you want à la carte when you can have buffet! Life is so much better when you can eat whatever you like, whenever you like! And all the people who like good food said... Amen!

> It is important to note that everyone has a worldview!

Apart from different cultures and foods, we are also exposed to different philosophies, faiths and ways of thinking. Nowadays, it is common to find people going to bible study one evening and doing yoga classes at the gym the next. At work, they go on a staff team-building session where they walk on hot coals chanting 'ice cold' to build confidence and focus. Over the weekend, they attend a New Age forum to help them become better people. They read selfhelp books to assist them achieve their full human potential. They practice the so-called 'laws of attraction' at the office. I mean, what is wrong with a Christian picking up these other practices, so long as they help them become a better person, right? Just like with cultures or foods, it is easy to ask ourselves, when it comes to spiritual things, 'Why settle for à la carte when I can have the buffet?' 'And anyway, who said one way is better than the other?' 'Isn't that just a function of where you were born?'

So we find ourselves living in world of buffet spirituality. In much of Africa, it was not uncommon to find earlier generation Christians going to church to pray for their issues on Sunday and then consulting a witchdoctor over the same issue during the same week. It is as if they wanted to make sure they covered all the eventualities, just in case one worked and the other didn't! Today's generation may not always visit a witchdoctor (though this practice is by no means uncommon) but they too seem to want to cover the eventualities!

At the root of our buffet spirituality is the issue of worldviews. What is a worldview? The dictionary defines it thus, 'A person's worldview is the way they see and understand the world, especially regarding issues such as politics, philosophy, and religion.'[142] A simpler definition of worldview is, 'Your view of the world used for living in the world.' In other words, what you think the meaning of life is and how that affects your day-to-day choices and actions.

It is important to note that everyone has a worldview! Whether we are aware of it or not, our worldview shapes and informs how we experience the world around us. Western civilization, since around the 4th Century, has been dominated by a biblical worldview, even though there have been individuals and groups who challenged it. But in the last couple of centuries, for reasons ranging from the technological to the theological, the biblical worldview has lost its dominance, and competing worldviews have

142 Collins English Dictionary

113

become far more prominent. Here is a list of major non-biblical worldviews that are popular today as well as what each one primarily teaches:

1. **Atheism:** There is no God.

2. **Deism:** There is a supreme being who however does not intervene in the universe.

3. **Naturalism:** There is no God. Humans are just highly evolved animals and the universe is a closed physical system. Nature is all there is and we are part of nature.

4. **Pantheism:** God is the totality of reality, thus, we are all divine by nature. Everything is interconnected and God is in everything.

5. **Secularism:** The material world is all that there is and a belief must be proven by science to show that it is true.

6. **Postmodernism:** There is no such thing as objective truth and moral standards. At best, we can only know what is true for ourselves.

7. **Pluralism:** The different world religions represent equally valid perspectives on the ultimate reality. There are many valid paths to salvation.

8. **Moralistic Therapeutic Deism:** God just wants us to be happy and nice to other people. He intervenes in our affairs only when we call on Him to help us out.

> People feel that because 'I worked for it, I can do whatever I want to do with it.'

Do any of these sound familiar? Even if they do not, we who today are consumers of western media are greatly influenced by these worldviews. Our passivity and unawareness in consuming entertainment is the reason these worldviews have come in, using Hollywood as a 'Trojan horse' to become widely accepted today. For example, popular T.V. series today show promiscuity as a light and casual activity and frequent sexual activity with multiple partners as normal behavior for people. Greed, adultery, rebellion, drunkenness and profanity are glamorized and celebrated. Gender is displayed as a matter of personal choice and feelings as opposed to being a beautiful God-assigned gift and responsibility.

What is the result of these worldviews? Let's take the example of marriage. It is common to find people today believing that marriage is all about them. Our generation enters marriage for what they can gain and when it no longer works for them, they find the fastest way out! People believe that 'if it feels good, I do it!' What they feel about an issue is the supreme guide for whether to do it or not. So if there is something that requires great sacrifice or patience or makes them uncomfortable, something that does not make them happy, they wonder why they have to put up with it. If watching porn or

BUFFET SPIRITUALITY

having sex with multiple partners works for me, then why should anyone interfere with my choices? When it comes to money, people feel that because 'I worked for it, I can do whatever I want to do with it.' And ultimately, it is common to hear a spouse justifying their leaving by saying, 'I just wasn't happy any more. I was no longer in love with her and couldn't imagine spending the rest of my life stuck in a loveless marriage.'

The consequences of these non-biblical worldviews on marriage, community, business ethics and friendships have been devastating, to say the least.

Question For My Journal

Which of the listed worldviews did you identify with? Which one may have affected how you think and act?

Verse To Remember

Isaiah 5:20 (NKJV). Woe to those who call evil good and good evil, who put darkness for light and light for darkness; who put bitter for sweet and sweet for bitter!

Prayer For Today

Lord, please reveal to me the ways that I have unquestioningly embraced worldviews that are contrary to my faith.

Sam's Journey

Yesterday, we spoke about different worldviews. Many of the worldviews that affect us today have a spiritual reality behind them. This was the discovery of our friend, Samantha. Sam was born into a Catholic family but her disillusionment with her faith saw her giving her life to Jesus in high school and joining a different church. But even there, she was unhappy with the hypocrisy that she began to see in people. She began to read widely in her spiritual search and ended up reading a bestselling book called "Conversations With God." This book really shook her up. It said many things that resonated with her, like money was not evil; there was nothing wrong with sex and Hitler went to heaven! It also said that God was not in the church and that you could find God on your own, which she thoroughly agreed with! Unknown to her, Sam was being introduced to the so-called 'New Spirituality'.

The tenets of this teaching is that we are all one. We should accept all religions because they are *all* paths to God that *all* lead to heaven. Neither was better than the other. Sam learnt to look at people involved in religious squabbles with pity. Spiritually, she considered them at a lower level and hoped that they too would one day evolve to a higher level of thinking that would enable them to realize that all paths led to God.

Another tenet of New Spirituality is that there is no good or evil, and there is no such thing as the devil. The bad things that happen to us are because we are vibrating at a lower energy level. We are stealing, lying, thinking negative thoughts and thus, attracting negative things. When we choose to have positive thoughts, we vibrate at a higher energy level and we do good things. These ideas were widely propagated by a book by Rhonda Byrne called, "The Secret" and are very popular across the world.

As she understood it, a third tenet of New Spirituality is that we are all gods. All of us have god-force within us and that is how we attract positive things we are actually creating them using the power of the god that is within us. There is an overall god or spirit who is also the Source. The thing though is that all of us, when we come together, form the Source; a bit like in the Hollywood movie, 'The Avatar'.

Sam eagerly consumed all these teachings and began to practice yoga for weight loss. In the process, she began to practice meditation to tap into the power in her. This is part of what is called the Human Potential Movement, which is the same as New Spirituality without the spiritual part. It is widely propagated by selfhelp books today, as well as various New Age forums that in Sam's words acted like a web, innocently drawing her in, getting her deeper and deeper.

With time though, Sam began to notice some major inconsistencies in her new beliefs. Her first problem was that anything goes; there is no right or wrong and you should live like there are no consequences. The problem however, was that she realized that life does indeed have consequences and when the consequences catch up with you, you find yourself very miserable and feel let down. All the positive thinking in the world cannot get you out of it! Secondly, for Sam, she felt that her compassion had become eroded. When bad things happened to her friends, she felt nothing for them. She thought that they simply needed to focus and be more positive. She stayed away from them so that she would not be drawn into their low energy levels. Sam's final issue is that she began to notice that, though at the beginning everything seemed all innocent, people would gradually move through the spectrum: From human potential to laws of attraction to white magic and into occultic involvement. The trajectory of the alternative worldviews she was consuming was a clear religious belief that stood against everything that the bible taught.

SAM'S JOURNEY

Sam was feeling rather disquietened by this when a friend dared her to visit Mavuno Church. On that first day, the preaching pastor talked about God being our Source, and that caught her attention as she had been learning about the Source from the New Age. Intrigued, she signed up for the *Mizizi*[143] discipleship course, and it was there that God convicted her about my beliefs. She realized that Jesus is the only way. In Sam's words, 'It may not be a popular view but it's the truth. You can't run away from the Truth!'

While we rejoice in Sam's story (today, she passionately serves God in the prayer ministry), we recognize that her story is all too frequent in our generation. Jesus said that we should love God with all our heart, soul, strength and mind.[144] Many of us have not begun to process what it means to love God with our mind. Loving God with your mind means intentionally developing a worldview that is obedient to Him. As the apostle Paul said, *'We demolish arguments and every pretension that sets itself up against the knowledge of God, and we take captive every thought to make it obedient to Christ.*[145] While we are consumers of the media, we have not learnt how to critique the ideas that are thrust upon us. That is how the enemy captures us with seemingly innocent ideas that gradually lead to our hearts hardening towards God's words and ways.

The consequences of engaging in alternative worldviews is a spirit of unbelief. With this kind of spirit, family members find it very difficult to become Christians. You may find yourself praying long for members to become Christians and when they eventually do, they still battle in their faith. They find it difficult to trust God but God is able to build their faith if they ask Him to. Another consequence of alternative worldviews is the inclination towards false religions. Alternative worldviews predispose subsequent generations to falsehoods so that the sin of idolatry continues into the next generation.

Question For My Journal

Which worldviews was Samantha being exposed to in the 'New Spirituality'?

Fill out the 'Non-Christian Spiritual Experience Inventory' in Appendix 6. Which alternative spiritual views have you sampled or experienced?

Verse To Remember

Exodus 20:2-3. '*I am the LORD your God, who brought you out of Egypt, out of the land of slavery. You shall have no other gods before me.*'

Prayer For Today

Lord, please reveal to me the lies of the enemy that have decieved me and my family. Please expose the spirit of unbelief in my life and in my family. Forgive us for holding on to other gods, and to ways of thinking that are not from You. In Jesus' name I pray. Amen.

---

143 *Mizizi* is a 10-week discipleship experience that helps people connect with God, connect with their purpose and connect with likeminded people on a journey of discovering and living out their purpose.
144 Luke 10:27
145 II Corinthians 10:5

Did God Really Say?

The bible story begins with the story of the first family. Adam and Eve lived in a perfect paradise that was custom-built for them. They had a perfect relationship with each other, with nature and with God. They were completely living out their purpose and all their work was meaningful and satisfying. They had full access to everything God had created, except one tree. God had warned them that they must not eat from this one tree. If they did this, then they would die. Now, why had God given them this command?

The bible does not bother to explain that and eventually, the only satisfactory answer is that He is God. As the Creator, He had every right to make things the way He had. He had every right to define how things should work. And that is where the enemy saw his opportunity. He approached Eve disguised as a snake, with a threefold strategy. The strategy was designed to make her...

1. Doubt God

The enemy's first question to Eve was, '*Did God really say, "You must not eat from any tree in the garden?"*'[146] This sounded like an innocent question from an objective observer who was really concerned for her wellbeing! Now clearly he was highly exaggerating what God said. God had never said that they should not eat from every tree in the garden of Eden, but the enemy was using a very clever distraction. He was trying to focus her attention on the fact of the prohibition so that she could forget the truth that God had given her family concerning every other tree in the place. The devil's question could be paraphrased as, 'Why would God want to deny you of something so unilaterally? He didn't consult you! Isn't that a bit restrictive? Don't you find that a bit strange? A bit unfair? Maybe even somewhat intolerant?'

> God had never said that they should not eat from every tree in the garden of Eden

Eve's reaction was, '*We may eat fruit from the trees in the garden, but God did say, "You must not eat fruit from the tree that is in the middle of the garden, and you must not touch it, or you will die."*'[147] Now, wait a minute! God nowhere said anything about not touching the tree! What Eve was saying here is, 'God is not all that unfair as you are insinuating, but you know what? I must concede that killing someone for eating a fruit¾that doesn't quite sound right to me either. In fact, it's somewhat intolerant!'

Now tolerance is a very interesting thing. Imagine you like bright colors like me. And so one day, dressed in your favorite brightly colored shirt, you are out having fun when your friend comes up and says, 'I've never liked how you dress.' Your eyes narrow and you ask, 'Why?' The person says, 'Bright colors are a sign that you're crying out for attention. You are clearly a very selfish and needy person! I suggest that you start wearing pale colors that blend in more. That's a sign of maturity.' What would you say to them? Probably something like, 'How dare you force *your* preferences on me! How intolerant of you!'

---

146 Genesis 3:1
147 Genesis 3:2

DID GOD REALLY SAY?

Suppose you have found a house that you love. This house is at the bottom of a hill and you are about to buy it. Your friend comes up to you as you are admiring it and says, 'Even though it's dry right now, this is actually a river bed. You'd be foolish to buy this house because when the river floods, you will have put your whole family in jeopardy. You'd better buy a house up the hill.' Would you call them intolerant? Probably not. You would research to find out if their words were true and if they were, you would rethink your buying decision. In this latter case, you would not call them intolerant but caring.

Some see religion as a crutch for weak-minded people

What the enemy does is that he takes a house-in-a-flood-valley decision and makes it a shirt-color decision so that God is no longer caring but intolerant.[148] And then why would you want to follow a God like that? For example, satan is asking many of us today, 'Did God really say that sex was bad?' Being good Christians we reply, 'No. He didn't, but... making me stay single so I may never enjoy sex!' or 'but forcing me to stay married to my wife when she's not meeting my needs... That sounds very restrictive and unfair!' And so you begin to doubt God and start to look for a second opinion.

The second thing the enemy does is he causes Eve to...

2. Reject God

Now that Eve is entertaining doubts, the enemy moves in. *'You will not surely die'* is his comeback.[149] Not only is God narrow and intolerant, He is trying to withhold from you information that will help you enjoy your life fully! How can you trust someone like that?

There are many reasons why people reject God. For some, it is because of the trauma and pain in the world. 'If God really existed, He would not have let it happen.' For others, it is because they feel God let them down. Maybe they prayed for His intervention in a difficult time and it never came. For others still, it is because of their experience with Christians. 'If Christians can be that petty and mean, I don't want anything to do with God.' Some see religion as a crutch for weak-minded people¾something that is not verifiable or supported by science. Others see religion as irrelevant to their lives¾not really adding value. Many do not like the idea of being submitted to yet another voice telling them what to do. It feels like giving up personal freedom for a set of "do's and don'ts." Why would anyone want to do that?

'You will not surely die'... The enemy continues to say that today. It is fashionable to reject God. I encountered this working in a government-run children's home in the US. I could teach the kids anything but would lose my job if I was even caught in the facility with a bible! In Africa, we are not yet at that extreme, but this is where we are heading. We do not like a God who puts any limits us. We want a positive, 'feel-good' Christianity that does not demand much from us. You'll find that on T.V. today, even on Christian channels. Such a faith helps us be all we can be, but it stops there. We reject anything that asks any more of us and follow only what

148   Illustration adapted from Andy Stanley's sermon.

149   Genesis 3:4

works for us.

And so the third thing the enemy does is he causes Eve to:

3. Replace God

His words were, '*For God knows when you eat of it, your eyes will be opened and you will be like God, knowing good and evil.*'[150] In other words, *you* can become like God and acquire the wisdom you need to determine your own destiny! Once we have rejected God, the next step is to replace God. The enemy is the master of half-truths. It is true that we are created in God's image and in that way, we are already like God. But he takes this truth and distorts it. Having rejected the God who made us in His image, we should now create God in our own image. Instead of us looking like God, now God looks like us!

And that is the role of religion. At the heart, it is true that all religions are the same. Religion is anything that helps humans connect with the divine. Religion is humanity's attempt to reach out to God, but the bible tells us that we do not have the capacity to discover God on our own terms. Our best efforts fall short of God's perfect holiness.[151] Religion does not work, and that is why the witness of the bible is that God comes to us and reveals Himself in a form we can understand.

> Buffet spirituality would be great if it were a shirt-color decision

When we insist on following our own spiritual path, it may feel good at first. It gives us control; it works for us. The bible says that when Eve looked at the fruit, it was 'good for food and pleasing to the eye and also desirable for gaining wisdom.'[152] It worked for her and so she and her husband ate it together. Instantly, their eyes were opened, but it wasn't what they expected. Instead of seeing themselves as gods, fully in control, they saw themselves as they really were – naked and exposed – and cut off from their real Source, who was their Creator.

Buffet spirituality would be great if it were a shirt-color decision, but not if it is a house-in-the-flood-valley decision. The bible tells us that it is the latter. The apostle John wrote to the early church, '*Dear friends, do not believe every spirit, but test the spirits to see whether they are from God, because many false prophets have gone out into the world. This is how you can recognize the Spirit of God: Every spirit that acknowledges that Jesus Christ has come in the flesh is from God, but every spirit that does not acknowledge Jesus is not from God. This is the spirit of the antichrist, which you have heard is coming and even now is already in the world.*'[153] Choosing our own spiritual path exposes us. Instead of bringing freedom, it enslaves us. It removes our spiritual cover. It gives the enemy the right to meddle in our lives. I believe that many of us have exposed themselves, often innocently, to alternative spirituality. While you are searching for the Truth, it is possible in your search to open spiritual doors that lead to death and not life.

---

150 Genesis 3:5
151 Romans 3:23 'For all have sinned and fallen short of God's glory'
152 Genesis 3:6
153 1 John 4:1-3

DID GOD REALLY SAY?

We recognize that it takes the Spirit of God to reveal this to you and that for some of you, this is so new that you need to process it. But we also suspect that there are many of you to whom God is revealing the ways that you have exposed yourself to teachings that have opened doors in your life to the enemy. We suspect that you would like to pray to close those doors.

Question For My Journal

In what ways have you doubted, rejected or replaced God?

Verse To Remember

I John 4:1. Dear friends, do not believe every spirit, but test the spirits to see whether they are from God.

Prayer For Today

Lord, please reveal to me and to my family the ways we have doubted, rejected and replaced you.

REPLACING THE LIE

The last few days have been spent talking about false worldviews that affect how we think, act and live. We live in a buffet world where even Christians will often hold on to views and practices that are completely contradictory to the faith that they strongly hold on to. The enemy uses our confusion to spread lies about God and about ourselves so that we gradually end up cutting ourselves off from the true Source of life.

Humans are created in God's image and are stewards of the earthn

As we said earlier, your worldview is "your view of the world, **used for living in the world.**" So, in daily living, it should be the dominant influence shaping your decisions and actions. Having a Christian worldview means living like an obedient Christian in all of life.

What does a biblical worldview teach? A biblical worldview believes that:

*   *God exists* (unlike the atheist);

*   *God actively "does things" in the world* (unlike the deist);

*   Humans are created in God's image and are stewards of the earth (unlike naturalists who say that nature is all there is);

*   God is the all-powerful, all-knowing Creator of the universe (unlike pantheists who worship nature);

*   God created an orderly world that can be studied scientifically and that science does not contradict but rather supports faith (unlike securalists);

*   Absolute moral truths exist as defined by God in His word (unlike postmodernists);

*   All religions are man's feeble attempts to reach out to God but that through Jesus, the Creator God intervened in history by coming to earth in human form, living a sinless life and then dying to take up the consequences of humanity's rebellion, and that reconciliation with God is only through accepting the gift of His salvation (unlike pluralists); and

*   Following God requires total surrender to His will, including becoming His agent to disciple the nations (unlike moralistic therapeutic deism).

Now, you could proclaim to believe all this, but if in your thinking and actions, you live as if God is not actively engaged in your world, then you are not living your view of the world for 'living in the world.' Instead, you are actually living out an atheistic or deistic worldview! Despite what you are professing with you mouth, that is actually what you truly believe!

Here are a couple of examples to demonstrate our point...

If you believe beauty is in the eye of the beholder (secular relative truth) as opposed to beauty is defined by God's purity and creativity (absolute truth), then any art piece, no matter how vulgar, or

REPLACING THE LIE

dehumanizing, is considered "art", a creation of beauty. Porn is a form of art then, and the porn video director is elevated to someone producing entertainment for adults. Watching steamy T.V. series' is okay, as it's simply entertainment.

A second example has to do with business ethics. Many churches are full on Sundays with people who lift up their hands in worship, and yet who during the week justify taking or giving bribes at work ('It's the only way to succeed in business in this country'), driving badly on the highway ('If I don't overlap, others will') and underpaying and overworking their employees ('It's nothing personal. It's how business is done').

A final example: Most Christians would readily agree that the Scriptures command us to avoid sexual immorality, but how often do you find born-again, church-attending Christians justifying habitual lust, premarital and extramarital sexual sin and divorce? I (Muriithi) remember as a young pastor in the early 2000s that when we conducted premarital classes, it was extremely rare to find a Christian, engaged couple living together before marriage. Today, it is the opposite. It is a lot more rare to find couples who have not slept together before marriage!

> Churches are full on Sundays with people who lift up their hands in worship, and yet...

In a research done in 2017, the Barna Research Group found that of Christians in the US who consider their faith important and attend church regularly, **only 17% held a biblical worldview!**[154] One of the biggest alternative worldviews held by Christians was postmodernism, especially among the young. Also known as 'New Spirituality', it teaches that:

There is no such thing as objective truth;

'All people pray to the same god or spirit' (no matter what name they use);

'Meaning and purpose come from being one with all there is'; and

'If you do good, you will receive good and if you do bad, you will receive bad' (karma).[155]

The research also pointed out that the results of not having a biblical worldview were most reflected in behavior choices. Those holding a biblical worldview held radically different views on morality and demonstrated vastly different lifestyle choices.

---

154 https://www.barna.com/research/competing-worldviews-influence-todays-christians/

155 The research found that among practicing US Christians:

61% agree with ideas rooted in New Spirituality.

54% resonate with postmodernist views.

36% accept ideas associated with Marxism.

29% believe ideas based on secularism.

It is, therefore, crucial that Christians be able to engage with unbelief at the worldview level. Christians need to understand not only what it means to have a biblical worldview, but also why they should hold fast to that worldview and apply it to all of life. They should be able to identify the major non-Christian worldviews that vie for dominance in our society, to understand where they fundamentally differ from the Christian worldview, and to make a well-reasoned case for what they believe.

Question For My Journal

In what ways have you doubted, rejected or replaced God?

Verse To Remember

Romans 12:2. Do not conform any longer to the pattern of this world, but be transformed by the renewing of your mind.

Prayer For Today

Lord, please forgive me because my conduct has often not reflected what I say I believe. Please help my life reflect my faith in You. Amen.

DEVELOPING A BIBLICAL WORLDVIEW

This week, we have learnt the key differences between a biblical worldview and the popular worldviews that are today propagated in the media. We have seen the dangers of mixing word-views and having a buffet sprituality. At its heart, buffet spirituality opens the door wide to the sin of idolatry. The very first of the Ten Commandments warns against this sin, '*I am the LORD your God, who brought you out of Egypt, out of the land of slavery. You shall have no other gods before me.*'[156] The picture that many of us may have of idolatry is of a person offering sacrifices to a grim looking statue. But at the core, the innocent sounding worldviews that are being peddled to us every day are seeds that, when full grown, will lead to practices that are just as opposed to the worship of the One True God!

So knowing this, how do we go about developing a biblical worldview? Before we answer that, here is a quote we really like about having a biblical worldview,

A biblical worldview is thinking like Jesus. It is a way of making our faith practical to every situation we face each day. A biblical worldview is a way of dealing with the world such that we act like Jesus twenty-four hours a day because we think like Jesus… At the risk of seeming simplistic, it is asking the question, "What would Jesus do if He were in my shoes right now?" and applying the answer without compromising because of how we anticipate the world reacting.[157]

> Read God's word and seek to make it my guide for everyday living

Developing a biblical worldview is about *learning to think like Jesus* to do what Jesus would do. You will find that your reaction to issues like fear about the future, suffering, disease and poverty are informed by our worldview. As followers of Jesus, we develop a biblical worldview by constantly engaging in these three practices…

1. Study The Word

King David wrote in the Psalms, '*your word is a lamp for my feet, and a light on my path.*[158]' As a follower of Jesus, I must regularly read God's word and seek to make it my guide for everyday living. The reality is that the more time you spend with someone, the more you learn about them, and the more you come to understand how they think. In the same way, the more you read God's word, the more you learn to think how Jesus would think! So make a daily habit of prayerfullly reading God's Word. You could use a bible app like YouVersion and either read through the entire bible every year or find a different bible reading plan that addresses a particular area you would like to understand. Your goal should be to ensure that the time you spend reading and thinking about God's word is not too far compared to the time you spend watching T.V. or browsing the internet!

---

156 Exodus 20:2-3
157 George Barna, 'Think Like Jesus'
158 Psalm 119:105

DEVELOPING A BIBLICAL WORLDVIEW

2. Study Your Culture

Moses wrote about the leaders of one of the tribes of Israel that was culturally aware. *'From the tribe of Issachar, there were 200 leaders of the tribe with their relatives. All these men understood the signs of the times and knew the best course for Israel to take.*[159]*'* That is so awesome! These men could offer excellent national leadership because they understood their culture and thus, understood the best decisions that their nation needed to take. As Christians, we must be aware, not just about what God's word says, but we must be aware of the opportunities and dangers our culture offers us so that we make the best decisions for our families.

One way to influence others is to read books together with those you lead

President Harry Truman once said, 'Not all readers are leaders but all leaders are readers'. To understand culture, we must become readers! As theologian Karl Barth put it, 'Take your bible and take your newspaper and read both. But interpret newspapers from your bible.' For Christians, that means, for example, that we should not just watch movies as a family but should search for Christian reviews for that movie (you can actually find those online) and discuss the movie together after we watch. That way, we learn to be critical consumers of media.

3. Be A Thought Leader

One way to influence others is to read books together with those you lead in order to shape a common understanding of the world. This is one of the most effective ways to build common culture and understanding for a team. This is unlike in our culture where many only read for exams! We love reading books with our children and have done so many times with our staff teams and with our pastors. A thought leader reads widely and has an opinion on current issues.

In three places in his second letter to the Corinthians, Paul reminded the believers in Corinth that they could not assume that their thinking was biblical or Christ-centered. He began by stating that the minds of the Israelites were hardened so they could not understand God's word, even when it was read to them.[160] Then he explained why their minds had been so dull. It wasn't because they were intellectual dwarfs, but rather, the enemy had completely blinded their minds so they could not understand God's word.[161] He then talked about how it was possible for the enemy to even ensnare these believer's thoughts.[162]

With that in mind, he challenged the believers strongly...

---

159 *I Chronicles 12:32*

160 *II Corinthians 3:14 (The Passion Translation). Their minds were closed and hardened, for even to this day that same veil comes over their minds when they hear the words of the former covenant.*

161 *II Corinthians 4:4 The god of this age has blinded the minds of unbelievers, so that they cannot see the light of the gospel that displays the glory of Christ, who is the image of God.*

162 *II Corinthians 11:3 But I am afraid that just as Eve was deceived by the serpent's cunning, your minds may somehow be led astray from your sincere and pure devotion to Christ.*

DEVELOPING A BIBLICAL WORLDVIEW

'For though we live in the world, we do not wage war as the world does. The weapons we fight with are not the weapons of the world. On the contrary, they have divine power to demolish strongholds. We demolish arguments and every pretension that sets itself up against the knowledge of God, and we take captive every thought to make it obedient to Christ.' [163]

As followers of Jesus, we must fight for not just for our thinking to be liberated, but for the thinking of those around us, including our family members. We must demolish the mental strongholds that seek to take us captive. This begins as we learn to take even our thoughts captive, protecting our mind from garbage and commanding it to be obedient to Jesus!

Question For My Journal

What do you sense God is saying to you through this week's readings?

Verse To Remember

Colossians 2:8. *'See to it that no one takes you captive through hollow and deceptive philosophy, which depends on human tradition and the elemental spiritual forces of this world rather than on Christ.'*

Freedom Prayer

Dear heavenly Father, I confess that I have not loved You with all my heart and soul and mind. I have sinned against You by violating the command not to have any other gods before You. I ask You to bring to my mind anything that I have done, knowingly or unknowingly, that involves the occult, cultic or non-Christian teachings or practices. I renounce all worship of false gods and choose to worship and serve only you. I cancel any ground satan may have gained in my life through my idolatry and renounce all satanic assignments for my life.

I recognize that there is only one true and living God who exists as Father, Son and Holy Spirit. He is worthy of all honor, praise and glory as the One who made all things and holds all things together. I recognize that in Jesus Christ, God came in human form to save us from the power of sin. I believe that He demonstrated His love for me, by dying for me while I was still a sinner. I declare that I am complete in Christ and that satan and his demons are subject to me in Him. Therefore, I obey God's command to submit to God and resist the devil, and I command satan in the name of Jesus to leave my presence. Amen. [164]

---

163   II Corinthians 10:3-5

164   Adapted from Neil Anderson, 'The Bondage Breaker'.

WEEK
-EIGHT-
WEAPONS OF SELF-DESTRUCTION

JACK'S STORY

Have you ever noticed that nobody ever wakes up one day and says something like, "Man, my life is going so great, I'm just bored with that. I am sick and tired of being blessed by God, and I'm sick and tired of having this great marriage and I'm also really tired of being a great parent and of living a life purpose where I am making a tremendous difference. So today, I think I am going to mess up my life by doing something stupid! Maybe I'll drink a bottle of alcohol, and one day if I am lucky, I'll become so addicted to the substance in this bottle, that it will cost me my marriage... ho, ho, ho! That would be so great! Or, maybe it will cost me my job or so much more!"

Nobody ever sets out and says, "Hmm, that sounds like a good plan!" Nobody says, "Hey! I think I'm going to go out with some buddies, and we'll place a little bet on a sports team. And then I want to get addicted to gambling and fall so much into debt that I won't be able to meet my family obligations!" Nobody in their right mind would say or want such a thing, right? And yet, wouldn't you agree that this happens all the time and people end up right there?

This week we will be talking about addictions. Allow us to begin with the sobering story (no pun intended) of our friend Jack. Jack was a middle child. It was clear to him growing up that his older sister was his

> ..things got so bad that his friends pulled away from him

father's favorite and his mother bonded with his younger brother who was named after her father. He felt rejected by his parents and felt he did not fit in. Jack started drinking in high school in a bid to fit in with his friends and find the acceptance he needed. By the time he was finishing high school, he was downing a bottle of vodka a day whenever he could. He went off to college in the UK and later moved to the US. His drinking steadily became worse because alcohol was cheaper and more available. As with every addict, he found he needed more and more stimulation to achieve the same high. In addition to alcohol, he became addicted to smoking and sex.

Jack told himself he could stop anytime he wanted, and he actually did several times. Once, he was even 'dry' for a whole year! But each time, after however long, all it would take would be a longing for one drink, and it would be as if he had never stopped at all. After several years, he returned home to Kenya, got a good job and got married. In his own words, the first five years of marriage were hell, and he and his wife even separated at one point. Things got so bad that his friends pulled away from him. His whole life now revolved around alcohol and his first thought every morning was where he could get his first drink! He hid bottles of alcohol around the house so that his wife couldn't find them. Jack knew that things were really bad when he began to drink cheap, local brews in order to get a quick high.

Jack soon became desperate to find help. One of his old buddies who had become a Christian, told him about Jesus and led him to accept Christ. This seemed to do the trick and he was dry for several months until, at a celebration event, he had one drink, and it was back to square one. His buddy faithfully stood by him and recommended that he check into a rehab center. Jack agreed, and they found an out-of-town Christian program where they helped people kick the alcohol habit using the scriptures. After an intense two mohths of imbibing God's word, it was as if God cleaned him out! Only a few weeks after that, Jack and his wife walked into a *Mavuno Church* service and found the community they had been looking for. They made good friends, began to grow in faith together and started serving in the marriage preparation class where they became a huge blessing to other couples. God is truly the God of a second chance!

You are not in control even if you think you are

When we asked Jack what he would say to someone caught in an addictive habit, he had this to say;

"I'd say, please acknowledge it and ask for help! You are not in control even if you think you are. Some of you drink every night and you excuse it by calling it social drinking. You need to understand it's not normal! You need to ask for help. Please talk to a friend and if you can't, at least talk to God and ask him to bring someone in your life that can help you. Believe me, if He could answer me, He can answer you!"

Question For My Journal

Have you or has someone in your family suffered an addiction of any kind? What do you learn from Jack's story?

Verse To Remember

Ephesians 5:18. Do not get drunk on wine, which leads to debauchery. Instead, be filled with the Spirit.

Prayer For Today

Lord, please open my eyes this week to ways that addictions could be affecting my family tree. In Jesus' name I pray. Amen.

ADDICTION CYCLE

This week, we are looking at addictions which is one of the ways that the enemy can gain legal access to harass us and our families. What are addictions? To put it simply, an addiction is the dependence on a substance or pattern of behavior to meet a legitimate, inner need.

There are generally two types of addiction. The first is substance addiction, where a person becomes dependent on a chemical to meet their need. Apart from alcohol, other substances include illegal drugs (as cocaine or heroin) or legal drugs (for example, nicotine or prescription drugs such as certain painkillers, cold medicine or antidepressants). Other addictive chemicals are sugar, caffeine (found in coffee and tea), and carbonated soft drinks. Many soft drinks contain large amounts of addictive sugar and caffeine.

The second type of addiction is behavioral addiction where one becomes dependent on doing a certain activity repetitively to calm their feelings or help them feel good about themselves. Many times these behaviors increase the level of adrenalin and other hormones in the body, providing a 'rush' to the person. In that way, they are really similar to substance addiction, as the net effect of the behavior is to release natural body substances that the body becomes addicted to! Some of the behaviors that people can become addicted to include gambling, gaming, overworking, shopping, internet use, watching T.V., crime, masturbation, watching pornography and sex.

> Most addictions come about because of internal factors, that is, a person trying to meet a legitimate, inner need

Addictions can be caused by external factors. For instance, someone may innocently take prescribed medication only to later realize that they are hooked to it. A child could be introduced to drinking by a parent before they have understood what they are doing, only to find themselves addicted as they grow older.[165]

However, most addictions come about because of internal factors, that is, a person trying to meet a legitimate, inner need. There are many different such needs. Some want to fit in they are extremely self-conscious or timid and are looking for a way to be accepted by others. Others want to calm their stress or anxiety at work or with life in general. For some, it is the need to forget trauma or to manage pain or loneliness. For others, it is a desire to prove to themselves that they can do what they want or to even punish authority figures who do not want them to act a certain way. For example, a teen who is resentful of the boundaries imposed by his or her parents could decide to take drugs as an act of defiance. For some, it is the need to be in control, for example, many people use sex with multiple partners to gain control. They may have been hurt or even sexually abused and because they felt weak and helpless at the time, they swore never to be vulnerable again. Each sexual encounter helps them feel in-charge of their lives and relationships, and then find that they cannot stop.

Regardless of the type of addiction, the addiction cycle is the same. Addictions normally progress along the following pattern:

---

165   The earlier young people start using drugs, the greater their chances of continuing to use them and becoming addicted later in life.

1. Rush

The cycle begins with an emotional or physical 'high' or feeling of wellbeing when the person first experiences the stimulant. After a little while, this high declines, often resulting in an emotional low a hangover or guilt and remorse.

2. Desire

In the next stage, the person is left with a longing to try the experience again so as to recreate the high. If they succumb or yield, the experience is repeated.

3. Habit

Over time, as they repeat the experience, they develop a habit. The substance or behavior becomes accepted as the way to cope. As they continue though, their body develops tolerance so that more and more stimulation is required each time to reach the same high.

4. Dependence

At some point, they cross the line so that they need the substance or behavior in order to feel normal. After this point, if they try to stop, they will react physically or psychologically in what are called withdrawal symptoms. By now, the person is in bondage, that is, controlled by the addiction. If they're a Christian, they are in the sin-confess-sin cycle. The behavior makes them feel guilty and so they confess it in prayer and promise not to do it again, until the next time. This is really a terrible place to be.

You see, the reality is, when someone is addicted, they can intellectually know, "I shouldn't be doing this," but the addiction continues to control and dominate them. For example, someone may have a problem with overeating, and intellectually they can say, "This is not good. This is bad for my body. I shouldn't do this," even as they take more bites. Or someone who gambles on their phone can be saying, "I know I'll probably lose my money and this is destroying my family," and yet go ahead and press 'send' to place the bet, knowing the whole time, "I shouldn't do this!" Or someone could be a workaholic and intellectually say, "I need to get home. I know my family needs me. This is too much. I shouldn't be doing this!" and the whole time she is saying this, she continues to work. Why? It is because we are mastered and we have become slaves to something else.

You might say, "Well, I'm not addicted." Let me ask six questions and if you answer 'YES' to three or more of these, it is very likely that you are on the road to addiction.

- Do your family and/or friends say that you have a problem?

- Do you continue even though you are hurting people?

- Do you arrange your schedule around 'it'?

- When was the last time you went a week without 'it'?

ADDICTION CYCLE

- Is it leading you to isolation, hurting your relationships?

- Are you trying to keep it a secret?

The greatest danger with addictions is that they are weapons of self-destruction. They have the power to sabotage your purpose, so that you will never accomplish the purpose for which God created you.

Question For My Journal

What did you learn about addictions from the reading? Which of the listed addictions are you vulnerable to?

Verse To Remember

II Timothy 1:7. For God has not given us a spirit of fear and timidity, but of power, love, and self-discipline.

Prayer For Today

Lord, please open my eyes this week to ways that addictions could be affecting my family tree. In Jesus' name I pray. Amen.

SABOTAGING PURPOSE

One of the most tragic examples in the bible of a person who sabotaged his purpose is King Solomon. His dad had been one of the most successful national leaders in the region. Solomon was one of those guys with huge potential. Right from birth, there was something special about Solomon and when he was a baby, a prophet came and gave him a special name, one given to him directly by God; a name that meant 'loved by the Lord.'[166]

Solomon grew up to be an exceptional and very gifted young man. Though only the seventh son, King David picked him as his successor, the next king of Israel. And although he had been brought up as a prince, Solomon was surprisingly humble, and pleased God by asking for wisdom and discernment, rather than riches for himself.[167] God not only gave him the wisdom he asked, but also gave him peace and economic prosperity. Solomon became known for many things. In addition to building a beautiful temple for God, he also built many public works. He reinforced the defence system. He made international trade treaties with all neighboring countries, bringing about major economic growth. He was a brilliant diplomat, politician, strategist and administrator who made Israel the envy of many nations. He was also a celebrity: Famous people from all over the world wanted to be seen with him! He was not only rich, but intelligent, charming and impressively handsome. You would have to agree that Solomon definitely had it made!

> ## Solomon seems to demonstrate well the addiction cycle

In light of all that, what the bible reveals about Solomon may come as a bit of a shock. It seems Solomon's problem was foreign women. He married hundreds of them. No African king would have had anything on him! Now the problem with this is that God had specifically warned his people against marrying foreign women. There was also a specific instruction in God's law that the king should not take multiple wives because they would lead his heart astray.[168] In light of that, it is not clear why Solomon decided to do it anyway. Perhaps he had felt under pressure to perform. After all, his predecessor had been the most famous and popular king in Israel's history and there could have been pressure to fit into his father's big shoes. Or maybe it had made him feel more powerful as a man they say older men often pursue young women to prove they are still virile. But most likely, it had been because of a more practical consideration; marrying foreign wives was common practice for kings in that day. As a standard practice, it helped to cement peace treaties and trade alliances.

Regardless of the reason, Solomon ended up with seven hundred wives of royal birth and three hundred concubines! Seeing how much time he spent in weddings, it is surprising he had time to do anything else! Solomon seems to demonstrate well the addiction cycle…

1. **Rush:**

   He marries a forbidden beauty, the daughter of the king of one of the most powerful nations in the region, Egypt. Nothing happens to him. In fact, it makes him appear quite in control, as he now has powerful friends. Perhaps he is wondering, 'What was the fuss about?'

---

166 II Samuel 12:24
167 I Kings 3:9
168 I Kings 11:2, Deuteronomy 17:17

SABOTAGING PURPOSE

2. Desire:

Because he enjoyed the excitement of flirting with the forbidden so much, Solomon decides to experiment again. A second then a third time. Each time, the resulting treaty actually seems to have worked, and rather than destroy him, he ends up with more money, power, control and sex. He still feels very much in control. Not bad! But now a barrier has been crossed.

3. Habit:

The bible seems to be speaking sarcastically when it says that he 'held fast in love' to his hundreds of wives and girlfriends. He was certainly not in love with that many women! With time, it seems the behavior spiraled out of control. He could stop himself! Think about it: If each wedding took one week to celebrate, he would have spent 19 years of his life in weddings! This is before we even get to his girlfriends. It seems clear that his habit distracted him from his work and sabotaged his relationship with God, but meanwhile, Solomon seems to have been in denial, probably blaming the women for any challenges he was facing (perhaps that's why he wrote several times about the problems of a nagging wife!)[169].

4. Dependence:

The costs become obvious to all. The safety of his empire depends on maintaining good relations with his wives and so they have power over him. He watches helplessly as they insist that he not only build temples

> God had a divine purpose in mind when He made you

for them to worship their gods, but that he accompanies them as they do so. He is clearly no longer in control. By the time Solomon realizes what he has done, it is too late; the damage is done. The man who has one of the most incredible intellects ever is wasting his precious gift in chasing women. The man with great potential, who could have been Israel's greatest king, instead becomes the reason why Israel is divided into two and eventually destroyed by their enemies. His addiction sabotages his purpose!

You were created for a great purpose. God had a divine purpose in mind when He made you and you will only achieve this purpose if you are dependent on God as your Source of life. Your enemy knows this. He will try to bring into your life dependence on anything except God, so as to sabotage the great purpose that God has created you for.

Back in the day, you would have had to work really hard to lay your hands on a pornographic magazine. Today, you can instantly get it on the internet for free and a huge percentage of young people today are porn addicts. Many in our generation are addicted to porn, masturbation or to casual sex. In our quest for control or intimacy, we are sabotaging our ability to ever enjoy a mutually satisfying relationship. For some, addiction is drugs or cigarettes, and we are destroying our bodies, robbing ourselves of the health and longevity we need to achieve our purpose.

---

169   Proverbs 15:17, 21:9, 21:19, 25:24

Others of us have more acceptable addictions. Workaholism, for example. You have convinced yourself that you work hard because you like excellence, but the truth is that in your insecurity, you need to overwork in order to feel good about yourself. But that is destroying your relationships and killing your purpose. Even the most 'innocent' addictions bring their own problems. That person who is addicted to tea or to a soft drink gets a headache every time they try to fast to hear from God.

Compulsive shopping is squandering our kingdom resources and compulsive T.V. or internet use is stealing years from our youth the time we should be using to make a difference. Truly, addictions are weapons of self-destruction!

Question For My Journal

Are there particular addictions you are vulneralble to? How can you ensure that they never sabotage your purpose?

Verse To Remember

James 1:13-15. When tempted, no one should say, "God is tempting me." For God cannot be tempted by evil, nor does he tempt anyone; but each person is tempted when they are dragged away by their own evil desire and enticed. Then, after desire has conceived, it gives birth to sin; and sin, when it is full-grown, gives birth to death.

Prayer For Today

Lord, please open my eyes this week to ways that addictions could be affecting my family tree. In Jesus' name I pray. Amen.

BREAKING THE CHAINS

One of our friends shared this testimony with us.

I came to know of my calling to be a pastor when I was eighteen-years-old after becoming a Christ-follower in high school. Though I passionately loved and served the Lord passionately, something was killing the life in me on the inside. I was only fifteen-years-old in high school when I began to feel drawn to pornography whenever I became frustrated or bored. Before long, I was solidly hooked on a secret, self-centered, shameful and seemingly irresistible habit. For the next several years, I wrestled against porn addiction with all my might. But I lost every battle because my willpower eventually proved no match for my desire for the passing pleasures of porn! In my early 20s, I simply gave up fighting and gave in. For almost six years, I simply stopped fighting it. It was a season that ended in the shattering of my self-esteem.

One morning, I looked in the mirror and what I saw I will never, ever forget. It was a sobering experience. I looked into the mirror and I looked into my eyes, and when I did, I saw the presence of evil. I don't know how to explain that, but it was there. It was like I was being consumed by evil. My life was destructive and out of control. I was hurting myself and everybody around me. I realized that something had taken control of me and was intentionally destroying my life and calling, and I cried out to God silently and asked Him to save me. Then one day soon after, I went to a conference and the preacher called out those addicted to porn and sexual sins. Though it was extremely embarrassing, I walked down to the altar and got my freedom.

> God is able to deliver us! He is the one who made us

Addictions can be shame-inducing and they can destroy you both on the inside and outside. But the worst thing about them is that they give the enemy legal access to oppress us and those we love. Thankfully, God is able to deliver us! As the one who made us, He is the Great Physician. He knows all our body chemicals and all our psychological pathways. He is able to bring complete and sustainable healing to all our addictions.

Here is what we must do to close the door the enemy is using and to deny him the use of these weapons of self-destruction against us.

1. **Acknowledge The Problem:**

   The first step we must take is to acknowledge that there is a problem. We must admit that we are addicted and that there is nothing we can do to free ourselves; we need God! This action takes a lot of humility. Before this point, many who are addicted will reason themselves out of this acknowledgement. They'll say to themselves, 'I can quit anytime I want,' or 'This is too embarrassing to share with others.' But as the apostle James encouraged the early church, *'Humble yourself before the Lord and He will lift you up.'*[170] So come to God and confess that things are out of control. Do not wait until you have destroyed your purpose to come to this stage.

---

170   James 4:10

2. Seek Accountability:

The bible calls the devil 'the accuser'. He loves to hold a secret over you. One of his favorite lines is, 'You'd better not share this. What will others think of you!' But the apostle James once more has a remedy for this, writing in his letter, *'Therefore confess your sins to each other and pray for each other so that you may be healed. The prayer of a righteous man is powerful and effective.'*[171]

3. Sin grows best in the dark.

Break the secret! King Solomon urged, *'People who conceal their sins will not prosper, but if they confess and turn from them, they will receive mercy.'*[172] If you are struggling with a potentially addictive behavior, you need to share about the issue with someone who can walk with you and help you. It could be your *Simama* partner, or perhaps a prayer counselor. Your accountability partner should be available so that any time you are tempted, you can give them a call and the two of you work out a pre-meditated plan. If you have not yet done *Mizizi*, please do so and surround yourself with friends who can help you. We often say at Mavuno Church that, 'You'll never be great alone.' I want to assure you that you will not succeed if you try to walk this journey alone.

> Find other healthy alternatives to substitute the addiction

4. Starve The Habit:

The third step is that you need to investigate what the triggers are that cause you to engage in the habit so that you can know how to deal with them. For some people, stress or loneliness gets them down the addiction road again. For others, it is when you feel anxious. Do whatever you can to avoid those situations. Jesus had some radical things to say about this. *'If your right eye causes you to sin, gouge it out and throw it away. It is better for you to lose one part of your body than for your whole body to be thrown into hell.'*[173]

While you may not literally cut your eye off, the point here is that desperate times call for desperate measures! To some of us it means breaking off that relationship, closing our WhatsApp or Instagram account, selling your T.V., maybe even changing your friends or quitting your job. It is better to enter another career than to destroy your purpose! Find other healthy alternatives to substitute the addiction, like working out in the gym, reading the bible or visiting a friend. Recognize that even though God has healed you, the enemy could try and nail you through the same spot again so you need to be on guard!

---

171   James 5:16
172   Proverbs 28:13 (NLT)
173   Matthew 5:29

BREAKING THE CHAINS

Question For My Journal

Do you or someone in your family or among your close friends need to take these steps? What would be this person's greatest hindrance to healing?

Verse To Remember

I Corinthians 10:13 (BSB). *No temptation has seized you except what is common to man. And God is faithful; he will not let you be tempted beyond what you can bear. But when you are tempted, he will also provide a way out so that you can stand up under it.*

Freedom Prayer

Dear Lord, I confess that you are able to break the chains of addictions. Please do so Lord, so that no one in my family, going forward, will ever be a slave to them again.

Father, You have told us to put on the Lord Jesus Christ and not to gratify the desires of the sinful nature (Romans 13:14). I acknowledge that we as a family have given in to sinful desires which wage war against our souls (I Peter 2:11). Please reveal to my mind the ways that we have transgressed Your moral law and grieved the Holy Spirit. As a family, we have sinned against Your holy law and given the enemy an opportunity to destroy our purpose (Ephesians 4:27, Ephesians 2:10). I come before Your presence to acknowledge our sins and to seek Your forgiveness (I John 1:9) that we may be freed from all bondage of sin (Galatians 5:1). I renounce our involvement in all sin and claim, through the blood of the Lord Jesus Christ, our forgiveness and cleansing. I cancel all ground that evil spirits have gained through our willful involvement in sin. I ask this in the wonderful name of my Lord and Savior Jesus Christ. Amen.174

---

174   Adapted from Neil Anderson, 'The Bondage Breaker'.

GOD IS ABLE!

What has mastered you? Our enemy wants to steal, kill, and destroy[175] and this week, we have been learning how he uses the weapons of self-destruction called addictions to do that. We have seen how he uses addictions to destroy us and our God-given purpose.

Are addictions disease or are they sin? Addiction to substances or to behaviors has been shown to literally rewire our brains so that they function differently. Addiction changes the brain, first by subverting the way it registers pleasure and then by corrupting other normal drives such as learning and motivation. Addiction is thus seen today as a chronic disease that changes both brain structure and function.[176]

That said though, there is an important distinction. Medically, the word 'disease' describes a diagnosable condition with a primary, physical cause. The cure is external to the patient and the patient is not able to heal himself. In the case of addictions however, the cure must come from within: The addicted person must make choices to reject, defeat, and forsake his addiction which is not a course of treatment that would work for a disease like cancer, malaria or even schiznoprenia.

We believe that even though it does end up changing our brains, requiring treatment, at the heart, addiction is a moral choice with moral consequences. The actions leading to addictions are usually learned behaviors (as opposed to imposed or inborn behaviors). Calling addiction a disease could prevent people from taking responsibility of their behavior. Ultimately though, the addict can and does get 'sick' because they cannot just stop once they are hooked. In the bible, drunkenness is referred to as sin, not sickness, and as an act of the sinful nature[177]. At their heart, addictions seek to fill the void within us that only God can fill and thus, become a form of idolatry.

You may know a family where addictions almost seem genetically passed on from one generation to another. We, for example, know a family in which in the past few years, the father and four of five brothers have all died from alcohol-related illnesses or accidents. This family owns a lot of land that could have made them quite wealthy, but it has not benefited them. Whenever they sold a piece of land, the money was dissipated in drinking and partying. The sad thing is that the remaining brother is also an alcoholic and believes that he too will have an early death. He does not seem worried about it though, and has accepted it as 'the way things are for us.'

But it does not have to be this way! What we see in this family is a spiritual stronghold introduced through the dad's abuse of alcohol and now decimating the next generation. Someone in that family needs to rise up and say, 'It stops with me!' The lie of the enemy is to make us believe that we are helpless to external forces. That's why the apostle Peter warned the early church, '*Be alert and of sober mind. Your enemy the devil prowls around like a roaring lion looking for someone to devour.*'[178] The devil is a fake lion! His greatest asset: His roar yet it makes you quake in fear. Hence Peter's next line, '*Take a decisive stand against him and resist his every attack with strong, vigorous faith.*'[179]

---

175   John 10:10

176   https://www.helpguide.org/harvard/how-addiction-hijacks-the-brain.htm

177   I Corinthians 6:9-10, Galatians 5:19-21

178   I Peter 5:8

179   1 Peter 5:9 (The Passion Translation)

GOD IS ABLE!

They say 'once an addict, always an addict.' We don't believe that! We know from experience that God can heal you and your family line completely of any besetting addictions. This healing could happen instantly and miraculously as we have witnessed on some occasions. But God could also choose to take you or your loved one through the slow process of getting help, seeing a counselor and maybe even going to a rehab center. We have seen God heal in both ways and it is not always clear why He chooses one path for one person and a different one for another. Bottom line though is that He is able to heal you, if you are ready to be healed. And He is able to cause you to be a source of freedom to your family so that addictions are not passed down the family tree as spiritual strongholds. But, you have to be willing to take the steps!

Question For My Journal

Are there any addictions or potentially addictive behaviors in your family?

What will it take for these not to be passed on to the next generation?

With your prayer partner:

a.   Acknowledge the problem: Confess your addictions to one another.

b.   Seek accountability: Work out what to do when temped (for example, call each other and pray together).

c.   Starve the habit: Identify the triggers that lead you into temptation, for example, loneliness, anger, stress, etc.

d.   Work out alternative coping mechanisms, for example:

When I am lonely, I will _____

When I am stressed, I will _____

When I am angry, I will _____

When I am (include any other trigger), I will _____

ACCOUNTABILITY COVENANT

ME

I, _____, covenant to call my prayer partner, _____, whenever I am tempted to indulge in my sin. I also promise to starve this habit my carrying out the alternative coping mechanisms I have worked out above.

_____

MY PRAYER PARTNER

I, _____, covenant to pray whenever _____ _____ calls. I recognize that prayer is powerful and through my action God will help my partner resist the temptation. I also promise to check on, a weekly basis (for the next month) that my partner is carrying out their alternative coping mechanisms. After this month, we will evaluate and see if to continue in this frequency or to make it twice a month.

GOD IS ABLE!

Verse To Remember

Galatians 5:1 '*It is for freedom that Christ has set us free. Stand firm then, and do not let yourselves be burdened again by a yoke of slavery.*'

Freedom Prayer

Dear Heavenly Father, You have told us to put on the Lord Jesus Christ and not to gratify the desires of the sinful nature (Romans 13:14). I acknowledge that I have given in to sinful desires which wage war against my soul (I Peter 2:11). I have sinned against Your holy law and given the enemy an opportunity to destroy my purpose (Ephesians 4:27, Ephesians 2:10). I come before Your presence to acknowledge my sins and to seek Your forgiveness (I John 1:9) that I may be freed from the bondage of addictions (Galatians 5:1).

I renounce my involvement in _____ (list all your addictions), and claim, through the blood of the Lord Jesus Christ, my forgiveness and cleansing. I cancel all ground that evil spirits have gained in me and in my family through my willful involvement in the sin of addiction. I ask Lord, not to be lead into temptation and for complete deliverance in this matter, I now choose to starve the habit by carrying out the alternative behaviors and also ask for your strength and grace to walk in purity and righteousness. In the wonderful name of my Lord and Savior Jesus Christ. Amen.

WEEK
– NINE –
HEALING OUR
RELATIONSHIPS

CONFUSED RELATIONSHIPS

Over the past 10 weeks, we have been walking together through the *Simama* experience in a bid to enforce the freedom that Jesus won for us and our families. The apostle Paul warned us that we should not give the enemy a foothold. Through this experience, we are identifying the major doors that the enemy uses to gain a foothold in our families, and then, through prayer, we are kicking him out and closing those doors. We have learnt to close several doors so far: The door of pride, the door of lies about ourselves and God, the door of rebellion, the door of bitterness, the door of spiritual strongholds and generational curses, the door of alternative spirituality and the door of addictions. Today, we want to look at the final doorway, which is in the area of dating and relationships.

> Most cultures in the world today, including our own, are greatly influenced by the social changes in the Western world.

People today enter into romantic relationships very casually. It is normal to have a series of temporal and convenient arrangements which remain as long as the fun lasts. Much as this is seen as fun, free, liberated and what normal people do, the casualty rate is very high. Many get hurt, lose trust and become hardened and cynical of relationships altogether. This cynicism is evident in singles who are dating, as well as among couples who are married.

The idea that two people can be faithful to each other, can abstain from sex before marriage and live faithfully in marriage as husband and wife until death, is a quaint ideal if not a pipe dream for many people today. But this has not always been the case. There was a time when the expectation was for couples to remain faithful to each other and to live together, all their lives. So, what caused the change?

Most cultures in the world today, including our own, are greatly influenced by the social changes in the Western world. Western media has played a huge role in spreading these social changes and making them a normal part of the globalized world we live in. Because we have been so influenced by the West, then to understand ourselves, we need to learn a bit about their social history.

The 1950s and 1960s witnessed huge social changes in the Western world that forever changed the landscape for families there. After years of being limited in their role as housewives, plus the perception of women as being naïve, less intelligent and emotionally unstable, women rightly rose up in arms to protest against these injustices. They demanded equal employment opportunities, equal pay and equal access to education, among other things. In tandem with this movement was the development of the contraceptive pill. The 'pill', as it was later to be popularized, was widely hailed as a great tool for opening up new opportunities for women. It not only promoted the sexual awakening of women, but with childbirth now under the control of women, they could explore education and careers in the same way as men could.

Other changes soon began to appear, chief among them the attack on the traditional emphasis on virginity and marriage. The introduction of *Playboy* (a magazine founded by Hugh Hefner) and Sex and the Single Girl (by Helen Gurley Brown) served to promote and celebrate the single life and sexual exploration so that now, unlike in prior generations, sex could be enjoyed by married and unmarried men and women, without any restrains.

Through the inflence of globalization and media, many of these changes spread across the rest of the world. In Africa, therefore, we observe some of the benefits of some of these social changes. Thanks to 'girl child' programs, women issues have been brought to the forefront and similar to the West, women are now re-engaged in the social, economic and political affairs of the society (We say re-engaged because in traditional or agrarian cultures, women were as equally engaged as men in all matters of the society).

> What started off as 'adult entertainment' nude magazines that were strictly regulated, has now grown into a global industry

What we might not always be aware of was the baggage also brought by these social changes. Families in the Western hemisphere were rapidly being unraveled by these changes. Wisdom calls for us to be aware and cautious of these effects over ourselves and our families. So, what has been the negative effect of these social changes?

A key negative effect has been the over-sexualization of men and women. With feminists calling for the sexual liberation of women and the surfacing of the singles' culture, forces combined to spark the sexual revolution of the 1960s. What started as a legitimate need for sexual fulfillment within marriage soon spiraled and sparked off many other enterprises, among them the porn industry. What started off as 'adult entertainment'¾nude magazines that were strictly regulated, has now grown into a global industry, with products readily accessible to anyone through mobile phones.[180] As pornography has moved from the periphery and into mainstream culture, many men and women, boys and girls, have got caught in its vice-like grip and find themselves enslaved to a habit that is extremely difficult to kick.

The problem with pornography is not just the introduction of addictive behavior; it has also been linked with criminal activities such as rape, acts of bestiality, child exploitation, degrading sexual acts and murder. Studies have shown that teen pornography consumption negatively impacts adolescents' self-esteem and mental health.[181]

Despite the fact that porn can be wildly unrealistic and often glorifies violence, sexism or racism, many young people believe that pornography is a realistic depiction of sex. Porn addiction does great harm to marriages, as living with a real-life human being pales in comparison to the airbrushed, drug-induced performances on the screen! Today, the average male college student is a consumer of porn. One can only imagine the impact that porn use will have on families as these young men begin the next generation of African families!

---

180 Every year, Hollywood releases roughly 600 movies and makes $10 billion in profit. And how much porn industry makes? 13,000 films and close to $15 billion in profit. The porn industry makes more money than Major League Baseball, The NFL and The NBA combined! (https://medium.com/@TheSBT/how-big-is-the-porn-industry-fbc1ac78091b)

181 https://fightthenewdrug.org/10-porn-stats-that-will-blow-your-mind/

Confused Relationships

The effects of pornography, plus the sexualizing of the fashion, music and film industry have had the net result of influencing the way we view ourselves. Unfortunately for us, we have embraced the message of media and have come to view ourselves primarily in sexual terms: The way we dress, talk, walk social poise is evaluated on sex appeal. Suitability of a partner is primarily based on chemistry how attractive (read sexually compatible) the person is. Sadly, character is no longer a part of the selection process and, because of this, many people today end up making poor relationship choices and yet have no clue where they went wrong!

Other effects of the sexual revolution and social changes have been:

1. **Impersonal Sex.**

As pornography and the whole sexual industry promotes pleasurable sex only, it removes the context of a lifelong, committed relationship. Without love, commitment, kindness and consideration for the other person, sex becomes a selfish act that ultimately does not satisfy. Consequently, people end up in serial relationships, looking in vain for happiness and satisfaction in 'pleasurable sex'.

2. **Rejection of Motherhood and Fatherhood.**

The rise of sexually uninhibited singles has also seen the increase of unplanned pregnancies. However, without the protection of marriage, children in these situations are often deemed as an unwelcome intrusion to personal happiness or an obstacle to career advancement. Even when wanted, they grow up without at least one of the protective roles that each parent is meant to play.

3. **Rejection of Marriage.**

It is not uncommon today to have single women preferring to have children without the 'baggage' of a man. Co-parenting is the new normal as more and more couples find themselves unprepared for the sacrificial commitment of marriage and preferring to separate or divorce. The impact on the next generation is catastropic.

> How one feels about their gender has now become a civil rights issue

4. **Gender Role Confusion.**

With the feminist movement minimizing, or obliterating male and female differences as defined biblically- or culturally, many people no longer have a clue what it means to be male or female. Girls are on one hand brought up to be assertive, while boys are brought up without any sense of responsibility or commitment. This has led globally to the 'hard-nosed blue woman' and to the 'spineless pink man' phenomena. In our context, it has resulted in many irresponsible young men who prefer to while away their days drinking and gambling, leaving their wives raising their children alone at home.

5. **Gender Identity Confusion.**

With gender roles confused, gender identity has followed suit. Today, gender is defined, not as a pre-assigned divine gift that allows a person to reflect God's image, but as a choice based on how one feels. How one feels about their gender has now become a civil rights issue and sex and marriage with someone of the same gender is seen as being a matter of choice and preference. Western governments, media and nongovernmental organizations (NGOs) are exerting a lot of financial and political pressure on governments across the world to ensure that these values become universal values. If we continue on the same trajectory as the West, it seems that it will only be a matter of time before those who do not agree with them will be ridiculed and labeled as out of touch with reality, intolerant, mentally ill or even criminally culpable!

6. Abortion.

Another sad result is that abortion on demand has become a major form of birth control. Much as abortions are marketed as an easy and convenient way of getting rid of unwanted pregnancies, they also come with baggage which, if not dealt with, can haunt a person for many years. The very act itself bears emotional, spiritual and physiological consequences. Some of the medical practitioners who perform the abortions suffer from nightmares, guilt and shame, sometimes resorting to alcoholism and drugs to numb the pain of these negative emotions. Others still, with all the killings, become calloused, lacking value for human life, and money, not the welfare of the patient, becomes the primary motivator. What this translates to is a less than professional handling of the patient and some patients have lost their lives when abortions have been done hurriedly or carelessly in order to get to other patients.

Those who have sponsored or handed out abortions often report overwhelming feelings of guilt and shame. Many resort to alcohol, drug use and other additions as a coping mechanism. At a physiological level, the consequences of abortion are:

- Miscarriages with later pregnancies;

- Malformation of births due to earlier cases of induced abortions;

- Infertility caused by damage to organs like ovaries;

- Abortion raises the chances of an ectopic pregnancy, where the baby grows in the fallopian tubes, causing a serious risk to the mother and almost certain death to the baby;

- Breast cancer: Pregnancy stimulates women's breast tissue. Abortion interrupts the growth process of the breast, increasing chances of a cancerous development;

- Haemorrhage: Blood loss during the procedure can result in other complications due to reversed blood flow. Most abortions are followed by severe haemorrhage as the instruments may at times injure the uterus and other organs;

- Internal infection of perforated organs as they are left exposed to bacteria; or

- Death has sometimes resulted from severe blood loss and internal infections.

In addition to the emotional and physiological consequences listed, abortion carries with it major spiritual consequences. The sixth commandment is, 'You shall not murder'182 and God

---

182 Exodus 20:13

CONFUSED RELATIONSHIPS

took murder so seriously that it carried the death sentence.[183] Abortion opens a major doorway for the enemy to operate in a person's life.

This is the context in which people are entering into dating relationships today, and no wonder then the devastation that we are experiencing in marriage!

Question For My Journal

Which of these negative social effects do you identify with and why?

Verse To Remember

Ephesians 2:1-5. As for you, you were dead in your transgressions and sins, in which you used to live when you followed the ways of this world and of the ruler of the kingdom of the air, the spirit who is now at work in those who are disobedient. All of us also lived among them at one time, gratifying the cravings of our flesh and following its desires and thoughts. Like the rest, we were by nature deserving of wrath. But because of his great love for us, God, who is rich in mercy, made us alive with Christ.

Freedom Prayer

Dear Lord, I confess I have been deceived by the Spirit of this world and conducted my relationships in the ways of the world and, as a result bear _____ (list all) as negative consequences. I renounce these works of satan in my life and destroy the spirits that have been operating in my life as a result. Cleanse me, with the blood of Jesus, from all the baggage I have been carrying. I declare to the heavenlies that I belong to Jesus and now choose to obey Him and follow His leading in the way I conduct myself in relationships. In Jesus' name. Amen!

If you have had or sponsored an abortion, pray this prayer...

Dear heavenly Father, I confess that I have conducted or sponsored or had an abortion (tick all that apply). I have sinned against You by violating the command not to murder. I renounce these actions in my life and now choose to honor life as sacred as unborn children are also created in Your Image. I cancel any ground satan may have gained in my life through my act of murder and renounce all satanic assignments for my life, including tormenting spirits of guilt, recurring nightmares, the spirit of death and (list all other emotional and spiritual consequences you have identified). I humbly ask that You bring healing and deliverance to my mind and body as the stronghold of satan is released by faith through this act of confession. In Jesus' name. Amen!

---

183   Leviticus 24:17 'If anyone takes the life of a human being, he must be put to death.'

BEYOND TALL, DARK AND HANDSOME

Yesterday, we spoke about the negative consequences of the sexual revolution, including the over-sexualization of men and women. God created us as sexual beings and as we saw earlier in this course, our gender is a deep part of what it means to be created in God's image. But one of the enemy's greatest tactics is to take something that is God's gift and to turn it into an idol. That way, we stop worshipping the Giver and begin to worship the gift. This surely is the case of our sexuality in today's over-sexed culture.

Through the influence of media and the fashion industry, it has become normal today for both men and women to believe that men are nothing more than sex-driven animals whose main drive is the sexual conquest of women. You will often here this sentiment expressed, 'All men are dogs,' or 'There are just no good men out there.' Many women know men as those people who lie, cheat, use and abuse you, saying they want a relationship, when they really don't. They will emotionally exploit you and then trade you up for a newer model as soon as they start becoming wealthy. And the reality seems to back this up! In practically every country worldwide, men are far more responsible for cases of spousal abuse, rape, family abandonment and crime in general.

> Conquering women is not a show of strength, but comes from a misguided definition of manhood.

Some of these are surely the effects of over-sexualization. In partnership with women, men were created to rule and have dominion over the whole earth. Conquering women is not a show of strength, but comes from a misguided definition of manhood. As we saw earlier, in the context of marriage, men were created to protect their families (not to exploit them), to provide for them (not take from them), to be spiritual leaders (not passive partners), and to be servant leaders (not self-centered dictators).

When men are sexualized, the following can be the consequences:

1. They see women as sex objects and pressure women to have sex;

2. They are driven to have multiple sexual partners;

3. They are unable to have genuine, non-sexual friendships with the opposite sex;

4. They are commitment phobic as they have not developed the ability to develop good friendships with the opposite sex that are not sexual;

5. They are obsessed with how they look. A natural desire to look good turns into an obsession with the gym, clothes, etc.; or

6. They live a life of insignificance, chasing women as opposed to their God-given purpose of changing the world!

Clearly, much as sexuality is a big part of us, it cannot be the sum total of who were are. We as men need to rediscover ourselves and what uniquely makes us male. In earlier weeks, we learnt that men

BEYOND TALL, DARK AND HANDSOME

were created to not only be protectors, providers and spiritual leaders of their families but also leave a mark in the world. Given these functions, what qualities then should men (married or single) be aiming to develop in themselves? Also, for the ladies, what should you be looking for in a man?

- **A Willingness to Grow Spiritually:** A man cannot offer spiritual leadership if he is not growing in his knowledge of God. No one is perfect, but there must be a willingness to grow, and an open and teachable heart. A man only accountable to himself has no other frame of reference except his own feelings and judgement. On the other hand, a man who is obedient to God can be trusted to keep his word and to act in honorable ways.

- **Self-Controlled:** In many circumstances, when sexual boundaries are broken in a relationship, it is as a result of a man pressuring the lady. Self-control will therefore help you keep off many harmful things. If a man knows and loves God, he will love you enough to respect you and treat you honorably. It will be an outpouring of his relationship with God.

> Godly men must learn to treat ladies with dignity.

- **Mission:** It is important for a man to have an idea of God's plan for his life. A man should be able to understand himself (his dreams, passions, gifts, abilities and experiences), and through prayer and courage, determine what his life is about. Even if these are at a rudimentary stage, a man who knows where he is going and who lives for something greater than just his own entertainment, will tend to lead well his family and those he is responsible for.

- **Financial Responsibility**: He may not be rich, but an important trait to have in your Mr. Right is somoene who is financially transparent and responsible. This is a man who is able to budget and plan well or, at the very least, is willing to work with his spouse if this is not an area of strength for him. Watch out for stingy or secretive men or careless investors.

- **Strong Relationships:** Watch how he relates with his family members. Does he honor his parents; love and respect his siblings? If he has sisters, how does he treat them? That might be how he will end up treating you. How about his friends? Who are they? Remember the saying, 'birds of a feather flock together?' If he hangs out with focused and responsible guys, he will most likely be the same as them. If he has strong relationships, then it is likely that he understands how to build and grow relationships.

- **Accountability:** Does he have anyone he is accountable to? An older friend, his father, a pastor, a group of friends or colleagues from work? A man who seeks accountability demonstrates that he is respectful of authority and values wise counsel.

Godly men must learn to treat ladies with dignity. They must learn how to treat women like their mothers, sisters and daughters, consistently respecting their boundaries, protecting them and desiring the best for them. It is the role of the man to create an environment in which his lady is able to flourish and shine. But ladies, if he is threatened by your success, treats you disrespectfully and is constantly pushing your boundaries, then see those as serious red flags!

Question For My Journal

Men, out of all the qualities listed, which one do you think if you took seriously would make the biggest difference in your life?

Ladies, what is the most important thing you have learnt about men from today's reading?

Verse To Remember

Ephesians 5:25-28. Husbands, love your wives, just as Christ loved the church and gave himself up for her to make her holy, cleansing her by the washing with water through the word, and to present her to himself as a radiant church, without stain or wrinkle or any other blemish, but holy and blameless. In this same way, husbands ought to love their wives as their own bodies. He who loves his wife loves himself.

Freedom Prayer

For Men

Lord, I confess that I have lacked _____ (list all of the above qualities that apply). As a result, I have influenced my girlfriend/wife/family to _____ which is not right in your eyes. I ask Your forgiveness and pray that by the shed blood of the Lord Jesus Christ, all ground gained by evil spirits in my life and that of my family because of my lack of character would be cancelled. I uproot and destroy the spirit of spiritual blindness and deceit within me in the mighty name of Jesus and pray that you will instead fill me with your Spirit of revelation and truth so that I may live a godly life. Amen!

For Married Women

Lord, I come before you on behalf of my husband, recognizing his character flaws as listed above. I confess that I too are not perfect and ask that you forgive me for any bitterness I may have harbored against my husband. I uproot and destroy the spirit of judgment against my husband and pray that you will instead give me a heart of empathy, compassion and mercy towards him. I pray that you will fill me with Your Spirit of revelation and truth so that I may exercise wisdom in my relationship with him. I invite You Holy Spirit to bring healing, reconciliation and a sense of oneness in my marriage. In Jesus' name. Amen!

For Single Women

Lord, my picture of a true man has been flawed by what I have consumed in the media and in our culture. Please forgive me for buying into the lie of the world. Help me not to conform any longer to the pattern of this world but instead to be transformed by the renewing of my mind (Romans 12:2). Amen!

BEYOND BEAUTY & MAKEUP

Yesterday, we looked at men and saw how the over-sexualization of our culture has led them to abdicate their role in family and society. Likewise, women too have been over-sexualized. Women are defined according to their ability to attract men. In agrarian settings, plump women were preferred because it showed that their husbands were wealthy enough to provide for them. It was also seen as a sign of their fertility and ability to produce many children. In modern times, the definition of attractiveness has changed. Nowadays, it is the color of the skin (the fairer the better, a really sad aspect of neo-colonialism), skin complexion, size of bust and buttocks, and ability to be visually attracting to men that seem to matter.

The fashion industry aims to assist women in reaching this sexual ideal and today, women's clothes are designed with this in mind. Women want to be sexy! Blouses and tops are created to:

- Reveal cleavage;

- Be so tight that buttons are about to pop;

- Be made of sheer fabric that makes them see through; or

- Reveal part or all of a women's back or abdomen.

- Trousers, shorts and skirts are designed:

- Tight;

- To ride low, revealing underwear in the back; and

- Short so that they ride exceedingly high above the knee such that when one is seated, they reveal as much flesh as possible.

Unfortunately, women have been so defined by their ability to be attractive to men that in some situations, women are advised to dress in a certain way in order to win contracts or get certain business. Some women have come to believe and see themselves only in these terms and so they dress and play the part of being men's sex toys.

> The fairer the better, a really sad aspect of neo-colonialism

Some of the consequences of this faulty belief about women are:

1. Many women dress in very provocative ways and thus attract the wrong kind of attention while all they want is to be appreciated and loved;

2. Many women mistake a man's physical attraction for her to mean he loves her, only to be disappointed when she realizes that all the man was attracted to was her body and his desire to have sex with her;

153

3. Many women become so desperate for acceptance by a man that they become clingy, even in abusive relationships; or

4. Many women now believe that they cannot be in a relationship with a man without being sexual.

A woman being valued only for her sex appeal is not only dehumanizing but is also a devaluation of her personhood. This is because women, being created in the image of God, have also been given qualities and characteristics that are unique to them and that can be used to positively influence people around them. If you ask people who has had the greatest influence on them, many of them will tell you it is or has been their mother. Women who are sure of themselves and confident in their unique gifts have the ability to greatly impact those around them and especially the next generation, for the better.

Like men, women were created to rule and have dominion over the whole earth! Agreeing to be objectified and seen as a sex object or using your feminine strengths to manipulate others only comes from a misguided definition of womanhood. As we saw, when it comes to marriage, wives are meant to be empowerers, nurturers, companions and culture setters. How should women (married or single) seek to embrace their femininity? And for those men who are not married yet, what qualities should you look for if you are seeking a potential life partner?

*   **A Heart for God:** A woman who finds her identity, value and guidance from God is priceless. As King Solomon wrote, *'Charm is deceptive, and beauty is fleeting; but a woman who fears the Lord is to be praised.'*[184] You You can be sure that such a lady will understand her role and strength as a woman. She understands that she is loved first by God, is valuable and of worth to God. You cannot give others what you do not have. Love can only flow from a source where it is abundant.

*   **Nurturing and Compassionate:** Women are naturally wired to be compassionate and are moved to meet needs in other people. So, how does she treat other people? Does she spend time to develop and nurture relationships? Is she caring towards her family and friends? The manner in which she treats people around her is the strongest indicator of how she will treat you, your friends and family.

*   **Takes Care of Herself:** It is a good value for a woman to dress well, be clean and elegant. This is the most visible thing about a woman. It does not mean spending huge amounts of money on or wearing expensive clothes, but rather having the ability to look good even on a shoestring budget. A decently dressed woman is the strongest message that she actually values herself and accepts that she is a woman worthy of respect!

*   **Beautiful Personality:** This has to do with being a person of character. No matter how stunningly and elegantly a lady dresses up, her character and personality are what will enhance her beauty. Some beautiful women whose character is an absolute turn off, have struggled to maintain relationships! Someone who has an optimistic view to life, and a light side or sense of humor often makes a good friend, while being a nag or whiner in a relationship can easily sap off energy and make dating or marriage a very draining experience. *'Better to live on a corner of the roof than share a house with a quarrelsome wife.'* Proverbs 21:9.

184 Proverbs 31:30

Beyond Beauty & Makeup

- **Self-Driven:** A woman needs to have a drive and passion for life. She needs to understand her God-given purpose and mission in life as this is what will guide her in knowing if the man she is with is compatible with where she is going. She does not wait to find a man to give her purpose or identity.

- **Supportive:** This is a person who is encouraging and not one who sees fault in everything others do. As a man wades through life, he faces many hard decisions and disappointments; the last thing he needs is his woman cutting him down to size!

- **An Ability to Provide Good Counsel:** Many women are intuitive and able to sense things beyond what the physiological senses can percieve. They often can tell how others are responding to an issue at a feelings or emotional level which makes them extremely valuable team members. Do not ever let people criticize you for being 'emotional'. There is absolutely nothing wrong with that!

- **Tenacity:** Women tend to have the persistence to go through difficult times and provide encouragement to those who are giving up hope.

Does this sound too ideal? Is it really possible to find such qualities in one person? Well, there are no perfect people. What this list does, however, is to show that a woman has so much more to offer other than her body. It is a list that can help a woman understand which areas to grow in and for a man to know what kind of woman to look for.

Question For My Journal

Ladies, out of all the qualities listed, which one do you think, if you took seriously, would make the most difference in your life?

Men, what have you learnt about ladies from today's reading?

Verse To Remember

Proverbs 31:10-12. A wife of noble character who can find? She is worth far more than rubies. Her husband has full confidence in her and lacks nothing of value. She brings him good, not harm, all the days of her life.

Freedom Prayer

For Women

Lord, I confess that I have lacked _____ (list all the qualities from the above list that apply). As a result, I have influenced my boyfriend/husband/family to _____ which is not right in your eyes. I ask Your forgiveness and pray that by the shed blood of the Lord Jesus Christ, all ground gained by evil spirits in my life and that of my family because of my lack of character would be cancelled. I uproot and destroy the spirit of spiritual blindness and deceit within me in the mighty name of Jesus and pray that You will instead fill me with your Spirit of revelation and truth so that I may live a godly life. Amen.

For Husbands

Lord, I come before you on behalf of my wife, recognizing her character flaws as listed above. I confess that I too are not perfect and ask that you forgive me for the bitterness I have harbored against her. I uproot and destroy the spirit of anger and bitterness within me in the mighty name of Jesus and pray that you will instead give me a heart of compassion and mercy towards my wife. I pray that you will fill me with your Spirit of revelation and truth so that I may exercise wisdom in my relationship with her. I invite You Holy Spirit to bring healing, reconciliation and a sense of oneness in our marriage. In Jesus' name. Amen.

For Single Men

Lord, my picture of a true woman has been flawed by what I have consumed in the media and in our culture. Please forgive me for buying into the lie of the world. Help me not to conform any longer to the pattern of this world but instead to be transformed by the renewing of my mind. (Romans 12:2). Amen!

RELATIONSHIPS PATHWAY

The last couple of days have been spent reclaiming our manhood and womanhood. We have learnt that God created us for so much more than sex. Having said this however, we need to understand that God is not anti-sex. He created it, for crying out loud! But, just like human manufacturers give their guide on how to use their products safely and effectively, God too has guidelines on where sex should happen within the confines of marriage. However, it is important to note that marriage does not guarantee good sex. Both married and unmarried people jump into bed thinking that good sex is a matter of technique and aphrodisiacs only to be disappointed when that is not the case. A good relationship based on truthfulness and trust trumps any technique or aphrodisiac!

> What you are about to read is completely counter-cultural! It will require you to swim upstream

How then do we develop a good relationship? The over-sexualization of our culture makes it difficult for men and women to get to know each other well without seeing each other as sex objects. The art of developing friendships has been lost in the din of a fast-paced life and the make-believe tales that bombard us with the messages that physical appearance, money and sex are the most important thing about relationships. There is so much more! God intended that we develop friendships first, and that romance would be the natural outflow of good friendships.

How then do we become friends? For those who are considering dating, the best place to start is putting yourselves in a no-pressure environment. Below is a schedule of a suggested process that will help a man and woman grow in a friendship while providing safety valves to quit amicably if the relationship is not working. If you are dating or planning to date, we hope you find this helpful, especially if you have realized that the world's way only leads to heartache and pain. If you are already married, we hope this will help you diagnose your own relationship and give you tools to help dating couples around you. A word of warning though: What you are about to read is completely counter-cultural! It will require you to swim upstream while everyone else around you is going with the current because it does not take much effort to do what everyone else is doing. Even a dead fish can float downstream. Only live fish swim upstream. So, are you ready? Here goes!

For The First Six Months

Take it slow. When you meet someone that you are interested in, realize that the more time you spend with him or her, the more you fan your emotions and heighten sexual desire. This quickly leads to infatuation which shortcircuits the entire 'become friends first' process. Slowing down can be done practically by:

- **Limiting your meeting time and talking time.** The less time you meet or spend time on lengthy phone calls, the less opportunity there is for heightening romantic feelings, thus increasing the chances of becoming 'just friends'.

- **Watch the subjects of conversation:** Avoid deep, emotional conversations or those that centre on sex. It is important to maintain emotional boundaries so that you do not get 'too deep, too soon.'

- **Go on group dates:** Join a small group at your church together. Doing activities with other people allows you to enjoy and observe the other person when their guard is down and their attention is not just on you. The things to observe are the lists we have been looking at in the last two days. For example, are they people of character and values? Are they sincerely seeking to know God? Do they have a teachable spirit? Do they have a good grip on their finances? Do they relate well with others (even those of different social standing)? Are your future plans compatible? As you make these observations, be as objective as possible.

Defining the Relationship

If at the end of the six to seven months you are satisfied that you are heading in the same direction (You are not looking for perfection; no one is perfect), then do what we call a DTR define the relationship. Come together and agree on the next steps of your relationship. If one of you is not ready to continue, then it is also okay to agree not to take the relationship beyond 'just being friends'.

Avoid being flirtatious through talk

If you decide to move the relationship beyond 'just friends' to 'special friend', then it will be helpful to still bear in mind a few facts.

1. **Keep Your Boundaries.** The relationship is still very exploratory and so, date in such a way that even if it broke up, yes, you would be hurt, but you would be able to make a clean break. This would involve dating with integrity. Men, in case you were not aware, women are easily influenced by the words we speak. Do not be too quick with your words if you are not ready to commit. In other words, do not rash to say, 'I love you' if your heart is not 100 percent committed to her. Similarly ladies, relating with integrity means avoiding being flirtatious through talk, body language and dress. Being flirtatious will certainly get a man turned on, but, unlike conventional wisdom would have it, it will not increase his commitment to you. A man is totally capable of having sex without engaging his heart, so be warned that sexy dressing may certainly be exciting but, if you want a man to respect and love you for who you are, then cover up!

2. **Men, Lead!** As a man, you should understand that you are the leader in the relationship. Use your strength, not to lord over or harass or even sexually prey on the girl, but to serve her. The goal of any relationship is to add value to the other person so that they are the better for having met you. Since the time of Adam, God holds men accountable for the state of their relationships. Lead by setting the standards of your sexual activities. Treat her with honor, respect and utmost purity by not engaging in sexual activities until marriage¾should the relationship end here. Seek accountability from your male friends to help sustain your commitment.

3. **Lead her by initiating spiritual conversations** and by ensuring you attend church and engage in courses that will help both of you grow spiritually. For far too long, women have led in these ways and yet it is the man's responsibility. In the matter of determining the pace of the relationship, take initiative. Pace your level of emotional engagement and match it with your level of commitment. In other words, do not act or speak in ways that are not commensurate with your

RELATIONSHIPS PATHWAY

level of commitment. In all your dealings, seek to protect and honor the woman.

4. **Ladies, Allow Him To Lead!** Girl, do not run ahead of the man and take leadership over the relationship. Guard your heart and only engage at the level of commitment of the man. Many times women fall into the temptation of thinking that the guy is romantically interested whereas he is only interested in a caring friendship with someone who is available to listen empathetically to his issues! Rein in your emotions and let the man pursue you at his pace. Many relationships end when the guy feels that he has been pushed to commit to something he was not ready for. It could be true that he takes forever to make decisions, but respect that and be patient. If it feels like he is taking too long, then reduce your availability or even move on. Let him see that though you enjoy his company, you have a life and that you enjoy hanging out with your friends and pursuing purpose.

5. **Also, give him space.** Recognize that he has a life outside of the relationship and give him space to engage with friends, family and work. Do not crowd his time, at the expense of these engagements. They are what built him to be who he is and taking him away from them may leave him worse off. However busy he might be, he will create time for you. This is one major sign that he actually values you. As he is busy doing his 'thing', go ahead and enjoy your own friendships and life. After all, there is nothing as exciting as pursuing a woman who has her life 'going'!

6. **Both of You, Remain Pure.** We like to say that sex before marriage is like eating your dessert before the rest of your food. The sweetness sears your tastebuds so that you cannot taste or enjoy the nutritious part of your meal. The dessert, which is meant to complement and complete the meal, will compete with it and even cause you to not eat it. Sex before marriage will often 'sear your tastebuds' so that it is impossible to build and enjoy the important parts of your relationship. There is a lot more to dating than sex! Going too fast physically will leave you unable to explore or enjoy growing together spiritually, intellectually, socially, financially and emotionally. You will be left with a purely sexual relationship which cannot sustain itself or stand the test of time. It will also, eventually, lower the level of respect in the relationship. If he walks away because you refused to give in, he will respect you for it later on. It is important to set a foundation in your relationship of honor for God. When you are willing to keep boundaries in your relationship because you honor God, you will be able to trust your spouse once you are married to guard those same boundaries in your relationship because he or she honors God. After all, if you could cheat on God with me, what will stop you cheating on me with others?

7. **Finally, Grow Together.** Read books together and engage in each others' social worlds by hanging out with each other's friends so that you are seeking to grow together intellectually, socially, financially and spiritually.

Safety Nets for This Period

1. Do not visit each other in your houses alone; do so with friends. Do not stay out too late alone.

2. Be especially vigilant in maintaining emotional and sexual boundaries.

3. Do not pair off by yourselves, but still be involved in the lives of your friends and family, inviting

them to engage with the both of you in your friendship.

If after another six months or so, if you both feel you are ready to make a lifetime commitment to each other, then declare your intentions to family, church small group members and close friends and seek out their counsel. If you have been open enough with the community around you, then often times they serve as good judges of character and give a pretty accurate assessment on the suitability of your intentions. It is quite telling that many times, during moments of candid reflection, couples who end up in divorce will admit having been warned about the suitability of their choice by their friends.

If a majority of your friends and family members are in agreement, then:

1. Start planning for a wedding;

2. Get a mentor couple to walk with you through the process of preparing for your marriage; and

3. Enter into a marriage preparation class.[185]

Question For My Journal

What is your first response to reading about the process described for growing a relationship? What felt right and what did you struggle with?

Verse To Remember

I Timothy 5:1-2. …treat younger men as brothers, older women as mothers, and younger women as sisters, with absolute purity.

Prayer For Today

Lord, I confess that I have lacked integrity in the way that I have related and, as a result, I have ended up wounding _____ (list all that apply). I ask Your forgiveness and pray that by the shed blood of the Lord Jesus Christ, all ground gained by evil spirits in my life because of my lack of integrity would be cancelled. I uproot and destroy the spirit of worldliness and deceit within me in the mighty name of Jesus. Amen.

---

185 A good course that we recommend is Ndoa, a 10-week marriage preparation experience by Carol & Muriithi Wanjau that will help you build a solid foundation for your marriage.

HOW FAR IS TOO FAR?

Acertain lady came to see me (Carol) over a matter that was troubling her. The background to her coming to see me was that a few months before that, she had attended a church service where a prayer had been made for single people who were hoping for a spouse. Soon after, she had met a man who was everything she had ever hoped for. He shared her faith, was involved in church activities just as she was and most impressively, was financially very responsible. He not only owned the apartment he currently lived in, but was engaged in various investment opportunities which made a future with him very attractive. To this lady, who was in her late thirties, all these factors made her convinced that this man was a direct answer to her prayers!

I was happy to hear her story and thought she wanted me to say a prayer of thanksgiving for the answered prayer. But she kept right on. "But now he wants me to move in with him!" I inquired whether she meant he had made a marriage proposal after only four months of dating, but the lady corrected me, saying that he was suggesting that they move in together because that was the only way they would truly know if they were right for each other. As I gently prodded to find out what her position was on the matter, I discovered that she was deeply troubled and confused. In addition, her friends were not only doing it but seemed to be enjoying themselves in the process. "Moreover", they reckoned, "How will you know if you are sexually compatible when you get married? If you don't agree, he will most definitely get someone else who will only be too happy to oblige and you will be left hanging, single all your life!" She ended with the advice one particular friend had given her. "Forget about being good. Good girls finish last!"

> God is not against sex! He not only created it, but also designed it so that it works best within the security of a marriage

What a sentiment! No wonder this lady was troubled. In a sexually-saturated world, where abstinence is seen as archaic, naïve and boring while being sexually active is seen as sophisticated and with the times, what is one to do when faced with such a situation?

Now, it is important to repeat again that God is not against sex! He not only created it, but also designed it so that it works best within the security of a marriage. Often times, the pleasures of illicit sex (sex outside the boundaries of marriage) are what we see shouted on T.V., in romantic novels, on the internet and social media, but seldom is the dark side of these pleasures disclosed. It is often within the privacy of pastors' and counselors' offices that the dark side is revealed, the victims by that time too ashamed to discuss their experiences with anyone else. But the scriptures are pretty graphic in their description of the dark consequences of illicit sex. For example, King Solomon had this to say on the matter.

At the window of my house I looked down through the lattice. I saw among the simple, I noticed among the young men, a youth who had no sense. He was going down the street near her corner, walking along in the direction of her house at twilight, as the day was fading, as the dark of night set in. Then out came a woman to meet him, dressed like a prostitute and with crafty intent. (She is unruly and defiant, her feet never stay at home; now in the street, now in the squares, at every corner she lurks.) She took hold of him and kissed him and with a brazen face she said: "Today I fulfilled my vows, and I have food from my fellowship offering at home. So I came out to meet you; I looked for you and have found you!

I have covered my bed with colored linens from Egypt. I have perfumed my bed with myrrh, aloes and cinnamon. Come, let's drink deeply of love till morning; let's enjoy ourselves with love! My husband is not at home; he has gone on a long journey. He took his purse filled with money and will not be hometill full moon!"[186]

From this passage, we can make several observations about illicit sex (sex outside the boundaries of marriage)

1. Illicit Sex is Very Alluring.

This passage feels like a scene straight out of a Hollywood movie! In the mind's eye, one can see a young man who is infatuated with his married colleague. They had hit it off at the office party, and there was such chemistry between them! He had told her about his last heartbreak and she had confided to him about her loveless marriage. They had had such a good time that they had agreed to meet for a date that next week, at a little, hidden restaurant not too far from her neighborhood.

> In our over-sexualized culture, there are also many who like this woman get addicted to recreational sex

When she shows up, the sight of her almost knocks him over! She is dressed extremely sexily, with an expensive-looking and very revealing dress. Her high heels give her an air of sophistication. Her makeup is perfectly applied and the smell of her perfume is intoxicating! Before he can compose himself enough to speak, she gives him a kiss and says, "My hubby took off yesterday on a long trip. So, let's just go to my house. I've set up the jacuzzi, made a dinner for two and put a bottle of wine in the fridge. I can't wait to share it with you!"

What a promise! Movies, magazines, porn, T.V., radio¾the messages all around us¾on every street, in every corner and square make this alluring promise, 'Come. Let's drink deeply of love till morning!' For some, like the young man, it starts very innocently. An accidental brushing of hands, a pop-up on your computer browser from a porn site, an exciting conversation between colleagues at an offsite teambuilding event, and the next thing you know, this other person is looking like the best thing that ever happened since sliced bread! But in our over-sexualized culture, there are also many who like this woman get addicted to recreational sex and who are constantly looking to make a sexual connection.

What happens next in the story seems inevitable, unless you have given this issue thought and made some prior decisions for yourself: *'With persuasive words she led him astray; she seduced him with her smooth talk. All at once, he followed her like an ox going to the slaughter.'* And that leads to our second observation...

---

186 Proverbs 7:6-20

HOW FAR IS TOO FAR?

2. Illicit Sex Always Seems to Make Sense.

The line spoken by the woman, *'My husband is not home'* seems like a rationalization. Perhaps this woman's reason for doing this is that her busy husband is never home for her. For many, illicit sex is often rationalized. It could be that your spouse no longer meets your needs. Or that porn is harmless as no one else is involved. Or that moving in together cuts costs and everybody is doing it anyway. Or that sex is the only way you can find out if you are suited for one another. Or that sex is a natural human need that needs to be satisfied. Or that nowadays, abstinence and virginity are such outdated concepts, does anyone even believe they are possible? We create our reasons and these reasons make sense to us.

3. Illicit Sex Always Leads to Death.
But finally, Solomon also warns us that regardless of how we rationalize it, there are significant negative consequences to illicit sex. Here's how his story ends...

'Like a deer stepping into a noose till an arrow pierces his liver, like a bird darting into a snare, little knowing it will cost him his life. Now then, my sons, listen to me; pay attention to what I say. Do not let your heart turn to her ways or stray into her paths. Many are the victims she has brought down; her slain are a mighty throng. Her house is a highway to the grave, leading down to the chambers of death.'[187]

Jesus, many years later, when referring to our enemy said, *"The thief comes only to steal and kill and destroy; I came that they may have life, and have it abundantly.*[188] *"* When it comes to illicit sex, the devil steals from, kills and destroys people in the following ways:

Lack of trust in a relationship introduces fear, suspicion, jealousy and hostility

- **Loss of Innocence:** Like Adam and Eve, your eyes are opened and you can no longer relate with members of the opposite sex without ulterior motives. People are reduced to sexual objects and are robbed of the joy of relating to the opposite sex with 'no strings' attached. In addition, memories of prior lovers and the inevitable comparison between different lovers often leads to guilt or sexual dissatisfaction in subsequent relationships.

- **Mistrust:** If you believe that sex is a natural urge that cannot be controlled but must be fulfilled at all times, how will you ever trust your spouse to be faithful to you? Lack of trust in a relationship introduces fear, suspicion, jealousy and hostility which, in almost all situations, leads to death of a relationship.

- **Inability to be Intimate:** The more you practice impersonal sex (that is, sex with no strings attached), the more you condition yourself to having meaningless sex. When a person finds themselves in this situation, then they try to make sex more sizzling by trying out different partners, trying different

187   Proverbs 7:22–27

188   John 10:10

sexual techniques, including having sex with members of the same sex, having sex orgies, swinging, using porn and so on. You are never able to enjoy a real, meaningful and lasting relationship with another person without viewing them as a sex object.

- **Literal Death:** 15 percent of women who depend on condoms for contraception will become pregnant within the first year of use and, if the woman is 15 years old, then the rates are higher with a 50 percent chance of falling pregnant. Abortion follows in many cases, including the widespread use of the 'emergency pill'. Basically an innocent life is taken because the person is not ready to take responsibility. Also, correct and consistent condom use can reduce, but not eliminate, the risk of sexually transmitted diseases like chlamydia, gonorrhea, herpes, human papillomavirus (HPV) and HIV/AIDS. These sexually transmitted diseases can cause infertility in both men and women, can affect the health of unborn children, and can cause actual death or reduce the ability of the infected person to to engage freely in future relationships.

- **Ungodly Soul Ties.** Out of all the dangers listed above, the worst of all, from a spiritual perspective, is that sex outside the protection of marriage exposes someone to an ungodly soul tie with the people or person involved. The apostle Paul posed the question, *'Or do you not know that he who is joined to a prostitute becomes one body with her? For, as it is written, "The two will become one flesh."* [189]

> When someone has sex with another person who has these spirits, they are transferred to them

In a godly marriage, God unites a couple both spiritually and emotionally through the sexual act. Spiritually, they become united, what scripture refers to as 'one flesh'. In the case of illicit sex then, this spiritual bonding still takes place, but instead of the Spirit of unity and oneness, illicit sex gives the enemy the legal right to introduce other spirits, for example, spirits of addiction, lust, adultery, fornication, masturbation and homosexuality. When someone has sex with another person who has these spirits, they are transferred to them and neither person can be truly intimate with their spouse because of the presence of such defiling spirits. In addition to this, even when two people break up, they still remain attached through a soul tie and if it is not broken, such a person will have difficulty receiving love from their spouse as spiritually, a spiritual attachment remains to their ex or ex'es.

The only way to break free is to confess the sin of fornication or adultery and to break off such soul ties. Soul ties can also be formed through non-sexual but deeply emotionally engaging relationships with your ex or with other people near or far, for example, an emotional affair with a colleague at work or cases of deep infatuation with superstars. All these need to be broken. Soul ties formed through prior marriages and also through non-consensual sex like rape and incest also have to be broken as must attachments to same sex relations, sex toys, sexually explicit movies, pornography and other addictive sexual behaviors.

---

189   II Corinthians 6:16

HOW FAR IS TOO FAR?

Question For My Journal

Which of the ways listed above (that is, the ways the devil kills relationships) have you practiced in the past or been in danger of practising?

Verse To Remember

I Corinthians 6:19-20. Do you not know that your bodies are temples of the Holy Spirit, who is in you, whom you have received from God? You are not your own; you were bought at a price. Therefore honor God with your bodies.

Freedom Prayer

Father, in the name of Jesus, I acknowledge that I have sinned against myself and against you by defiling my body through the sexual sin of fornication. I repent and ask forgiveness of my sin. I am also repenting that I have defiled _____
(fill in the name of those you have had illicit sex with) by agreeing with him/her to commit the sin. I ask for the blood of Jesus to cleanse me from the sin of fornication. Father God, I receive your forgiveness and I receive the power of the blood to cleanse me from every defilement that comes with fornicating.

Breaking Soul Ties

I break the soul ties to all my former sexual partner(s) _____
(if there are several, you should break the soul ties by praying this prayer for each one) in the name of Jesus. I also break all romantic and sexual memories of _____
that are attached to my emotions and my mind in the name of Jesus. I cast down all residue of fantasy with my sexual encounter with _____ in the name of Jesus. I forgive _____ for defiling my body, my mind and my spirit in the name of Jesus. Father, forgive me for defiling him/her as well. I ask God that you will bring healing and cleansing to my emotions, my mind and my body.

Once you have prayed the above for every former sexual partner, then conclude with this prayer...

In the name of Jesus, I bind every unclean spirit of lust, impurity, immorality, as well as any other spirit that entered into my body through fornication and I command them to be cast out and thrown directly to you, where you may deal with them as you choose. I ask for the blood of Jesus to cover these doorways as I totally put a closure to all sexual sins in my life. Father God, starting today, I declare that I will value purity and walk in holiness, in the name of Jesus. Thank you for your love, for your forgiveness, for the cleansing and the protecting power of the blood and my newly-found freedom in the name of Jesus! I BREAK THE CURSE of fornication in my life, in the name of Jesus! Completely renew my mind. Thank you for healing my mind from the tormenting memories of my past. In the name of Jesus. Amen!

Breaking the Curse of Barrenness Because of Sexual Sin

Lord, I thank you that You have forgiven my sins and that you will never hold them against me. I want to start my future marriage on the right foundation. And so Lord, I now pray against any curse that I have opened myself up to, either in my womb (for ladies) or in my loins (for men) because of fornication. I ask for the blood of Jesus to remove the power of the curse. I break this curse in the name of Jesus. I ask for your blessing instead over my womb (for ladies) or loins (for men) in the name of Jesus. Amen.

Confessing and Repenting the Sin of Pregnancy Before Marriage and the Breaking Off of the Spirit of Illegitimacy

Father, I also would like to ask for forgiveness of the sin of fornication that produced a life in my womb (or produced a life in my girlfriend's or fiancé's womb). Forgive us for getting pregnant outside of the protective covering of marriage. Father, I now dedicate this child to you in the name of Jesus. I break the spirit of illegitimacy that came into him/her because of our sin, in Jesus' name. I ask that this child will be reclaimed for your glory. I break the pattern of fornication in his/her life in Jesus' name. Bless this child in the name of Jesus. May he/she be a branch grafted into the True Vine, which is Jesus, and may his/her life be one characterized by the fruit of righteousness. In the name of Jesus. Amen.

HOW FAR IS TOO FAR?

Breaking the Curse of Fornication or Rape on a Child

Father God, in the name of Jesus, I thank you for the life of this baby. I dedicate him/her to you in the name of Jesus. Set him/her apart for the purpose of honoring and glorifying your name. I confess the sin of fornication/rape through which this baby was conceived. I ask forgiveness for this sin in the name of Jesus. I break the power of this sin and instead I ask God that you will sanctify this child in the name of Jesus. I declare that the curse is broken by the blood of Jesus! I close the door against any spirits that the enemy may ever use to harass this child because of his/her conception. May this child become great and my his/her future be a glorious testimony that God can take what the enemy meant for evil and turn it into the most beautiful good. Lord, use this child to bless our family and to bless the world. Thank you for your great love for him/her. May he/she experience this love and know that they are loved, admired and wanted by our family and by You. And thank you for giving this baby a different life and a new slate. In Jesus' name. Amen.

WEEK
– TEN –
IN CONCLUSION

HELP! THEY ARE BACK!

This week's chapter is written in form of a dialogue between a graduate of the *Simama* course and their pastor. Let's use it to prepare ourselves for life after Simama!

Mike: Pastor, I don't think I can make it.

Pastor: Uh, huh…

Mike: You see, after taking the class, life was really good! Somehow I felt lighter, as if certain weights had been lifted off my shoulders. The world looked brighter, our meetings at life groups were real, we were all so excited about the new things we had learnt and the changes we had seen in our lives. But, after the 10 weeks were over, I wondered how long the illusion would last and I was right. Things have begun to fray at the ends: Work is very fast and I have gotten a new boss who is literally from hell! I thought things would improve between me and my wife but she has now moved into the next room. In addition, I have this headache that will not go away. There is this weight and heaviness that I have every morning that makes waking up and being civil to people very difficult. Man, I don't know if this thing really works. To be honest, the beers, my boys and the club are making a lot more sense now. At least in that other life, I could drown away my sorrows and have fun in the process! Pastor, what do I do? Was what I felt real or just an illusion?

Pastor: Wow! That sounds like a lot for one person! If these things were to happen to me, even I would begin to think that what I had gone through was an illusion! But what I would like for us to do is to first of all step back, just like doctors do, and look back to what could have possibly gone wrong with the 'treatment' you received as a result of going through the course. It is true that sometimes, when people go through a course such as *Simama*, there are some prevailing issues that might prevent them from breaking free from destructive thought patterns or behaviors. So, I want us to go through a few of these issues and then offer some prescriptions that hopefully will help. Is that ok?

Mike: Honestly, I do not know… after 10 weeks, surely you are not asking me to do another course, are you?

Pastor: No, not at all. What I am saying is that breaking old traits and habits is like a science. When something is not quite working as it should, then we need to trace back to see if there is a step that was missed out and correct it.

Mike: Oh well. I am very sure I was quite diligent in class… but let me hear you out.

Pastor: Breaking old destructive habits begins by first of all being willing and open to facing issues, then repenting of them and asking for God's forgiveness. Now the interesting thing is that this is an ongoing process. A 10-week course cannot possibly solve everything. It only shows the key areas or ways in which we give the devil an opening in our lives and the methods of 'kicking' him out.

Breaking sinful habits can fail if these situations remain true in our lives: Bitterness and unforgiveness; unresolved pain or guilt; unconfessed sin that one wants to keep hidden, ungodly soul ties still in place, being under or using ungodly domination or control; when one's life is out of balance; when…

Mike: Whoa! Wait a minute! I can understand bitterness, unforgiveness, guilt, pain and all that. I recognize I was full of this stuff and I genuinely prayed about it, but life out of balance? How does that make the breaking of my past habits ineffective?

Pastor: Have you ever heard people say that the word, BUSY, is an acronym for bustling under satan's yoke?

Mike: Not really…

Pastor: Well, leading an out-of-balance life means that we are not taking the time to recharge and renew ourselves physically through exercise and proper diet, emotionally through healthy friendships or relationships or even spiritually through spending time with God. When we fail to recharge, our bodies easily get fatigued and, with that, our emotions become raw and brittle, making us highly irritable and prone to anger. When we fail to connect with God, our perspective gets off balance and circumstances easily get us down and depressed, unlike say other people around us. Does that sound familiar?

Mike: Man, it's like you're reading off a page from the book of my life! I remember early in the course being told about eating right and being made to exercise with my *Simama* partner. Are you for real? I thought that was just for the course duration?

Pastor: No. Leading a balanced life is a lifestyle, not a course requirement.

Mike: But my life is so hectic. Doing the daily readings was hard enough but making it a lifestyle… I've just gotten a boss whose motto in life is 'no pain, no gain!'

Pastor: But you now understand that leading an out-of-balance lifestyle is not good for you…

Mike: Yes.

Pastor: Can I go on with the other ways?

Mike: Sure.

Pastor: Well, the other ways in which breaking of sinful habits is not successful are if there is still deeper healing that is needed; when inner vows have not been renounced; when one is in disobedience over something God has said not to do; when one does not know Jesus as their personal Savior or when there is doubt and lack of faith that God is able to break a sinful habit and bring about full healing and deliverance.

Mike: You know Pastor, as I hear you speak, two things stand out for me: My out-of-balance lifestyle and my unbelief that even what happened during the course was for real. How do I deal with these two things?

Pastor: Let me first of all assure you that what happened during the course was real. As we prayed and

HELP! THEY ARE BACK!

canceled all the ways in which the devil had taken hold over our lives, it really did happen, and that is why you felt 'lighter'. But, just as in any war, the devil does not easily give in or not try to take back what he has already lost. This is why the apostle Peter taught us to 'stand firm and resist the devil.'[190]

Mike: Hey Pastor, I must admit this is getting spooky. I thought we were finished with all this devil stuff after we were done with Simama?

Pastor: The reality is there are two spiritual kingdoms operating on the earth today: The Kingdom of Light and the kingdom of darkness. God is the ruler or king of the Kingdom of light and satan is the ruler or prince of the kingdom of darkness. After Jesus was baptized, we are told that "from that time on Jesus began to preach, 'Repent for the kingdom of heaven is near.'"[191] In other words, an invasion or intrusion of another kingdom had begun. Up until this time, the 'ruler of the prince of the air', that is, Satan, had the legal authority to rule the earth and dominate humans¾a right he had stolen from Adam and Eve after leading them to rebel against God. Remember, God had entrusted this right to Adam and Eve when he told them to multiply, fill the earth and rule over it.[192] But the enemy snatched this right away when he led mankind in rebellion against God by sowing seeds of mistrust, hatred and suspicion towards God and, as a result, many destinies were destroyed.

Mike: Okay – that's really interesting! But how does all this connect with my issues?

Pastor: You see, as a descendant of Adam and Eve, you too were meant to rule over God's world. There is a unique purpose that God created you for![193] But the enemy's ploy, through all the issues that are plaguing you, is to destroy you and keep you from realizing this purpose. Anybody seeking to enter into their God destiny must change kingdoms. They must move from the kingdom of darkness and into the Kingdom of Light, which is what we do when we get saved. And whereas the kingdom of darkness keeps people in bondage by lying to them that true freedom is found in doing as you wish,[194] being in God's Kingdom requires total surrender¾it is through surrender that we experience the life of freedom that we were created for![195]

Mike: So, I remember the chapter on surrender during Mizizi, but I can't quite remember now what the details were. I'm supposed to surrender...

Pastor: Everything. Your right to control your destiny, your marriage and children, your right to determine your career, your ambitions, achievements, accomplishments, money... everything![196]

Mike: Yeah, I remember now. But doesn't that make me a zombie? I mean, can I no longer think for myself?

---

190 I Peter 5:9
191   Matthew 4:17
192 Genesis 1:28
193 Ephesians 2:10. 'For we are God's handiwork, created in Christ Jesus to do good works, which God prepared in advance for us to do.'
194 Genesis 3:4, The enemy's lie is, 'You will surely not die!'
195 John 10:10. 'The thief (that is, the devil) comes only to steal and kill and destroy; I have come that they may have life, and have it to the full'
196 Philippians 3:8 'What is more, I consider everything a loss compared to the surpassing greatness of knowing Christ Jesus my Lord, for whose sake I have lost all things. I consider them rubbish, that I may gain Christ.'

Pastor: No. What it means is that you now have a ruler or boss whom you take instructions from but also whom you consult with before making major decisions.

Mike: What if I make mistakes and do the wrong things or what if God asks me to do something I do not want to do?

Pastor: Be careful not to fall for that classic lie of satan. He deceived Eve into thinking that God was holding out on her and He did not have her best interest at heart! As the prophet Jeremiah promised, God's plans for you are for good and not for evil; they are for peace and not disaster, plans to give you a future filled with hope.[197]

Mike: Okay. I get that. So, what about the issues I came to you about?

Pastor: Let's do first things first. Let's first pray the prayer of surrender as this will help us once we begin tackling your issues. Is this ok?

Mike: Okay.

Question For My Journal

What do you resonate with or struggle with when it comes to the concept of total life surrender to God?

Verse to Remember

Matthew 16:25 (NLT). If you try to hang on to your life, you will lose it. But if you give up your life for my sake, you will save it.

Prayer

I recognize that there is only one true and living God (Exodus 20:2, 3), who exists as Father, Son and Holy Spirit. I recognize that He alone deserves all honor, praise and worship as He is the Creator, Sustainer, Beginning and end of all things (Revelation 4:11; 5:9, 10; Isaiah 43:1, 7, 21). I recognize Jesus Christ as the Messiah, the word who became flesh and dwelt among us (John 1:1, 14). I, therefore, relinquish all rights to my life, my desires, achievements, accomplishments, ambitions (list any others) and declare that from now on, it is no longer I who lives but Christ who lives in me. The life I will live from now on, I choose to entrust it to Jesus who loved me so much that He gave His life for me (Galatians 2:20). I thank you God for delivering me out of the kingdom of darkness and transferring me into your Kingdom of Light. Amen!

---

197 Jeremiah 29:11

HELP! THEY ARE BACK!

Pastor: Hey Mike! The last time we met, we ended with a prayer of surrender. How is that going for you?

Pastor: Hey Mike! The last time we met, we ended with a prayer of surrender. How is that going for you?

Mike: That prayer was actually quite scary. The thought of giving up on my ambitions was quite tough and my greatest fear is not living out what I prayed.

Pastor: You know you are right. None of us has what it takes to keep such commitments, but the amazing thing about God is that He not only gives us the desire to make the commitment; He also helps us keep it!

Mike: Oh, yeah? What does that mean?

Pastor: Remember telling me how tempting it has been to go back to your old ways? Well, God is able to help you overcome this temptation.

Mike: Okay, I get that and don't get me wrong, I'm glad I finally prayed that prayer. It wasn't as bad as I thought it would be! So, my question today is, how come, even after I surrender my life to Jesus, I still struggle with issues in my life and in my relationships? Why hasn't God taken them away, despite the fact that I have prayed and asked Him to?

Pastor: Well, there are different reasons. The first that I can think of is that we have an enemy! The last time we talked about the two kingdoms and about transferring from one to the other. However, when someone moves from satan's kingdom, the enemy does not easily give up on his prize and he does all that he can to keep someone in his grip. As the apostle Paul said, 'For we wrestle not against flesh and blood, but against principalities, against powers, against the rulers of the darkness of this world, against spiritual wickedness in high places.'[198] In other words, behind the daily events that occur in our lives, there are spiritual forces that we do not see.

Mike: So, basically, the devil is fighting me? I thought it was impossible for the devil to possess someone who is a follower of Jesus…

Pastor: I believe that a believer cannot be possessed by the enemy in the same way an unbeliever can! You see, Jesus won the victory back for us from the enemy, and we received that victory when we accepted Christ. We are no longer fighting for victory, but we are fighting from victory¾-from the position that we are on the winning side. The enemy no longer has authority over us because we belong to a different kingdom. The beautiful thing is that God has given us authority to resist the enemy. That's why the bible teaches us to 'resist the devil and he will flee from you!'[199]

Mike: So, how do I resist the devil?

Pastor: You basically do it through prayer. St. Paul wrote, 'The weapons we fight with are not the

---

198   Ephesians 6:12
199   James 4:7

weapons of the world. On the contrary, they have divine power to demolish strongholds.'[200] You need to understand that prayer is a very powerful weapon! God created the world through His words and since we are made in His image, our words too have power. For example, remember the freedom prayers you learnt in your Simama book? Whether or not you felt their effect, in the spiritual realm, something was happening when you prayed them aloud! You can continue to pray them regularly over your life and over your family, and especially the doctrinal affirmations in the appendix. But the bible also tells us to 'put on the full armour of God so that you can take your stand against the devil's evil schemes.'[201] We put on God's armor by regularly and prayerfully practicing the attributes you find in Ephesians 6, such as reading God's word, faith in His word, trusting in His salvation and so on.

Mike: Man! I really need to set aside some time regularly to pray for my family! You said there were some other reasons for my struggle?

Pastor: The other reasons are both related. The first is your sinful nature. As we learnt during Simama, it is possible for a believer to give back legal access to the enemy by reopening certain doors through sin in their life. The enemy can then use this to harass and intimidate them.

I've just been reading through the book of Judges and it demonstrates this truth powerfully. Whenever God's people would rebel against God and turn to idols, God would release them to the consequences of their rebellion by removing His protection over them which would allow the neighboring nations to oppress and colonize them. When they cried out to God to save them, God would send a leader, also called a judge, who would easily displace the enemy's hold over their nation. In the same way, God never forces Himself on us and our recurring rebellion can open the door to the enemy's oppression. But when we ask God to save us, His Righteous Judge, Jesus, removes the enemy's work from our lives so we can live as we were created.

Mike: That one really makes sense! After Simama, I made a resolution to change the way I relate to my wife and kids, but I still found myself messing up and being nasty to them. Like this morning; my wife was late, as usual, getting to the car and I found myself hooting the horn angrily. I know Pastor; not too smart! It sure made for an awkward ride to school and work and I ended up feeling really guilty! I was telling a friend at work that sometimes I feel like God just tempts us so He can see if we're really serious!

Pastor: It's interesting you should say that! Just this morning I read this scripture from the book of James, 'When tempted, no one should say, "God is tempting me." For God cannot be tempted by evil, nor does he tempt anyone; but each person is tempted when they are dragged away by their own evil desire and enticed. Then, after desire has conceived, it gives birth to sin; and sin, when it is full-grown, gives birth to death.'[202] James was writing to believers, and I believe the 'evil desire' he refers to is the sinful nature. Some theologians

---

200 II Corinthians 10:4
201 Ephesians 6:10
202 James 1:13-15

WHY I STRUGGLE

teach that Christians no longer have a sinful nature; that it was destroyed at the cross. Others teach that even though we are saved from sin, we still have a sinful nature that will be fully redeemed once Christ returns, and that, in the meantime, we must wage war against it. While both positions can be argued from scripture, I believe that there are several scriptures that lead me to the conclusion that the believer must still be alert and not imagine that sin can no longer influence them. Let me pull some out and let's read them together...

I John 1:8-9. If we claim to be without sin, we deceive ourselves and the truth is not in us. If we confess our sins, he is faithful and just and will forgive us our sins and purify us from all unrighteousness.

Galatians 5:16-18. So I say, walk by the Spirit, and you will not gratify the desires of the flesh. For the flesh desires what is contrary to the Spirit, and the Spirit what is contrary to the flesh. They are in conflict with each other, so that you are not to do whatever you want. But if you are led by the Spirit, you are not under the law.

Romans 8:12-13. Therefore, brothers and sisters, we have an obligation—but it is not to the flesh, to live according to it. For if you live according to the flesh, you will die; but if by the Spirit you put to death the misdeeds of the body, you will live.

Ephesians 4:22-24. You were taught, with regard to your former way of life, to put off your old self, which is being corrupted by its deceitful desires; to be made new in the attitude of your minds; and to put on the new self, created to be like God in true righteousness and holiness.

Philippians 3:20-21. But our citizenship is in heaven. And we eagerly await a Savior from there, the Lord Jesus Christ, who, by the power that enables him to bring everything under his control, will transform our lowly bodies so that they will be like his glorious body.

Romans 13:14. Rather, clothe yourselves with the Lord Jesus Christ, and do not think about how to gratify the desires of the flesh.

I Peter 2:11. Dear friends, I urge you, as foreigners and exiles, to abstain from sinful desires, which wage war against your soul.

Matthew 15:18-20. But the things that come out of a person's mouth come from the heart, and these defile them. For out of the heart come evil thoughts—murder, adultery, sexual immorality, theft, false testimony, slander. These are what defile a person...

Mike: Oh wow! I see what you mean! I definitely agree. Being a Christian doesn't mean I don't struggle with sin! But I suspect you're going to tell me that God is able to help me!

Pastor: Hehe... that's right. The bible tells us that even though we are tempted by sin, just like everyone else, we are no longer slaves to sin.[203] Before you accepted Christ, you had no choice but to sin. But when you accepted Christ, you received the Holy Spirit who now gives you the power to say no to sin.[204] And on those occasions when you do sin, the bible says that when you confess it to God or call it what it is without pretending, God not only forgives you, but He completely restores you as if you never sinned.[205]

---

203 Romans 6:6-7
204 Romans 6:8-14
205 1 John 1:9

Question For My Journal

Do you have a small group of people with godly values that you are committed to meet with regularly?

Verse to Remember

James 4:7. Submit yourselves, then, to God. Resist the devil, and he will flee from you.

Freedom Prayer

Thank you, Lord, for your work on the cross through which I am no longer a slave to sin. Thank you too for Your Holy Spirit who helps me to say no to sin and to resist the devil. I confess that I have often been deceived by the father of lies into believing that I am the captain of my ship and the one who determines the destiny of my life. Because of this I have often lived my life without acknowledging you or even giving you honor for the things you have done in my life. I ask for your forgiveness and pray that by the shed blood of the Lord Jesus Christ, all ground gained by evil spirits because my pride and deception be canceled. I acknowledge you as my Father who grants me healing and health *(Exodus 15:26);* who enables me to prosper *(Proverbs 28:25);* who disciplines me when I go wrong *(Hebrews 12:6);* who gives me knowledge and wisdom *(Daniel 1:17),* who gives me counsel *(James 1:5);* who is able to restore me, no matter how difficult my past has been *(Psalm 71:20);* who rebukes the enemy on my behalf *(Deuteronomy 28:7)* and who has also given me authority over satan and his demons because I am God's child *(Ephesians 1:19-23).* I therefore rebuke every evil spirit that is causing me to feel down and defeated because I choose to believe the word of God that says, I have the victory.

I am confident that God is on my side. He will never leave me or forsake me *(Isaiah 43:1, 2).* I pray, Lord, that you will give me a community of friends that I can walk with and with whom we can be in the habit of meeting regularly together. And I pray that You will give me the power to serve you and walk with you faithfully, for the rest of my life. Amen!

DEVOTIONAL LIVING

Mike: Now Pastor, thanks for being available to have coffee with me. Today, I want us to get real!

Pastor: Oh, yeah? I thought we have been real all this time!

Mike: True. I appreciate the change in my world view. You got me praying to surrender my life fully and showed me that I need to understand my everyday circumstances according to what scripture says. I must say that I was also quite encouraged when you shared with me how God is on my side and that He has assured me victory over all the issues surrounding me. But this has not solved all my issues!

Pastor: Oh, yeah? How so?

Mike: There are these two women who are making my life a living he… Well, you get the picture!

Pastor: Okay. Uou mean your wife and another woman?

Mike: No! No! My wife and my boss!

Pastor: What seems to be the problem?

Mike: My wife nags me about not spending enough time with her and the kids, while my boss pushes for unrealistic deadlines which means I have to work overtime. Man! I'm fed up with feeling unappreciated all around!

Pastor: So, how do you respond when criticized?

Mike: You know, I don't need anyone telling me I am stupid and inadequate. I got all that when growing up!

Pastor: Sounds like a real sore issue. What do you do when you feel unappreciated?

Mike: That's when my beers and boys come in. At least there I get respect and…

Pastor: Whoa! Wait a minute… I remember you mentioned that you stopped drinking during *Simama*!

Mike: Yes… I don't drink much nowadays. Just a beer every now and then when I'm with my boys. That's not a sin, right?

Pastor: That's not even the issue right now. What I'm trying to say is that you are in a vicious cycle. You feel poorly about yourself; then you get criticized; then you reach out for alcohol, work, porn, a relationship to soothe you and so on, but the core issue is not dealt with. You see, life is full of joys as well as disappointments. You will encounter situations where you will be misunderstood, falsely accused, jeered and even maligned. Think about, when Jesus was betrayed by a trusted friend, who or what did He reach out for?

Mike: His pals?

Pastor: Not exactly! Even they failed Him at His greatest hour of need. They could not stay awake to pray for Jesus in the excruciating moments before His crucifixion.[206] Jesus turned to His Father to give Him the strength to face the most difficult assignment He ever did while here on earth. The problem with us believers is that we carry on with life, only calling on God during emergencies and then, when we do not 'feel' Him or do not see Him answering our prayers, we turn our backs on Him saying that prayers don't work!

Mike: Mmm... much as I hate to admit it, I have said the same thing.

Pastor: Even as we talked about praying and understanding life through scripture, you cannot succeed in your Christian walk if you do not cultivate a close relationship with God. Just like Jesus, we need to learn how to both love and receive love and comfort from our Father.

Mike: Okay. So, how does that work exactly?

Pastor: It involves developing a lifestyle of hanging out with your Heavenly Father as one does with a friend.

Mike: But Pastor, how do I do that when God is invisible?

Pastor: Sounds weird, huh? Well, when I first began to 'hang out' with God, I wasn't quite sure what was expected of me. I mean, was I supposed to pray for long hours using complicated English? Then there was reading the Bible. Was I to read it like a normal story book from the first page to the last? How about when the bible didn't make sense and I had an exceptionally crazy schedule, was I still expected to 'hang out' with God?

Mike: Wow, I thought it was only non-pastors like me who thought like this!

Pastor: You'd be surprised Mike that just as there is an initial awkwardness with a new friendship, our initial times of 'hanging out' with God may seem that way. But, as with every new friendship, that awkwardness doesn't stop us from continuing to 'hang out' and getting to know the new person. So, we too need to push through this awkward phase with God as it is the only way to know Him.

Mike: I guess when you put it that way it makes sense... but how do I start?

Pastor: A good place to start is reading the Bible. When you're getting to know someone, reading stuff they've written like their journals would reveal to you what they think. As you chat on email with a friend, you get to know what they think about different issues and you get to know their heart more. Similarly, as you read the bible, you get to hear from God and understand who He is, how He acts, and what He desires of you.

Mike: But sometimes it does not seem to make sense!

Pastor: Why not try starting with reading a book from the New Testament like Matthew and use

---

206   Luke 22:39-46

DEVOTIONAL LIVING

a version of the Bible that is easier to understand like the New Living Translation, or one I really enjoy, 'The Passion Translation'. You can actually get both of these on an app on your phone called the YouVersion app. It also has different daily reading plans that can help you read through the bible or different segments of the bible.

Whichever method you decide to use, remember that it will take a deliberate effort to build the discipline and you will have to work towards moving it from an unfamiliar activity to a habit and, finally, a lifestyle.

Mike: So, loving God through having devotions daily means reading the bible daily?

Pastor: That is part of it, but loving someone also means making time to spend time with them in conversation, and that is what prayer is. It is having conversations with our loving Father who longs to hear from us, as well as share His heart with us. That means that prayer is not a one-way conversation. You must allow God to speak to you as you listen to Him. Do you know that it's possible to know God so intimately that you can know His heart on an issue without Him saying a word to you about it? That is what happens when you hang out with someone long enough you get to know them so well that you can start sharing private, nonverbal communication.

Mike: But how do you have this conversation with someone you can't see?

Pastor: Well, as you carry on a phone conversation, are you seeing the person at the other end of the line?

Mike: No, but at least you know who it is you're talking to.

Pastor: Exactly. Think of beginning your journey in prayer as beginning to know someone, only in this case that someone is God. In the same way that with time you learn to recognize someone's voice on the phone even if their number doesn't reflect on your phone, God's voice will begin to grow more familiar to you. Can you see how we're having this conversation? That is exactly what you do. You tell God what's on your mind and allow Him to do the same. It doesn't even have to be spoken, you can write down your prayers in a journal as conversations with God.

There are times when I share my thoughts regarding my day in a conversation like this: 'Good morning, Father. Thank You for a lovely evening yesterday. I really enjoyed that play. Thank you that I slept well and that I'm feeling pretty fresh right now, especially because today will be rather long, full of meetings. Which reminds me, I'm still trying to finalize my presentation and it isn't flowing yet. Please help me so that it flows and I'm able to clearly convey why I'm proposing these changes in our department…' And so on. I'll pray through my entire plan for the day and also for my friends and relatives. I'll also ask God to show me how to pray for different situations that we're facing in the world.

Mike: Hmm…when you put it that way, it doesn't sound so 'out there' or impossible.

Pastor: It isn't. It just takes making the time to do this. Begin by choosing a time in the day that you are freshest. I happen to be a morning person and so, I love getting up early and spending some moments with God before I have to get to work. For some people, evenings work best while yet for others, they get to the office 45 minutes or so earlier and have their devotions there, before everyone else comes in.

Mike: So that's what having devotion is all about?

Pastor: Yes, basically, that's it, but, before I forget, remember that during *Simama* we had introduced the idea of connecting with God through worship music?

Mike: Ah, yes… I had never done that before and yet I found that I was able to connect with God even easier than reading the bible.

Pastor: Precisely. Music has a way of touching us in very powerful ways.

Mike: Yes. It had a very calming effect that helped me arrive at work in a very good mood.

Pastor: And now?

Mike: Well, I am back to my favorite radio station and, somehow, the effect is not the same.

Pastor: Mmm… so what do you want to do?

Mike: I don't know… I really do want to stay current and I find the station really entertaining… but I know it's complete gossip and the language is not very clean… I know it's not helping me much, but, like I said, it's entertaining!

Pastor: Can I tell you what I did?

Mike: Mmm..

Pastor: I let it all go. It was entertaining and funny, but some of that stuff left me feeling corrupted, empty and hollow while, on the other hand, listening to this other music left me feeling clean, fulfilled and in touch with God.

Mike: Man! This is rough.

Pastor: Yes, it is and we need to be ruthless to get rid of anything that the devil will use to get us back to where we were before. The good news though is that God is more than willing to help us overcome the alluring draw that these things have on us. Which of these things would you like me to pray for you this week?

Mike: Definitely the music thing and my depressive moods. I also need God's help in prioritizing this whole devotion thing.

DEVOTIONAL LIVING

Question For My Journal

In which areas do you think you might struggle after the *Simama* experience is done? What do you intend to do about it?

Verse To Remember

Hebrews 12:1. Therefore, since we are surrounded by such a great cloud of witnesses, let us throw off everything that hinders and the sin that so easily entangles, and let us run with perseverance the race marked out for us.

Prayer For Today

Lord, I confess that I still have an attraction towards (apply your list) which are evil desires that are leading me away from You. I renounce, break and loose myself from these demonic allurements and attachments and declare in the heavenlies that I now belong to Jesus. I wash myself in the blood of Jesus and command evil spirits assigned to me to lead me into temptation, to depart from me and never return again. I ask you now to fill with your Holy Spirit and I submit my affections, emotions and desires to the Lord Jesus. I pray that you would quicken my spirit to love you and to enjoy spending time with you so that devotions become my lifestyle. I remove the distractions that satan has put my way to prevent me from spending time with you and I pray that in Jesus' name, you will open my eyes and help me plan my times with you. In Jesus' name. Amen.

SOWING THROUGH SERVING!

Pastor: Last week, you said that you want us to get completely real, right?

Mike: Eh... I did?

Pastor: You mentioned the challenges that you're having with your wife and boss and how they are driving you up the wall.

Mike: Well, that's an understatement!

Pastor: So, let me ask you, when the drama begins with your wife what normally happens?

Mike: I put her in her place. Times have changed, man! Nowadays it's difficult to get respect in your own home, but I still make sure that she knows exactly what I think.

Pastor: And by that, do I take it that there's a shouting match that ensues... does the term 'fits of rage' describe it?

Mike: Oh, yeah! Then I drive off and join the boys for a drink or two or three... At least with them, I can vent my anger with people who get me... But, then, we said boys and drinks are gone...

Pastor: You're right. That's what we said. Are you willing to try something different?

Mike: What do you mean? You mean like pray about it?

Pastor: No, this will sound radical but I want you to hear me out. Serve them. Serve your wife and serve your boss, regardless of their response or behavior.

Mike: Come on! Let's be real here, Pastor! What do you mean, serve them? I'll end up being taken advantage of and being 'sat on'. You must be kidding me!

Pastor: I am pretty serious, Mike. Let me read you something the apostle Paul wrote: 'People's desires make them give in to immoral ways, filthy thoughts, and shameful deeds. They worship idols, practice witchcraft, hate others, and are hard to get along with. People become jealous, angry, and selfish. They not only argue and cause trouble, but they are envious. They get drunk, carry on at wild parties, and do other evil things as well. I told you before, and I am telling you again: No one who does these things will share in the blessings of God's kingdom.'[207]

Mike: Do you mean that because I am a Christian I'm not supposed to get angry? That's impossible, I may be saved, Pastor, but I am clearly not Jesus!

Pastor: Well, you got that right! You're not Jesus! The truth is, none of us is! Remember though that we have been working towards helping you deal successfully with your issues post the *Simama* course? We've talked about surrender to God, understanding the spiritual battle we are in and creating a habit of daily devotions. All these will help you greatly, but there is another important habit we need to develop and that is service. Serving others plays the crucial role of bringing up issues that are still within our heart; issues which, if not dealt

---

207 Galatians 5:19-21 CEV

SOWING THROUGH SERVING!

with, will continue to plague us and cause us to live miserably or unfulfilled. We not only grow in our character, but we also become holy which is pleasing to God and is indeed His will for us.

Mike: Hmm… You got that right. I do not want to continue in my misery, but I still don't get it. Are you saying that I pretend that I'm not angry. Isn't that just being hypocritical?

Pastor: No, Mike. Denial is not what I'm talking about. How do I explain this? Let me use my family's story. It might just help explain what I mean.

Growing up, I was close to my father. He was a fun-loving and cool guy, but when I was 12 years old, he abandoned us. He left my mum to completely fend for the five of us on her own and it was not an easy time. With only a single income, my mum found it difficult to make ends meet and we lived with the embarrassment of being sent away from school due to lack of school fees, or having dark nights or no running water when our electricity and water were disconnected due to lack of payments. All this time, my dad was living it up. He was into wild living, partying, drinking and womanizing and, because he had a good job, he could easily afford this lifestyle.

Because of all this, I was angry and bitter toward my dad and this did not change even after I become a Christian. I constantly battled with unforgiveness and just when I thought I had forgiven him over some grievance, he would go and do something else that would hurt and disappoint us. I would again be down the path of anger, bitterness and unforgiveness. I wanted nothing to do with my dad and lacked basic respect and honor for him. You can, therefore, imagine our pain and outrage when he got a terminal illness and we were called upon to care for him! His so-called friends and family had abandoned him at his greatest hour of need and there was no one else to care for him except us!

Mike: You're kidding…

Pastor: Actually, I'm not. Many times when I looked at him in his helpless state, I ached, both from the wounds of my childhood, but also from the seemingly unfairness of the situation. What pained me most was that we now had to foot his health bill, especially when I remembered how much we had suffered due to his abandonment of us. My constant prayer was for God to give me kindness for my father as, humanly speaking, that was the furthest thought from my mind!

Mike: That's rough, man…

Pastor: Well, God never promised that it would be easy, but do you know what happened to me as I learnt to serve my dad, even on those occasions when he didn't seem appreciative? I began to change in ways I had never imagined. God began to grow the fruit of the Spirit in me. In other words, I began to realize that I was becoming more *loving, joyful, peaceful, patient, kind, good, faithful, gentle, and self-controlled!*[208]

208 Galatians 5:22

SOWING THROUGH SERVING!

As I wrestled in my heart while serving Dad, issues that lay deep in my heart were dealt with. I can genuinely say that I forgave my father and came to love him so much such that by the time he passed away, I genuinely grieved our loss. Not only that, because of our example of lovingly serving him despite all had done, he too made his peace with God before he died.

Mike: Man! You are strong! I don't know if I would have been able to do that.

Pastor: Mike, you're wrong about that. I'm not that strong! Remember how Jesus taught his disciples to ask God for 'daily bread'? Well, in those days, I literally learnt, on a daily basis, to ask God to pour into my spirit the virtues I desperately needed. Many times I asked Him to give me the love and desire to do good and serve my dad. I asked God to give me kindness towards my dad; at other times, love for him and a lot more times, for a good attitude! Psyching ourselves to do good when we have been wronged never works! It is only God who pours into our spirits these virtues since it is only Him who can make us holy.

Mike, God is the one who is *working in you to make you willing and able to obey Him.*[209] His perfect plan is to make you perfect, to make you holy and, as you obey Him and serve your wife and boss even in difficult circumstances, He is able to make you more like Himself holy.

Mike: So, are you saying that if I choose to obey God and serve my wife and my boss, it's a guarantee that things will become better and that all the drama will stop?

Pastor: The situation may or may not turn out as you expect, but that is not ours to determine.

Mike: So, how do I gather the psych to do this?

Pastor: Well, during those days as we looked after dad, there is one saying by the apostle Paul that really encouraged me: *'Whoever sows to please their flesh, from the flesh will reap destruction; whoever sows to please the Spirit, from the Spirit will reap eternal life.*[210]*'* In other words, I came to understand that if I continued to do things 'humanly', for example, being vengeful, unforgiving, etc., then the situation would only deteriorate leading to destruction, strife and conflict. But, if I resisted doing evil and instead started doing good, then that evil would get pushed back and good, leading to eternal life, would result.

There were many times when I could not see any immediate results in my father's situation and, in those times, I chose to apply this verse by faith. I would chant to myself several times, 'I am sowing in the spirit. I am sowing righteousness that good will result in this situation!' I thank God that today I can say that God's word is true!

Mike: Wow! What a story!

Pastor: This can be your story too, if you choose to serve and not pay back evil with evil.

Mike: But, how do I start?

---

209 Galatians 6:8-9
210 Philippians 2:13

SOWING THROUGH SERVING!

Pastor: Let's start with prayer. What evil thoughts overcome you when you are engaging with your wife and what virtues do you want God to replace them with?

Mike: I can immediately think of quite a few! As I think about it, I think the main ones are anger, self-defensiveness and fear of lack of respect.

Pastor: What virtues would you want God to replace these with?

Mike: Hmm... Let's start with the ability not to kill someone! Seriously though, I need to pray for patience and the ability to serve even when I don't want to.

Question For My Journal

Which family relationship brings you down the most and what evil thoughts overcome you when you are engaging with this particular person?

What virtues do you need in order to interact with this person in a godly way?

Verse To Remember

Matthew 15:11 (NLT). It's not what goes into your mouth that defiles you; you are defiled by the words that come out of your mouth.

Prayer For Today

Lord Jesus, I confess that in my interactions with _____ (name of person or people, family member), I have defiled myself in my thoughts and words. I confess having the following (list all negative emotions that apply) which wage war in my spirit and cause me to be ungodly. I renounce (list all negative emotions that apply) as works of satan that I want nothing to do with. I command these (your list above) evil spirits assigned to defile me, to flee from my presence and never return again and I wash myself in the blood of Jesus that makes me clean. I now ask you to heal me from any spirits of sickness and infirmity that lay claim to me because of these evil spirits. I also ask you to fill me with your Spirit and infuse me with love, joy, peace, forbearance, kindness, goodness, faithfulness, gentleness and self-control *(Galatians 5:22-23)*. In Jesus' name. Amen.

(Combine this prayer with service whenever issues come up in the relationship you are struggling with).

PRAYING WITH AUTHORITY

Mike: Hey Pastor! Thanks for making the time! I've really enjoyed these coffee dates!

Pastor: So have I, Mike. It's been really good getting to know you better.

Mike: I've got to say, I was really discouraged when we began. But you know what, I'm learning to fight for my family as opposed to fighting with or in my family. As much as we still have some issues, I can tell you I'm really enjoying this season of our marriage! We were even saying last week that we want to do *Simama* again in a few months' time. The last time we did it with my side of the family my parents, siblings and their spouses. This time we want to do it with her side of the family. After that, we also plan to take our kids through it when they're home on holiday from school.

Pastor: That's awesome, Mike! And that really is an awesome introduction into what I'd hoped we'd talk about today. What comes to mind when you hear the word 'evangelism'?

Mike: Well, I remember sharing the 'Four Spiritual Laws' booklet with guys around the neighborhood during the evangelism week at *Mizizi*, plus of course the crusades that are held everywhere.

Pastor: Yes. Those indeed are some of the ways in which evangelism is done, but I want to take this a notch further and look into another aspect of evangelism that is rarely talked about and yet one that is really relevant to helping you succeed in life after *Simama*.

Mike: I'm listening…

Pastor: Remember how early this week we referred to the reality that there are two spiritual kingdoms at work in the world; the kingdom of light and the kingdom of darkness?

Mike: Yes, I remember…

Pastor: Remember we said that the kingdom of darkness seeks to enslave us, to keep us in bondage through addictions, bad family or work relationships, etc. and also fights to prevent us fulfilling our God-ordained destinies?

Mike: Yeah that's correct.

Pastor: We also said that the habits of surrender, prayer, daily devotions, and serving others all work to push back the kingdom of darkness. Well, evangelism, takes this a notch higher by taking an offensive against the kingdom of darkness!

Mike: I'm not sure I get where you are going with this…

Pastor: Okay, let's look at an actual life situation and break it down. Mike, as you examined your family tree, what issues did you identify?

Mike: Well, I discovered that there was polygamy, witchcraft, greed and a lot of infighting within the family. In fact, currently, there's a lot of tension between my step-siblings who are from my dad's first wife and my family (Mum was his second wife). My father is quite elderly and they have threatened us, saying that they alone will inherit his property since they are the children

PRAYING WITH AUTHORITY

from the first wife. It's almost as if they are waiting for the old man to die! It has been really crazy visiting my parents since each interaction with them is treated with such suspicion!

Pastor: So, what are you going to do about this?

Mike: We have engaged a lawyer for my mother and we are going to fight them! If they even try anything shady, they will be in for the fight of their lives! I will not allow my family to lose out on what is our rightful inheritance!

Pastor: I hear you, but have you been praying about the situations you noted in your family, and here I am not just talking about the inheritance battle, but the generational issues you mentioned of witchcraft and polygamy?

Mike: Well, we prayed for them during *Simama*! I've been praying for God to help me because right now I am the only Christian in my family apart from my mum and being her oldest son, I am looked to quite a bit for leadership.

Pastor: I'm glad that you have been praying. In taking the step to engage a family lawyer, it tells me that you are not content to sit back but are taking an offensive legally. Am I correct in stating it that way?

Mike: Yes, that absolutely correct!

Pastor: Well, just as you are taking the offensive through legal action, I want to show you how through evangelism you can also take the offensive spiritually, not just in this situation of the inheritance, but also in the other areas of brokenness that you noted in your family.

Mike: Through evangelism? How? Are you saying that I shouldn't engage the lawyer?

Pastor: No, that is not what I am saying. I am just showing you an additional way of taking the offensive by owning and walking in the authority that God has given you. The apostle John wrote that when we received Jesus, and believed in His name, He gave us the authority to become children of God[211]. As God's children, we walk in God's authority.

Mike: Honestly, Pastor. I'm not quite sure I'm following you!

Pastor: Okay, let me break it down for you. What I'm simply saying is this: God has given us power through prayer and sharing His word to take back ground that the kingdom of darkness has gained over our families.

Mike: So, are you saying that I should be praying for my step-siblings? And by doing so, I am taking authority over that family situation and battling for my family?

Pastor: That's exactly it! As a son of God in that family, as you pray scripture over your siblings, you are taking the offensive in battle spiritually. God desires to have your siblings know Him just as you know Him. He desires to deliver your whole family, not just your mother's children, but also your step-siblings. By choosing to stand in the gap for them in prayer, you are taking

---

211   John 1:12

spiritual authority over your family and denying the kingdom of darkness opportunity to continue messing around with you guys!

Mike: Does that mean that they will stop fighting us eventually?

Pastor: Again, just as in the situation with serving your wife and boss, the outcome is not ours to determine. But what is guaranteed is that we are fighting from a point of victory because Jesus has already defeated satan. Remember Mike that according to the bible, you are *'seated with Christ in high places.*[212]*'*

Another version says it nicely, *'He (Jesus) raised us up with Him to rule with Him in the heavenly world.*[213]*'* This means God has raised you spiritually to a vantage point, a high place that enables you to look down below at what the devil is doing in your family. From this high position, you have the authority to trample the works of satan and to bring down the Kingdom of God into your family!

So, take your place of authority with Christ and declare and decree God's word over your family. Take back, through prayer, the territory that the kingdom of darkness has gained in your family! [214]

Mike: That kind of prayer sounds different from the one we were talking about two days ago. It sure doesn't sound like conversational prayer!

Pastor: You've got that right. I have prayed this way for my family and have seen almost all my family members come to Christ. I have found fasting and exposing my family members to the word of God especially useful.

Mike: I remember fasting during the *Simama* experience. How does fasting work?

Pastor: In the Old Testament, people used to fast during times of repentance or as an indication of their sincerity when praying through a critical situation. In the New Testament, Jesus also seemed to imply that there are some situations that can only be resolved through prayer and fasting.[215] I personally decided to own all these contexts and apply them to my family situation. I therefore fast to show that the situation is critical and I desperately want my family saved. I also fast like Nehemiah[216] to repent of sins for myself and family. I also fast to release God's power into those situations that Jesus said required fasting. I take the matter of my family so seriously that I fast once a week for them and have done so for several years. I must say I have seen the power of God working in my family!

Mike: Wow! I hear you and your sincerity over your family, but my family is different. I cannot say I sincerely want them to get saved. My step-brothers have been very mean to us!

Pastor: Mike, it's not about you. God has chosen you to be a light in your family! Had He not saved you, where would you be?

Mike: Honestly, in a few years I would be dead, if not from drinking, then from HIV.

---

212 Ephesians 2:6
213 Ibid Good News Bible
214 Luke 10: 19 'I have given you authority to trample on snakes and scorpions and to overcome all the power of the enemy; nothing will harm you'
215 Mark 9:29
216 Nehemiah 1:4-6

PRAYING WITH AUTHORITY

Pastor: Precisely! God has had mercy on you and now wants you to extend this same mercy to your family. The hatred you have towards your step-brothers is an 'arrow' from the enemy to keep your mind diverted from the real issue of your family's salvation. Remember, as you go on the offensive, the enemy is also on the offensive and in his arsenal are 'arrows' or 'darts' of resentment that are directed at you!

Mike: Man! This is deep! So,- the feelings I have towards my step brothers are 'arrows'?

Pastor: Yes.

Mike: Oh my! So, how do I pray?

Pastor: Did you go through the *Steps To Freedom* Appendix when you were doing the *Simama* course?

Mike: Em... no! I don't think so!

Pastor: Well, that's a great place to start. I seem to remember that your prayer partner as you did the course was your younger brother. Why not recruit him and each of you can lead the other through praying the different prayers there? It takes about two hours to go through it so maybe one of you can do the praying the first week and then you switch the following week. I've seen some tremendous changes come over my family as I have prayed these spiritual warfare prayers for myself and for them!

Mike: I'll definitely give it a try. Let me call my bro and see if he's available this Saturday. I'll let you know how it goes next time we meet!

Question For My Journal

As you look back to your family tree, what are the strongholds in your family?

What 'arrows' are directed at you and about which particular family member?

Verse to Remember

Ephesians 6:10-17. Finally, be strong in the Lord and in his mighty power. Put on the full armor of God, so that you can take your stand against the devil's schemes. For our struggle is not against flesh and blood, but against the rulers, against the authorities, against the powers of this dark world and against the spiritual forces of evil in the heavenly realms. Therefore put on the full armor of God, so that when the day of evil comes, you may be able to stand your ground, and after you have done everything, to stand. Stand firm then, with the belt of truth buckled around your waist, with the breastplate of righteousness in place, and with your feet fitted with the readiness that comes from the gospel of peace. In addition to all this, take up the shield of faith, with which you can extinguish all the flaming arrows of the evil one. Take the helmet of salvation and the sword of the Spirit, which is the word of God.

Freedom Prayer

I thank you Lord that though we are human, we don't wage war as humans do. We use God's mighty weapons, not worldly weapons, to knock down the strongholds of human reasoning and to destroy false arguments. We destroy every proud obstacle that keeps people from knowing God. We capture their rebellious thoughts and teach them to obey Christ (II Corinthians 10:3-5).

With this regard, I take captive _____ (list your arrows) as thoughts that are not obedient to you, which are keeping me from praying for my family. I recognize these as arrows from the evil one and, in the authority of Jesus, I bind these spirits and command them to flee from my presence and not return again, in Jesus' name. Lord, I confess that my family has been deceived by the evil one and, as a result, have lived in active rebellion against you. I plead your mercy over them and ask that You forgive their sins. As a result of their rebellion, the devil has taken position over my family and is waging war against us. Have mercy upon us and deliver us from this evil!

I, therefore, take my position in the heavenlies with Jesus and command that the strongman attached to my family, barricading the minds of my family members from receiving the Lord Jesus, be pulled down, in Jesus' name. Every spirit of _____ (list all family vices as seen in the family tree) be loosed from my family in Jesus' name. I bind every spirit of bondage and addictions, of spiritual blindness, of lukewarmness, of death and destruction and command them to be loosed from my family members, in Jesus' name.

Give my family members the desire to seek after you. Indeed, send them people who will encourage them to go to church and even read the bible.

I take captive the spirits of infirmity (list the diseases common in the family) that have been operating in my family and command they be bound and loosed from my family members in Jesus' name. The reason the Son of Man came to earth was to destroy the works of satan and diseases are such works. I release healing into these family members as evidence of the presence of the Kingdom of God manifesting in my family. I decree the Kingdom of God, of justice and righteousness, be established in my family as the perfect will of God over my family. I decree, nullify and render impotent weapons of retaliation against me and my family. I surrender my family to the Lord Jesus Christ so that He can complete the work of salvation in the life of my family members. In Jesus' name. Amen!

FURTHER RESOURCES

We pray that you have been blessed by the *Simama* course. Through this course, you have learnt how to fight for, as opposed to fighting your family. Each week you have said freedom prayers, taking back any legal authority that the enemy may have had in the past over your family. Already, we believe that there has been a spiritual shift in the atmosphere over your family, and that significant victories have been won. The next generation of your family will be different, because you prayed!

in this final section, you will find some useful resources that will further help with what you have learnt in the course. Please look through them. We also recommend that you plan to pray through the '*Steps To Freedom*' with your prayer partner, each person taking turns to pray aloud and close the different doors that the enemy may have used to harass your family. Then, continue in battle over your family and let fasting be an integral part of your arsenal. There might be times when you see no progress and therefore feel discouraged to continue. Some of the strongholds over our family members are quite strong and require persistent prayer. If you feel discouraged, remember that this might be an 'arrow' lodged against you so, refuse it through prayer, and ask God for faith and persistence to carry on. As this can sometimes be a long-term process, continually reach out to your family members by openly telling them that you are praying for them, plus sending them encouraging verses, especially when they are discouraged.

Constantly look out for ways that you can support your family members through prayer, encouragement and help. If you did the *Simama* course as a small group, consider organizing visits to each of your families so that you can bless them with a meal and/or a gift and say a prayer over them. Perhaps you can do such a visit once a month until you have visited each family. If you did the course with family members, consider planning a regular time of prayer and fellowship as a family going forward. And do not give up prayerfully inviting them to church or to specific programs like *Mizizi*. Through you, our prayer is that your entire family will be transformed into a joyful and caring space, full of God's freedom; a space where everyone is living a life of effectiveness and purpose. With God's help, it is not just possible, it is inevitable!

God bless.

Muriithi and Carol Wanjau

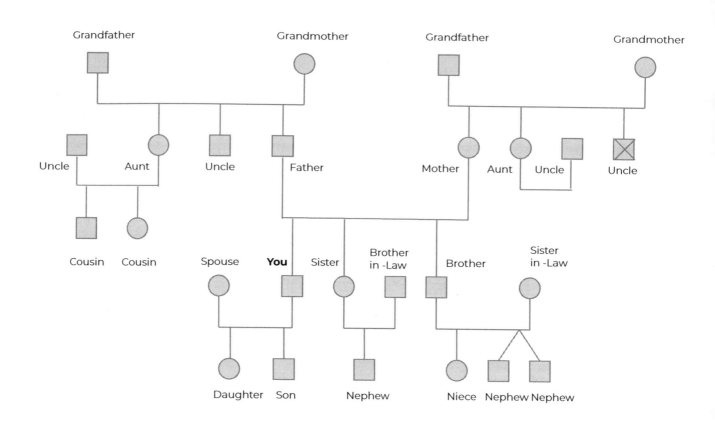

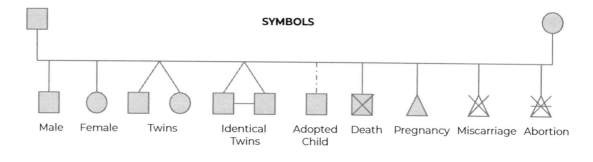

SYMBOLS

Male   Female   Twins   Identical Twins   Adopted Child   Death   Pregnancy   Miscarriage   Abortion

217   This form of family tree is called a genogram. It is "a pictorial display of a person's family relationships and medical history. It goes beyond a traditional family tree by allowing the user to visualize hereditary patterns and psychological factors that punctuate relationships." It was invented by American psychiatrist and pioneer of family therapy, Murray Bowen.

EATING HEALTHY

SOME EATING DISORDERS AND UNHEALTHY ATTITUDES

Too much focus on weight has had some detrimental effects on our health as well as our eating habits. On one hand, it has led to life-threatening eating disorders such as anorexia nervosa and bulimia nervosa and obesity on the other hand.

Anorexia Nervosa: An affected individual refuses to maintain the minimal body weight because they have an intense fear of becoming fat. They diet, fast or exercise excessively. Weight loss is viewed as an impressive achievement whereas weight gain is an unacceptable failure of self-control. His or her self esteem is highly dependent on body shape and weight.

Bulimia Nervosa: Individuals with Bulimia Nervosa engage in binge eating then use inappropriate methods to prevent weight gain. Binge eating is eating more food than most people would eat during a similar period of time and under similar circumstances. One does not feel in control during such an episode, they cannot stop eating or control what or how much they are eating. Afterwards they purge through self-induced vomiting, misuse of laxatives, diuretics or other medications, fasting or excessive exercise. One gets this diagnosis if these behaviors occur on average at least twice a week for three months. Just as in Anorexia Nervosa, the self-esteem of individuals with Bulimia Nervosa is also highly dependent on their body shape and weight

These two examples represent extreme eating disorders. There are other conditions and habits that still miss the point on the importance of healthy eating.

SOME TIPS ON EATING HEALTHY

Meat, Fish and Pulses, that is, beans, peas, green grams, chickpeas, etc.

- Saturated fats are found mainly in the meat of cows, pigs and sheep, and products which include their meat, such as sausages, meat pies and beef burgers. Eating too much saturated fat can lead to coronary heart disease and being overweight.

- Unsaturated fats are found in oily fish, chicken, eggs, turkey, duck, beans and lentils and foods made from these. Unsaturated fat is better for you, but still eat it in moderation.

- It is wiser to buy a small amount of lean meat rather than fatty meat or solid fat.

- Cut down on eating meat and instead obtain your protein from legumes such as beans, peas, black beans, green grams (*ndengu*) and chickpeas.

- Eat more fish of all kinds.

- Increase your iron intake by eating liver.

- Cut down on fat by steaming, grilling or boiling instead of frying your food. If you use any fat or oil in any of your recipes, use less of it than you would ordinarily do.

- Eat bread without spreading butter on it.

- Cut down on sugar as it causes dental decay and increases your weight and does not give you any nutrients.

- For everyone: where fat is involved, less is better.

Milk and Dairy Produce

- Milk, cheese and yoghurt are good sources of protein, vitamins and minerals, but they are also high in animal fat. Drink some milk and dairy produce. If semi-skimmed or skimmed milk is available, this is better for adults as it contains less fat.

- The best milk for babies and young toddlers is breast milk which contains everything they need for up to six months of age for a healthy start in life and can be continued for up to two years.

Potatoes, Bread, Rice and Cereals (Carbohydrates)

Some carbohydrates are better than others. Good carbohydrates are those that break down in the body slowly and gradually release glucose into the bloodstream. One cause of diabetes is eating foods that release glucose into the bloodstream too quickly, overworking the pancreas. Eating good carbohydrates prevents diabetes and heart disease as well as assists in weight loss.

Good carbohydrates have a lower glycaemic index (GI) whereas foods that are rapidly absorbed in the body have a higher GI value. High GI foods still have a place in our diet. They are, however, best consumed by athletes during periods of competition when rapid energy boosts are required. For the rest of us, when tempted to reach for a soda or other beverage to get an energy boost, remember that it is wiser to reach for an alternative with a lower GI value since sugar has a very high GI.

Foods with a High GI Rating (eat these sparingly)

- Watermelon, dates, glucose and white sugar.

- White rice, white bread, white maize, white wheat flour and white potatoes (as much as it is possible, eat potatoes with the skin on as the skin is a rich source of vitamin C.

- Soda and energy sport drinks.

- Pumpkins and broad beans.

Foods with a Low GI Rating (eat plenty of these)

- Brown rice.

- Oats, millet, sorghum, amaranth (*terere*), unsifted maize flour and unsifted wheat flour.

- Carrots, peas and corn.

- Chickpeas, black beans, red beans, peas, soy beans and other soy products.

- Apples, pears, oranges, bananas, pineapples, plums, grapes, raisins and mangoes.

Vegetables and Fruit

- Vegetables are the main source of minerals and vitamins in our diet. Many of us do not eat enough of either.

- Try to eat what is in season and what is locally produced (that is, spinach, amaranth (*terere*), kale (*sukuma wiki*) black nightshade (*managu*), pumpkin leaves, etc.) as they are the cheapest and full of flavor. If you can, grow your own vegetables as you are then assured of their freshness.

- Fruit is also a good source of minerals and vitamins. Try to eat the fruit in season as it is more affordable. Eat portions of fruit and vegetables at least two times each day.

GI Tips for Healthy Cooking

- To receive the full benefit of the food's fiber content, do not chop or cut food too finely. The smaller the pieces of food, the less fibrous they are and the higher their GI rating.

- Use vinegar or lemon juice instead of salt to add flavor to your food.

- Choose seeded or whole-grain brown bread over soft-textured, plain white bread.

- Eat brown rice, arrowroot, sweet potato, cassava or pasta in preference to ordinary white potatoes and ordinary rice.

- Add legumes such as beans, peas, black beans, green grams, split peas, lentils and chickpeas to soups.

- Serve a green salad with every main meal. Keep it simple so that it is not a chore to make.

- Grill or roast vegetables as carrots, pumpkin, yams, eggplant, green peppers and red onions.

- Stir frying reduces the amount of oil used while cooking and the food does not get overcooked. Stir fry vegetables such as broccoli, cauliflower, sugar snaps, snow peas and mushrooms.

Activity

Make a list of the food you ate in the last 24 hours (or typically eat over a similar period of time) and give a GI rating for each of the items. Also note if the food was fatty or non-fatty, boiled, grilled or fried. An example is provided below.

BREAKFAST	SNACK	LUNCH	DINNER
Tea (high GI cause of sugar)			
White bread (high GI)			
Fried egg			
Watermelon (high GI)			

Question For My Journal

If you were to eat food with a lower GI rating, or lower in fats, what food and methods of cooking would you have to adapt?

THE SPIRIT OF REBELLION

In pairs of *Simama* partnerships, that is, in fours, share the following:

1. The adventures you had as a riotous teen;

2. The ways in which you felt your parents may have contributed to your rebellion; and

3. Now that you are older, which authorities do you struggle to submit to and why.

From our reading, we learnt that rebellion is actually a condition of the fall. From Adam, we inherited a nature that does not like to submit to authority and so it is not so much what our parents did to us, but rather that we have a nature that is naturally rebellious. Because of this we refuse to yield to God's will and opt instead to do things our way. For some of us, what started as cool and fun has landed us into trouble as we now find ourselves trapped in all manner of addictions that have been difficult to get rid of.

Look at the list below and identify the manner in which rebellion has manifested itself in your life. Put a tick on all that apply

Identifying the Character of the Spirit of Rebellion

1. Arrogance.

2. Open defiance.

3. Self-righteousness, that is, not able to see one's mistakes.

4. Unbelief – not able to accept God's word.

5. Pride. As a result of the fall, we are all infected with pride and rebellion. We want to do things our way.

6. Individualism. Pride and rebellion are at the root of individualism. When we are individualistic, we want to do things our way and cannot take instruction from others, much less from God.

7. Rejection of God's approved leadership.

8. Murmuring against God and His appointed leaders over us.

9. Having a contentious disposition.

10. Stubborn – not being able to receive the ideas of others.

11. A defiant spirit – not able to follow instructions.

12. Unteachable or stiff-necked.

13. Uncorrectable.

14. Being unable to submit to God in worship.

15. Self-seeking and attributing to self honor due to God.

16. Controlling of others by manipulating them to do things our way by using tactics such as violence, anger, temper tantrums, crying, withdrawing and being emotionally unavailable.

17. Undisciplined living where people cast off restraint and engage in the licentious lifestyle of free sex, alcohol, drugs, pornography, masturbation, etc.

Share with your *Simama* partner (that is, in twos), what is true about yourself from the list above. Explain to them how the circumstance(s) came about.

As we learnt during the week, the problem of rebellion is that it opens the door to the enemy's attacks. The only way to close this door is to confess the sin of rebellion and to repent by choosing to submit to authority instead.

Remember that we have said that choosing to submit is both a matter of the will and a matter of faith – faith that as we honor our parents, it will go well with us (which includes a long life; Ephesians 6:1-3); faith that when we humble ourselves like Jesus at our workplace and in our family, God Himself, in due time, will lift us up (I Peter 5:6) and, finally, faith that humility is the path to true greatness (Matthew 23:11-12; the greatest among you will be your servant. For those who exalt themselves will be humbled, and those who humble themselves will be exalted)!

Activities

- With your *Simama* partner, share with one another how you are going to practically honor those you have been rebelling against.

- Work out a plan for how you will practically honor your parents this week and with your *Simama* partner, keep each other accountable.

- Debrief, as a class, the highlights of this session and then end the session with a concluding prayer.

RESPONDING TO PAIN AND HURT

The prophet Isaiah has this amazing message from the Father for us. *'The Spirit of the Sovereign Lord is upon me, for the Lord has anointed me to bring good news to the poor. He has sent me to comfort the brokenhearted and to proclaim that captives will be released and prisoners will be freed.'* Isaiah 61:1 (NLT).

Bring to your Father all those who have hurt you.

Write a list of all your family members you need to forgive.

Next, taking turns with your *Simama* partner, lead each other to pray aloud as follows:

Thank You, Jesus for dying that I might be forgiven. By an act of my will, I now choose to express the desire of my heart and forgive the following members of my family.

Lord, I forgive _____ (name each one in turn)
for _____ (what he/she did or failed to do).

I also ask that in your mercy You will forgive them as well for in their circumstance they did not know to do any different.

Next, look at the table below (that is, common ways that people respond when hurt) and circle only the headlines that apply.

APPENDIX 4

Common Ways that People React When Hurt

<u>Circle all</u> that apply.

BITTERNESS	REBELLION	CONTROL	REJECTION	WITHDRAWAL	DEPRESSION	HEAVINESS
Resentment	Self-will/Stubbornness	Possessiveness	Fear of Rejection	Pouting	Despair	Gloom
Hatred	Disobedience	Dominance	Self-rejection	Daydreaming	Despondency	Burden
Unforgiveness	**STRIFE**	Witchcraft	**INSECURITY**	Fantasy	Discouragement	Disgust
Violence	Contention	**RETALIATION**	Inferiority	Pretension	Defeatism	**WORRY**
Temper	Bickering	Destruction	Self Pity	Unreality	Dejection	Anxiety
Anger	Argument	Spite	Loneliness	**ESCAPE**	Hopelessness	Fear
Retaliation	Quarreling	Hatred	Timidity	Indifference	Suicide	Dread
Murder	Fighting	Sadism	Shyness	Stoicism	Death	Apprehension
		Hurt	Inadequacy	Passivity	Insomnia	**NERVOUSNESS**
		Cruelty	Ineptness	Sleepiness	Morbidity	Tension
		ACCUSATION	**JEALOUSY**	Alcohol		Headache
		Judging	Envy	Drugs		Nervous habits
		Criticism	Suspicion			Restlessness
		Faultfinding	Distrust			Excitement
			Selfishness			Insomnia
						Roving
SENSITIVENESS	Schizophrenia	Fears	Confusion	**PHOBIA (All kinds)**	**PERFECTION**	Adultery
Self-awareness	Paranoia	Confrontation	Forgetfulness		Pride	Fornication
Fear of man	Hallucinations	**CONFUSION**	Indifference	Hysteria	Vanity	Incest
Fear of disapproval	**VOWS**	Frustration	**SELF-DECEPTION**	**FEAR OF**	Ego	Harlotry
PERSECUTION	Declarations made in hurt e.g. I will never allow myself to come close to this person again, etc	Incoherence	Self-delusion	**AUTHORITY**	Frustration	Rape
Unfairness		Forgetfulness	Self-deduction	Lying	Criticism	Exposure
Fear of judgment			Pride	Deceit	Irritability	Frigidity
Fear of condemnation				**PRIDE**	Intolerance	**GLUTTONY**
Fear of accusation				Ego	Anger	Nervousness
Fear of reproof				Vanity		Compulsive eating
Sensitiveness				Self-righteousness		Resentment
SELF-ACCUSATION				Haughtiness		Frustration
Self-hatred				Importance		Idleness
Self-condemnation				Arrogance		Self-pity
GUILT						Self-reward
Condemnation						
Shame						
Unworthiness						
Embarrassment						

Once you have done so, pray over each one in the following way:

Father, I confess that, as a result of being hurt, I have allowed myself to hold (list the headlines) in my heart against (insert specific names). I acknowledge this as sin, and I now repent and turn from this behaviour. I ask that you will forgive me and cleanse me. In Jesus' name. Amen

Prayer of Renunciation (take turns)

I now speak directly to every evil spirit that has taken advantage because of the way I responded in sin to hurt and pain in my family. You (refer to list of the ways you respond when hurt) *no longer have any rights here, and I order you to leave now without hurting or harming any of my family members or even going into any other members of my family. I renounce this vow* (state decision, if any, made as a result of woundedness and hurt) *as ungodly and repent of it. I commit to no longer act in accordance to the vow but in accordance to the word of God. I rebuke and cast out spirits of infirmity and disease that entered my life as a result of my sin and command them never to enter my life again. Lord Jesus, I give my entire being–spirit, soul, body into your hands, that you may heal me. I also invite you now to fill me with your Holy Spirit that I may be totally yours. In Jesus' name. Amen.*

Debrief, as a class, the highlights of this session and then, end the session with a concluding prayer.

APPENDIX 5

IDENTIFYING GENERATIONAL PATTERNS

PART A

We shall begin to free ourselves from harmful generational patterns by first of all denouncing ungodly soul ties. Ungodly soul ties in families are those bonds that are not fashioned according to the way that God intended. For example, bonds that are characterized by manipulation, violence, incest or even too close an attachment to one parent in place of or above the other parent or other siblings (that is, in cases of favoritism mama's or daddy's boy or mummy's or daddy's girl) are all ungodly. These ties, being sinful, give the devil a foothold in the lives of those involved such that negative characteristics in one person, for example, a foul temper, moodiness, diseases, etc., flow from one person to the one they are connected with.

The table below helps identify such bonds.

Situation	Issues That Develop	What It Should Be
One parent dominating, controlling or even being violent to the other	Domination, control, fear	Dad is the leader, mum submits, children submit to both parents
Parents emotionally manipulate and control children and, sometimes, abuse them	A sense of being suffocated by the parent and even though an adult, not having the freewill to say no to parents' requests. Domination, control, fear results	Children should be free to love their parents, even as God allows us to choose to love Him
When a child takes the place of spouse, that is, mummy's boy or daddy's girl, or becomes a confidant of the parent at the exclusion of the parent's peers	Parental burdens become too heavy to bear. Parent should cultivate peer relationships	Priority should be the husband-wife relationship and then the parent-children one. Parents should seek peer counsel and not depend exclusively on their child
Siblings fighting each other with distant relationships amongst each other	Strife, conflict, sibling rivalry that could be carried on to the next generation	Siblings are meant to be good friends since this is the one bond that lasts the longest
Lack of sexual boundaries in families	Incest, sexual abuse and rape could occur	Children should be taught to respect each other's privacy and be made aware of the dangers of sexual experimentation
Parents demanding of or treating grown adult children like children	Anger, resentment, manipulation and control; adult child distances themselves from their parents	The relationship is supposed to change so that parents and adult children relate at peer level

In the name of the Father, the Son and the Holy Spirit, I ask God to break all ungodly spirit, soul and body ties that have been established between me and (speak the name of the individual) which were brought on by (name the activity you have identified from the table above). I supernaturally sever that linking and ask God to remove all the influence that (name the person again) has had. I now draw back to myself every part that has been wrongfully tied. I also speak directly to every evil spirit that has taken advantage of this ungodly soul tie. You no longer have any rights here, and I order you to leave now without hurting or harming (name the above person again) or any other person and without going into any other member of the family. I rebuke and cast out spirits of infirmity and disease that entered my life as a result of this soul tie and command them never to enter my life again. Lord Jesus, I give my entire being spirit, soul, body into your hands that you may heal me. I also invite you now to fill me with your Holy Spirit in this area of my life that I may be totally yours. In Jesus' name. Amen.

LEAVE

God's intention is that adult children need to leave their parents,[218] which involves severing physical (i.e. moving out of parental home) emotional, financial and psychological attachments before one can function independently as an adult. We may move out of our parents' houses but then continue having dependent child like attachments that make it difficult to form an attachment with a potential spouse. We need to sever these needy dependent child like attachments and transform these to adult interactions that are more peer in character. If you have never spiritually delinked yourself in this way then go ahead and do so through this prayer.

Lord, I thank you for my parents and the role they played in raising me. I recognize that as an adult, my relationship now needs to move from a dependent one to one where we relate as adults. I now sever these dependent attachments (list all that apply, that is, physical, emotional, financial, psychological) that are characteristic of my childhood and instead ask that by the power of the shed blood of Jesus, you will transform them into mature interactions so that I can relate at a peer level with my parents. Increase my level of faith and give me wisdom and guidance on how to relate with my parents from this day on. In Jesus' name. Amen.

Look again at table, but, this time, identify the <u>negative patterns</u> that flow through the family. After you identify the patterns, taking turns with your *Simama* partner, pray the following prayer of renunciation.

---

218 Genesis 2:24 (Berean Study Bible). For this reason a man will leave his father and mother and be united to his wife, and they will become one flesh.

PRAYER OF RENUNCIATION

I thank you Lord that according to *II Corinthians 5:17 (BSB) (… if anyone is in Christ, he is a new creation. The old has passed away. Behold, the new has come)*, I am a new person. I therefore sever supernaturally the link that connects me spiritually to the old which includes (list all the negative family patterns identified). I ask for your forgiveness and renounce (mention vows, curses or ungodly rituals you have participated in, especially surrounding death and birth) as sinful and offensive to you. I speak directly to every evil spirit that has taken advantage of these vows, oaths, curses, rituals and negative family patterns and declare that because I am a child of God, you no longer have any rights here. I order you to leave now without hurting or harming any other member of the family. I rebuke and cast out spirits of infirmity and disease (specifically name the ones identified from the table) that entered my life as a result my family background. Lord Jesus, I give my entire being¾spirit, soul, body into your hands that you may heal me. I also invite you now to fill me with your Holy Spirit in every area of my life that I may be totally yours. In Jesus' name. Amen!

Debrief, as a class, the highlights of this session and then, end the session with a concluding prayer.

STEPS TO FREEDOM [219]

As part of the *Simama* experience, we encourage each course member to verbally pray through the *Steps To Freedom*, with the help of your prayer partner. Counseling, which is what we call taking these prayers, should take approximately two hours per person. The following is an explanation of the prayer counseling process, which is adapted from Neil Anderson's book, "The Bondage Breaker."

Before we came to Christ, the Bible tells us we were in the dominion of darkness. We were under the domain controlled by God's enemy satan. When we accepted Christ, we changed "management" and defected to a new authority. We are no longer under satan's control but under God's *(Ephesians 1:1-10)*.

Of course the old 'landlord' is not happy with his loss of business! Think of our lives as a house. We have kicked out the previous owner and replaced him with a new owner, God's Holy Spirit. But the previous owner wants to hold on to any part of the building that he can. If he can just entice us to open the door, even a bit, then he can have a small claim on it. He will then use this small claim to try and gradually win himself back to total ownership. That is why the Bible tells us, "do not give satan a foothold!" *(Ephesians 4:27)*.

We are thus, in a battle and prayer is one of the ways we engage in that battle *(Ephesians 6:12, 18)*. In your time of prayer, you will be led by another person on a 'walk' through each 'room' of your life. Under their guidance, you will explore each one in prayer to make sure that you have not left a foothold there for the enemy. And together you will shut each door firmly. Their role is actually more like that of a partner in prayer, not a counselor; you will be the one who does most of the prayer!

There are seven different 'doors' you will pray together about in the session. These include false teachings and religions, wrong beliefs about God and yourself, bitterness against others, habitual sins and addictions, rebellion, pride and family curses. The net effect of this time of prayer is that you will be spiritually breaking any ties with the kingdom of darkness and allowing God total rule over your life. You will be effectively getting rid of the 'baggage' and 'issues' that you carried with you from your past life!

Over the years, we have prayed with many Christians, both new and older in this way and have never ceased to be amazed at how much freedom, confidence and victory this exercise has inevitably brought. You will be equipped during this time to walk in freedom, to resist the enemy and to pray boldly about your life. And after you are done, we pray that God will also use you to pray in the same way with others who have been set free by Christ as you have.

---

219   Adapted from Neil Anderson's 'The Bondage Breaker'.

APPENDIX 6

Note: There are some 'pre-existing conditions' that might prevent one from receiving full healing and deliverance: Some of these are:

a. When one does not know Jesus as Lord and Savior;

b. Bitterness and unforgiveness;

c. Lack of faith that God is willing or able to heal;

d. Unresolved pain or guilt;

e. Unconfessed sin that one is not willing to let go;

f. Life out of balance;

g. When one is either under or is using ungodly domination or control;

h. Presence of ungodly soul tie;

i. Unbroken occult powers;

j. Hidden or unrecognized abuse or emotional damage that needs healing;

k. Denial of issues;

l. Generational sin and/or demonization that has not been dealt with;

m. Inner brokenness through trauma and where deeper healing is needed;

n. The presence of ungodly vows that need to be renounced;

o. Not ready to be healed; and

p. No yet God's timing.

Which ones do you think are still operational in your life? Confess them to one another (your *Simama* partner) and then pray the following prayers to close all doors.

STEP ONE: THE DOOR OF FALSE TEACHINGS AND RELIGIONS

As you go through this step, pray aloud in the following way:

> Dear heavenly Father, I ask You to guard my heart and my mind to reveal to me any and all involvement I have had, either knowingly or unknowingly, with cultic or occultic practices, false religions and false teachers. In Jesus' name I pray. Amen.

Non-Christian Spiritual Experience Inventory

(Circle any of the following activities in which you have been involved in any way.)

OCCULT	CULTS	OTHER RELIGIONS
Astral projection	Christian Science	Zen Buddhism
Ouija board	Unity	Hare Krishna
Table lifting	Scientology	Bahaism
Speaking in a trance	The Way International	Rosicrucianism
Automatic writing	Unification Church	Science of Mind
Visionary dreams	Church of the living word	Science of Creative Intelligence
Telepathy	Jehovah's Witnesses	Hinduism
Ghosts	Mormonism	Transcendental meditation
Materialism	Children of God	Yoga
Clairvoyance	H.W Armstrong (Worldwide church of God)	Theosophical Society
Fortune-telling	Unitarianism	Islam
Tarot cards	Masons	Black Muslim
Palm-reading	New Age	Other_____
Astrology	Other_____	
Amateur hypnosis		
Blood pacts		
Fetishism		
Incubi & succubi (sexual spirits)		
Black & white magic		
Magic charming		
Mental suggestion		
Healing magnetism		
Other____		

For each practice, cult or religion circled, pray:

> *Lord, I confess that I have participated in* _____
> *I ask Your forgiveness, and I renounce* _____ *as a counterfeit to true Christianity.*

Note:

- Do not feel bad if you must confess in several categories.

- If anyone in your family was involved in any of the categories, you may want to renounce the activity anyway, just in case you unknowingly gave satan a foothold in it.

- Do not be surprised if you encounter some resistance as you complete this step. satan does not want you to be free and will try his best to keep you from obtaining freedom!

STEP TWO: THE DOOR OF LIES ABOUT GOD AND ABOUT MYSELF

Before beginning this step, pray aloud this prayer:

Dear heavenly Father, I know that You desire truth in the inner self and that facing this truth is the way of liberation (John 8:32). I acknowledge that I have been deceived by the father of lies (John 8:44). I pray in the name of the Lord Jesus Christ that You, heavenly Father, will rebuke all deceiving spirits by virtue of the shed blood and resurrection of the Lord Jesus Christ. And since by faith I have received You into my life and I am now seated with Christ in the heavenlies (Ephesians 2:6), I command all deceiving spirits to depart from me. I now ask the Holy Spirit to guide me into all truth (John 16:13). I ask You to "search me, O God, and know my heart; try me and know my anxious thoughts; and see if there be any hurtful way in me, and lead me in the everlasting way" (Psalm 139:23,24). In Jesus' name I pray. Amen.

Read aloud the following affirmation of faith and do so again, as often as necessary, to renew your mind and take your stand according to the truth. I recommend that you read it daily for several weeks, especially if you recognize that you have been deceived by specific lies about God and yourself.

DOCTRINAL AFFIRMATION

I recognize that there is only one true and living God *(Exodus 20:2-3)*, who exists as the Father, Son, and Holy Spirit, and that He is worthy of all honor, praise and worship as the Creator, Sustainer and Beginning and End of all things *(Revelation 4:11; 5:9,10; Isaiah 43:1,7,21)*.

I recognize Jesus Christ as the Messiah, the Word who became flesh and dwelt among us *(John 1:1, 14)*. I believe that He came to destroy the works of satan (1Jn.3:8), that He disarmed the rulers and authorities and made a public display of them, having triumphed over them *(Colossians 2:15)*.

I believe that God has proven His love for me, because when I was still a sinner, Christ died for me *(Romans 5:8)*. I believe that He delivered me from the domain of darkness and transferred me to His kingdom, and in Him I have redemption, the forgiveness of sins *(Colossians 1:13-14)*.

I believe I am now a child of God *(I John 3:1-3)* and that I am seated with Christ in the heavenlies *(Ephesians 2:6)*. I believe that I was saved by the grace of God through faith, that it was a gift and not the result of any works on my part *(Ephesians 2:8)*.

I choose to be strong in the Lord and in the strength of his might *(Ephesians 6:10)*. I put no confidence in the flesh *(Philippians 3:3)* for the weapons of my warfare are not of the flesh *(II Corinthians 10:4)*. I put on the whole armor of God *(Ephesians 6:10-17)* and I resolve to stand firm in my faith and resist the evil one.

I believe that Jesus has all authority in heaven and on earth *(Matthew 28:18)* and that He is head over all rule and authority *(Colossians 2:10)*. I believe that satan and his demons are subject to me in Christ because I am a member of Christ's body *(Ephesians 1:19-23)*. I therefore obey the command to resist the devil *(James 4:7)* and I command him in the name of Christ to leave my presence.

I believe that apart from Christ I can do nothing *(John 15:5)*, so I declare my dependence on Him. I choose to abide in Christ in order to bear much fruit and glorify the Lord (John 15:8). I announce to satan that Jesus is my Lord *(I Corinthians 12:3)*, and I reject any counterfeit gifts or works of satan in my life.

I believe that the truth will set me free *(John 8:32)* and that walking in the light is the only path of fellowship *(I John 1:7)*. Therefore, I stand against satan's deception by taking every thought captive in obedience to Christ *(II Corinthians 10:5)*. I declare that the bible is the only authoritative standard *(II Timothy 3:15-17)*. I choose to speak the truth in love *(Ephesians 4:15)*.

I choose to present my body as an instrument of righteousness, a living and holy sacrifice, and I renew my mind by the living Word of God in order that I may prove that the will of God is good, acceptable and perfect *(Romans 6:13; 12:1, 2)*.

I ask my heavenly Father to fill me with His Holy Spirit *(Ephesians 5:18)*, to lead me into all truth *(John 16:13)*, and to empower my life so that I may live above sin and not carry out the desires of the flesh *(Galatians 5:16)*. I crucify the flesh *(Galatians 5:24)* and choose to walk by the Spirit.

I renounce all selfish goals and choose the ultimate goal of love *(I Timothy 1:5)*. I choose to obey the greatest commandment, to love the Lord my God with all my heart, soul and mind, and to love my neighbor as myself *(Matthew 22:37-39)*.

STEP THREE: THE DOOR OF BITTERNESS AGAINST OTHERS

Before beginning this step, pray aloud this prayer:

Dear heavenly Father, I thank You for the riches of Your kindness, forbearance, and patience, knowing that Your kindness has led me to repentance (Romans 2:4). I confess that I have not extended that same patience and kindness toward others who have offended me, but instead I have harbored bitterness and resentment. I pray that during this time of self-examination You would bring to mind all those people that I have not forgiven in order that I may do so *(Matthew 18:35)*. I also pray that if I have offended others You would bring to mind all those people from whom I need to seek forgiveness and the extent to which I need to seek it *(Matthew 5:23-24)*. I ask this in the precious name of Jesus. Amen.

Make two lists: One of people you need to forgive and the other of people you need to seek forgiveness from. For each person on the lists, pray:

Lord, I forgive, _____

for _____

(be detailed as possible and allow yourself to remember and deal with all the pain they have caused you).

OR

Lord, please forgive me for _____
I promise to confess my sin to them and to seek to be reconciled.

STEP FOUR: THE DOOR OF REBELLION AGAINST AUTHORITY

Make a list of God-ordained authorities against whom you have been rebellious. These could include God, parents, national leaders, teachers, employers, church leaders, etc. After you have confessed any willful rebellion to God, pray the following prayer aloud:

Dear heavenly Father, You have said that rebellion is as the sin of witchcraft and insubordination is as iniquity and idolatry *(I Samuel 15:23)*. I know that in action and attitude I have sinned against You with a rebellious heart. I ask Your forgiveness for my rebellion and pray that by the shed blood of the Lord Jesus Christ, all ground gained by evil spirits because of my rebelliousness would be cancelled. I pray that You will shed light on all my ways that I may know the full extent of my rebelliousness and choose to adopt a submissive spirit and a servant's heart. In the name of Christ Jesus, my Lord. Amen.

STEP FIVE: THE DOOR OF PRIDE

Before beginning this step, pray aloud this prayer:

Dear heavenly Father, You have said that pride goes before destruction and an arrogant spirit before stumbling (Proverbs 16:18). I confess that I have not denied myself, picked up my cross daily, and followed You *(Matthew 16:24)*. In so doing I have given ground to the enemy in my life. I have believed that I could be successful and live victoriously by my own strength and resources. I now confess that I have sinned against You by placing my will before Yours and by centering my life around self instead of You. I now renounce the 'self' life and by so doing cancel all the ground that has been gained in my members by the enemies of the Lord Jesus Christ. I pray that You will guide me so that I will do nothing from selfish ambition or empty conceit, but that with humility of mind, I will regard others as more important than myself *(Philippians 2:3)*. Enable me through love, to serve others and in honor prefer others *(Romans 12:10)*. I ask this in the name of Christ Jesus, my Lord. Amen.

Having made this commitment, now allow God to show you any specific areas of your life where you have been prideful such as:

- A stronger desire to do my will than God's will;

- Being more dependent on my strengths and resources than God's;

- Sometimes believing that my ideas and opinions are better than others';

- Being more concerned about controlling others than developing self-control;

- Sometimes considering myself more important than others;

- A tendency to think I have no needs;

- Finding it difficult to admit I was wrong;

- A tendency to be more of a people-pleaser than a God-pleaser;

- Being overly concerned about getting the credit I deserve;

- Being driven to obtain the recognition that comes from degrees, titles, positions;

- Often thinking I am more humble than others; or

- All other ways that I may have thought more highly of myself than I should. (List them).

- For each of these that has been true in your life, pray aloud:

Lord, I agree that I have been prideful in the area of _____
Please forgive me for this pridefulness. I choose to humble myself and place all my confidence in You. Amen.

STEP SIX: THE DOOR OF BONDAGE TO HABITUAL SIN AND ADDICTIONS

Before beginning this step, pray aloud this prayer

Dear Heavenly Father, You have told us to put on the Lord Jesus Christ and make no provision for the flesh in regard to its lusts (Romans 13:14). I acknowledge that I have given in to fleshly lusts which wage war against my soul (I Peter 2:11). I thank You that in Christ my sins are forgiven, but I have transgressed Your holy law and given the enemy an opportunity to wage war in my members *(Ephesians 4:27, James 4:1, I Peter 5:8)*. I come before Your presence to acknowledge these sins and to seek Your cleansing (I John 1:9) that I may be freed from the bondage of sin (Galatians 5:1). I now ask You to reveal to my mind the ways that I have transgressed Your moral law and grieved the Holy Spirit.

Prayer for Sexual Sins (pornography, masturbation, sexual promiscuity) or sexual difficulty and lack of intimacy in your marriage

> Lord, I ask You to reveal to my mind every sexual use of my body as an instrument of unrighteousness. In Jesus' name I pray. Amen.

Renouncing Sexual Sins

> Lord, I renounce (name the specific use of your body) with (name the person) and ask You to break that bond.

Now commit your body to the Lord by praying:

> Lord, I renounce all these uses of my body as an instrument of unrighteousness and by so doing ask You to break all bondages that satan has brought into my life through that involvement. I confess my participation. I now present my body to You as a living sacrifice, holy and acceptable to You, and I reserve the sexual use of my body only for marriage. I renounce the lie of satan that my body is not clean, that it is dirty or in any way unacceptable as a result of my past sexual experience. Lord, I thank You that You have totally cleansed and forgiven me, that You love and accept me unconditionally, therefore, I can accept myself. And I choose to do so, to accept myself and my body as cleansed. In Jesus' name. Amen.

SPECIFIC PRAYERS

Homosexuality

Lord, I renounce the lie that You have created me or anyone else to be homosexual, and I affirm that You clearly forbid homosexual behavior. I accept myself as a child of God and declare that You created me a man (or woman). I renounce any bondages of satan that have perverted my relationships with others. I announce that I am free to relate to the opposite sex in the way that You intended. In Jesus' name. Amen.

Abortion

Lord, I confess that I did not assume stewardship of the life You entrusted to me, and I ask Your forgiveness. I choose to accept Your forgiveness by forgiving myself, and I now commit that child to You for Your care in eternity. In Jesus' name. Amen.

Suicidal Tendencies

I renounce the lie that I can find peace and freedom by taking my own life. Satan is a thief, and he comes to steal, kill and destroy. I choose life in Christ, who said He came to give me life and to give it abundantly.

Eating Disorders Or Cutting On Yourself

I renounce the lie that my worthiness is dependent upon my appearance or performance. I renounce cutting myself, purging, or defecation as a means of cleansing myself of evil and I announce that only the blood of the Lord Jesus Christ can cleanse me from my sin. I accept the reality that there may be sin present in me because of the lies I have believed and the wrong use of my body, but I renounce the lie that I am evil or that any part of my body is evil. I announce the truth that I am totally accepted by Christ just as I am.

Substance Abuse

Lord, I confess that I have misused substances (alcohol, tobacco, food, prescription or street drugs) for the purpose of pleasure, to escape reality, or to cope with difficult situations resulting in the abuse of my body, the harmful programming of my mind, and the quenching of the Holy Spirit. I ask Your forgiveness, and I renounce any satanic connection or influence in my life through my misuse of chemicals or food. I cast my anxiety onto Christ who loves me, and I commit myself to no longer yield to substance abuse but to the Holy Spirit. I ask You, heavenly Father, to fill me with Your Holy Spirit. In Jesus' name. Amen.

After confessing all known sin, pray:

I now confess these sins to You and claim through the blood of the Lord Jesus Christ my forgiveness and cleansing. I cancel all ground that evil spirits have gained through my willful involvement in sin. I ask this in the wonderful name of my Lord and Savior Jesus Christ. Amen.

STEP SEVEN: THE DOOR OF FAMILY CURSES AND SPIRITUAL ASSIGNATIONS

This step involves denouncing ancestral and generational sin or curses that may have been passed on to us.

Dear Heavenly Father, I come to You as Your child, purchased by the blood of the Lord Jesus Christ. I here and now reject and disown all the sins of my ancestors. As one who has been delivered from the power of darkness and translated into the kingdom of God's dear Son, I cancel out all demonic working that has been passed on to me from my ancestors. As one who has been crucified and raised with Christ and who sits with Him in heavenly places, I reject any and every way in which satan may claim ownership of me. I declare myself to be eternally and completely signed over and committed to the Lord Jesus Christ. I now command every familiar spirit and every enemy of the Lord Jesus Christ that is in or around me to flee my presence and never to return. I now ask You, heavenly Father, to fill me with Your Holy Spirit. I submit my body as an instrument of righteousness, a living sacrifice, that I may glorify You in my body. All this I do in the name and authority of the Lord Jesus Christ. Amen.

MAKING A FAMILY COVENANT

Some of your reading this are heads of families. As we've learnt during Simama, you have spiritual authority over your family members. Perhaps you are the father of the home or the only parent in a single parent home, or maybe even the oldest sibling in the absence of responsible parental figures. In this appendix, we want to share a covenant prayer that you can make to God on behalf of your family.

What is a covenant? A covenant is a relationship between two parties that has been formalized through binding promises that the parties make to each other. There are different types of covenant in the bible, including those that a person with more authority (e.g. God or a king) made with those having less authority or power, and those made between people with equal status. Marriage is seen as an example of a covenant, when a man and a woman enter into a lifelong relationship premised on promises they make to one another.

The bible shows God as a covenant making and covenant fulfilling entity. God establishes covenants with different people through the bible narrative, and these covenants are the way God unfolds his redemptive plan. They include the Noahic Covenant (made between God and Noah after the flood)[220], Abrahamic Covenant (made between God and Abraham through which God would bless Abraham and through him all of humanity)[221], the Mosaic Covenant (between God and the people of Israel after He had delivered them from slavery)[222], the Davidic Covenant (between God and David where God promises that a descendant of David would always rule His people)[223] and the New Covenant (between God and His people that is first spoken of by the prophet Jeremiah who spoke of a coming day when God would bring forgiveness of sin, internal renewal of the heart, and intimate knowledge of God to His people. This was inaugurated by Jesus at the Last Supper with his disciples.)[224]

These are all examples of God initiating and making a covenant with people on behalf of themselves and their families. The scriptures also have many examples of people formally making a vow to God or affirming the covenant that God had made with them or their ancestors. Here are a few examples…

Genesis 28:20-22 - Then Jacob made a vow, saying, *"If God will be with me and will watch over me on this journey I am taking and will give me food to eat and clothes to wear 21 so that I return safely to my father's household, then the Lord[a] will be my God 22 and[b] this stone that I have set up as a pillar will be God's house, and of all that you give me I will give you a tenth."*

God appeared to Jacob and reaffirmed the covenant that He had made with his grandfather Abraham. In turn, Jacob committed himself to serve God.

Joshua 24:14-15 - *"Now fear the Lord and serve him with all faithfulness. Throw away the gods your ancestors worshiped beyond the Euphrates River and in Egypt, and serve the Lord. 15 But if serving the Lord seems undesirable to you, then choose for yourselves this day whom you will serve, whether the gods your ancestors served beyond the Euphrates, or the gods of the Amorites, in whose land you are living. But as for me and my household, we will serve the Lord."*

---

220 Genesis 9
221 Genesis 12 and 15
222 Exodus 19 and 24
223 2 Samuel 7
224 Jeremiah 31:31-34 and Luke 22:14-23

Joshua reminded the Israelites of God's covenant with them and challenged them to be faithful to it. But even if they didn't, he made a commitment that he and his family would remain faithful to serve God.

1 Samuel 1:10-11 - In her deep anguish Hannah prayed to the Lord, weeping bitterly. 11 And she made a vow, saying, "Lord Almighty, if you will only look on your servant's misery and remember me, and not forget your servant but give her a son, then I will give him to the Lord for all the days of his life, and no razor will ever be used on his head."

Hannah desperately wanted a child. She vowed to God that should He answer her prayer, she would dedicate her child to God's service all the days of his life.

Job 1:5 - When a period of feasting had run its course, Job would make arrangements for them to be purified. Early in the morning he would sacrifice a burnt offering for each of them, thinking, "Perhaps my children have sinned and cursed God in their hearts." This was Job's regular custom.

Job, the righteous man, took personal responsibility for his children, confessing their sins (intentional and unintentional) to God and offering a sin offering to God on their behalf.

Acts 13:30-34 - He then brought them out and asked, "Sirs, what must I do to be saved?" They replied, "Believe in the Lord Jesus, and you will be saved—you and your household." Then they spoke the word of the Lord to him and to all the others in his house. At that hour of the night the jailer took them and washed their wounds; then immediately he and all his household were baptized. The jailer brought them into his house and set a meal before them; he was filled with joy because he had come to believe in God—he and his whole household.

This particular experience shows the spiritual authority of a parent. When this prison official in Philippi decided to become a follower of Jesus and to commit himself to God, his whole family followed suit!

With all this in mind, read through the following prayer and if it is the desire of your heart, then pray it out aloud on behalf of your family. If you are a couple, you could change it from singular to plural and pray it together. If you are praying in your house or compound, you could also have some anointing oil with you to symbolize the presence and power of the Holy Spirit. You can use cooking oil or olive oil if you have some.

FAMILY COVENANT PRAYER

Heavenly Father, as the head of this family, I come before you to surrender my family to You. On the basis of the spiritual authority that you have given to me, I confess the sins of all the members of my family against You. Please forgive us Lord, and through the blood of Jesus, wipe away all our transgressions. Reveal to me any doors that the enemy may use to legally oppress any member of my family, and through Your grace, show me how to close it in prayer. I dedicate my children to You, thanking You by faith for their salvation. I choose life, so that my children and I will live *(Deuteronomy 30:19)*.

By the power of the Holy Spirit who dwells in me, I tear down any strongholds that the enemy may have used to oppress me and my family. I raise up a spiritual altar to You in our home. May our home be a place of worship. May all who dwell here, and those who visit us, experience the power of the Most High God. May Your Presence always tangibly dwell among us. *(If you have oil, pray, I dedicate this oil to you and pray that its use will be acceptable to you. I now pour it on my home to symbolize that your power and presence dwell here)*

I now affirm the covenant that You have with me and with my family. I declare that my family belongs to You. May this family never depart from serving You, O Lord. I declare by faith that we, in view of God's mercy, will offer our bodies as living sacrifices, holy and pleasing to God—as our true and proper worship *(Romans 12:1)*. We will not conform to the pattern of this world, but we will be transformed by the renewing of our minds and thus be able to test and approve Your good, pleasing and perfect will *(Romans 12:1-2)*.

Lord, I covenant that with Your help, I will train up my children in your ways so that they will not depart from it *(Proverbs 22:6)*. I will model to them what it means to walk in righteousness and to treat those weaker than them with compassion and justice. I declare by faith that as a family, we have been crucified with Christ; and it is no longer us who live, but Christ who lives in us. Because of this, we will live our lives by faith in Jesus, who loved and gave Himself up for us *(Galatians 2:20)*. I make invalid any claims that the enemy may have on any of my family members. We resist the enemy and he has no choice but to flee from us *(James 4:7)*.

I declare by faith that we are blessed because we fear the Lord and find great delight in His commands. I declare that because of that, my children will be mighty in the land and the generation of the upright will be blessed *(Psalm 112:1-3)*. My children will not just be saved and make it to heaven; they will be 'mighty in the land'! While on earth, they will fulfill their God given purpose and be a blessing to their generation (Acts 13:36). I declare that in this family, all children will be taught by the Lord, and great will be their peace *(Isaiah 54:13)*.

I further declare by faith that it is You who gives us the ability to create wealth, thus fulfilling Your covenant with us *(Deuteronomy 8:8)*. I speak over my household the blessing of the Lord, which brings wealth and has no sorrow added to it *(Proverbs 10:22)*. We will be blessed in the city and blessed in the country, blessed when we come in and blessed when we go out *(Deuteronomy 28:3,6)*. Our enemies will come at us from one direction but flee from us in seven *(Deuteronomy 28:7)*. The Lord will open the heavens, the storehouse of his bounty, to send rain on our land in season and to bless all the work of your hands. We will lend to many nations but will borrow from none. We will be the head, not the tail, always at the top, never at the bottom *(Deuteronomy 28:12:13)*. And with Your help, we will give generously to Your work *(Genesis 28:22)* and be a blessing to the poor *(Proverbs 19:17)*.

So Lord, arise now and take Your place as the true Leader of this home. As for me and my household, we will serve the Lord *(Joshua 24:15c)*!

Made in the USA
Las Vegas, NV
13 September 2022